Germany and the Approach of War in 1914

The Making of the 20th Century

Series Editor: GEOFFREY WARNER

Germany and the Approach of War in 1914

Second Edition

V. R. Berghahn

To reform Prussia is impossible; it will remain
the *Junkerstaat* it is at present, or go to pieces
altogether. . . . I am convinced we are on the eve
of the most dreadful war Europe has ever seen.
Things cannot go on as at present, the burden
of military expenditure is crushing people and
the Kaiser and his government are fully alive to
the fact. Everything works for a great crisis in
Germany.

AUGUST BEBEL, 1910

St. Martin's Press   New York

First published in the United States of America in 1993

Reprinted 1997

Printed in Hong Kong

ISBN 0–312–10076–0 (pbk.)
ISBN 0–312–09993–2 (cl.)

Library of Congress Cataloging-in-Publication Data
Berghahn,.Volker Rolf.
Germany and the approach of war 1914 / V.R. Berghahn.
p. cm.
Includes bibliographical references and index,
ISBN 0–312–09993–2 (cl.) – ISBN 0–312–10076–0 (pbk.)
1. Germany–Politics and government–1888–1918. 2. Bethmann
Hollweg, Theobald von, 1856–1921. 3. World War, 1914–1918–
Germany.
1. Title.
DD228.8.B38   1993
940.3'112–dc20   93–7850

                                                                              CIP

To E. M.

Contents

Abbreviations

A.A.	Auswärtiges Amt (German Foreign Office).
A.H.R.	*American Historical Review.*
B.A.	Bundesarchiv Koblenz.
B.A.–M.A.	Bundesarchiv-Militärarchiv Freiburg.
B.D.	*British Documents on the Origins of the War, 1898–1914.*
B.d.I.	Bund der Industriellen.
C.d.I.	Centralverband der Industriellen.
D.D.F.	*Documents Diplomatiques Français.*
D.Z.A.I.	Deutsches Zentralarchiv Potsdam.
G.P.	*Die Grosse Politik der Europäischen Kabinette, 1871–1914.*
H.J.	*Historical Journal.*
H.St.A.	Hauptstaatsarchiv Dresden.
H.Z.	*Historische Zeitschrift.*
J.C.H.	*Journal of Contemporary History.*
M.G.M.	*Militärgeschichtliche Mitteilungen.*
Ö.U.	*Österreich–Ungarns Aussenpolitik.*
P.A.A.A.	Politisches Archiv des Auswärtigen Amts Bonn.
P.& P.	*Past and Present.*
P.V.S.	*Politische Vierteljahresschrift.*
R.D.M.V.	Reichdeutscher Mittelstandsverband.
R.M.A.	Reichs-Marine-Amt.
S.K.	Senats-Kommission Hamburg.
S.P.D.	Sozialdemokratische Partei Deutschlands.
St.A.H.H.	Staatsarchiv Hamburg.
V.f.Z.G.	*Vierteljahrshefte für Zeitgeschichte.*
Z.f.G.	*Zeitschrift für Geschichtswissenschaft.*
Z.f.R.u.G.	*Zeitschrift für Religions- und Geistesgeschichte.*

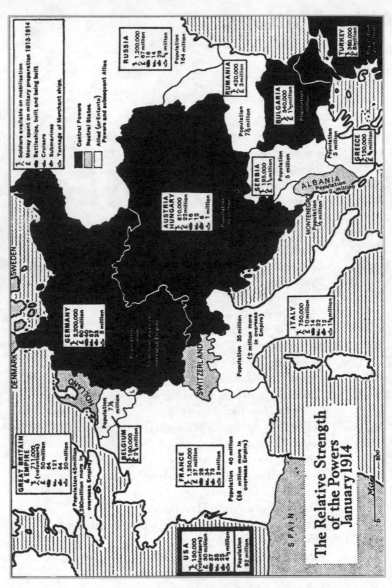

The Relative Strength
of the Powers
January 1914

Map I

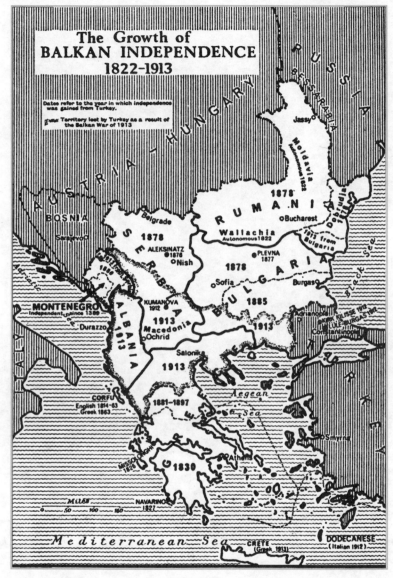

The Growth of
BALKAN INDEPENDENCE
1822–1913

Dates refer to the year in which independence
was gained from Turkey.

Territory lost by Turkey as a result of
the Balkan War of 1913

RUSSIA

AUSTRIA - HUNGARY

BOSNIA
Sarajevo

BESSARABIA

Jassy

Moldavia
Autonomous 1822

1878
RUMANIA
Bucharest

Dobrudja
1913 from
Bulgaria

Belgrade
1878
ALEKSINATZ
1876
Nish

SERBIA

Wallachia
Autonomous 1822

PLEVNA
1877
1878
Sofia

Burgas

Black Sea

MONTENEGRO
Independent since 1389
Durazzo

KUMANOVA
1912
1913
Macedonia
Ochrid

ALBANIA
1913

BULGARIA
1885

1913

Adrianople
KIRK-KILISSE 1912
LULE-BURGAS 1912
Constantinople

1913

Salonika

1913

TURKEY

ITALY

Aegean
Sea

1881–1897

Smyrna

CORFU
English 1814–63
Greek 1863

MISSOLONGHI
1826

1830
Athens

MILES
0 50 100 150

NAVARINO
1827

Mediterranean Sea

CRETE
(Greek 1913)

DODECANESE
(Italian 1912)

Map II

Acknowledgement is due to Martin Gilbert and Weidenfeld &
Nicolson Ltd for permission to reproduce Maps I and II, taken from
Recent History Atlas 1860–1960.

Introduction to the Second Edition

The first edition of this book was published in 1973 as a synthesis of the new research on Wilhelmine Germany that had been produced in the wake of Fritz Fischer's controversial books on the origins of the First World War.[1] As a relatively concise treatment of a crucial period of modern European history it is apparently still finding enough readers twenty years later for my publishers to develop the idea of putting out a second edition now that Samuel Williamson's parallel volume on Austria-Hungary has finally appeared.[2] Knowing that the Wilhelmine period has remained a major area of research, I had many doubts and hesitations about the project. Would a book on Germany's foreign and domestic policies and politics not have to be completely rewritten, all the more so since its basic framework and lines of argument have not gone unchallenged? Let me, by way of this introduction, deal with the most important debates that have been taking place more recently in order to assess the present state of play in the historiography of the Wilhelmine period and the origins of the First World War.

As far as I can see, a fundamental challenge has come from the diplomatic historians, among whom some had become increasingly sceptical of the structural analyses of the Wilhelmine Empire that were published in the wake of the Fischer Controversy. What they found particularly objectionable was the attempt to explain the pre-war crisis in terms of a 'primacy of domestic politics', as first formulated in the 1920s by Eckart Kehr in opposition to the then dominant 'primacy of foreign policy' school.[3] Although initially arguing, as does this study, for a middle way, that is the interdependence of foreign and domestic politics, historians of international politics such as Andreas Hillgruber, Klaus Hildebrand, Michael Stürmer and most recently Gregor Schöllgen had, by the 1980s, reverted back to a 'primacy of foreign politics' position.[4] They thereby revived the argument, last advanced in the 1950s,[5] that the history of Wilhelmine Germany can only be understood in

1

terms of the country's geopolitical situation among the Great Powers right in the heart of Europe. Her moves within an anarchic international system, in which the principle of cut-throat power politics obtained, were said to be reactions to the pressures exerted on her borders by others. Bismarck's 'nightmare of internal revolution' that, according to Hans-Ulrich Wehler,[6] had guided the first Reich Chancellor's foreign policy, was once again countered by the view of the 'nightmare of hostile foreign coalitions'. Extending this interpretation to the Wilhelmine period, Hildebrand and Schöllgen finally went so far as to place the main responsibility for the growing pre-war crisis not on the Kaiser's *Weltpolitik* and rearmament programme, but on the inability and unwillingness of the other Great Powers, notably Great Britain, to accommodate the highly dynamic and politically restive Reich within the existing international order.[7] Accordingly, the outbreak of the First World War is once again seen in a very different light from what many people thought had become the firmly established findings of the 1960s and 1970s.

After this, the old question is still on the table: were the primary determinants in the development of Wilhelmine foreign and armaments policy domestic or external? Was Tirpitz's ambitious naval building programme a response to, and copy of, what other powers were doing in the 1890s; or was it produced by a unique constellation within Germany and its perception by William II, his advisers, and the political forces supporting the Prusso-German monarchy in its traditional shape and form? Did, once *Weltpolitik* and the Tirpitz Plan had run into growing trouble abroad and opposition at home, German anxieties about the country's deteriorating international and domestic situation feed upon each other, with armaments policy acting as the hinge? And finally, did all this unleash a crisis out of which an 1866-style war appeared to offer the only way out, as this book argues? Or should we, as Schöllgen has done, put a question mark behind this 'escape into war' position, because the crisis was in effect an outgrowth of Social Darwinist rivalries among the Great Powers? Was the root problem the failure of the non-German statesmen to recognise the dangers and to appease, in time, Germany's defensive concern with geopolitics instead of trying to contain her?[8] It is important to realise that Hildebrand, Schöllgen and others do not base their revisionism on the discovery of new sources, but rather present it as a reinterpretation of known documents. The fact that they have also chosen to ignore readily accessible published material on certain calculations behind the Kaiser's naval and world policy has no doubt helped their case. Thus they conveniently fail to deal with the anti-parliamentary intentions of Tirpitz's '*Dreiertempo*' whose significance is explained in Chapter 2 below. Ultimately the rejection of the findings of the 1960s as 'wrong', and the false labelling, against better knowledge, of earlier research as Marxist must probably be seen in the larger context of a resurgence of more conservative and benign interpretations of modern German history, which first found their way into the professional literature from the mid-1970s onwards, before they finally exploded onto the public stage in the bitter *Historikerstreit* of the 1980s.[9] In the light of these developments which show that the question of continuity in German history has never stopped casting its long shadows right into the present, the debate on the motivating forces and the exact course of Wilhelmine policy at home and abroad continues, and the following chapters contain what I would still see as the more plausible line of argument.

At the same time as the diplomatic historians mounted their challenge, a group of British scholars around Geoff Eley and David Blackbourn began to find other problems with the studies of the 1960s and 1970s. To be sure, they had little sympathy with the revival of geopolitical interpretations. Like Wehler and others, they, too, were concerned to explain the dynamics of Wilhelmine politics in terms of the country's internal development. But inspired by grass-roots approaches to History and by E. P. Thompson's cultural Marxism, they were unhappy with the 'history from above' as practised by the 'Bielefelders'.[10]* To them Germany was no longer a securely patriarchal society that could be run and manipulated from the top by strategic elites and by the agrarian *Junker* in particular. They saw a society in an age of universal suffrage and mass politics that from the 1890s onwards, if not before, had begun to organise itself 'from below'. Autonomous self-mobilisation became their central explanatory category. The early objections of this group to what was polemically labelled a 'new orthodoxy'[11] are probably best summed up in the words of Richard Evans, who wrote in 1978:[12]

---

* For an explanation of this term see below, note 3 of the Introduction.

Political processes, changes and influences are perceived as flowing downwards—though now from the elites who controlled the State, rather than from the socially vaguer entity of the State itself—not upwards from the people. The actions and beliefs of the masses are explained in terms of the influence exerted on them by manipulative elites at the top of society. The German Empire is presented as a puppet theatre, with Junkers and industrialists pulling the strings, and middle and lower classes dancing jerkily across the stage of history towards the final curtain of the Third Reich. ... British historians have come increasingly to emphasise the importance of the grass roots of politics and the everyday life and experience of ordinary people.

This critique has spawned much fruitful and imaginative research. Eley's notion that the 1890s witnessed a 'seismic shift' at the grass-roots of German society, first stimulated fresh empirical work on a large variety of organisations that proliferated at this time. Studies appeared on nationalist associations and political parties, economic pressure groups and, eventually, on the organisational efforts of women and minorities.[13] Responding to a further shift of emphasis that, from the 1970s onwards, affected the writing of social history in the Western world more generally, other scholars soon began to look at the unorganised. Accordingly we now also have studies dealing with the conditions of daily life in Wilhelmine Germany—patterns of housing, of health and illness and of migration.[14] No less important than retrieving the actual realities was the task of examining how they were experienced by different categories of ordinary Germans and how they shaped individual and collective perceptions of their social environment. The world of industrial workers became a major focus.[15] But work on the professions and the middle classes did not lag far behind.[16] Eventually the boundaries between social history and cultural history began to disappear, once traditional definitions of culture as 'high culture' had been expanded to include popular culture, that is the traditions and customs of local communities and specific social groups, rather than merely the works of intellectuals and artists.[17] Catholicism and Protestantism were rediscovered in order to uncover patterns of popular piety.[18] Opposing the Prussocentric view of the 'Bielefelders', the 'new' social history also turned to the non-Prussian regions of the Reich.[19] As a result of all this research, we now have a much better understanding of how German society 'ticked' at the grass-roots, how people lived, what their responses to the world around them were. The picture has become richer and more colourful. If there was ever a dominant view that this society was authoritarian and militaristic from top to bottom, such notions have been effectively undermined by the findings of recent social history.

Now while Evans, as quoted above, had a point when criticising the 'top down' approaches of the 'Bielefelders', it is worth remembering first of all that they had not been quite so one-sided. They, too, had pointed to the emergence of forces that had begun to challenge, 'from below', the established constitutional order and distribution of wealth and power in Germany; they, too, saw these forces as having a destabilising effect on the existing system. But they located them on the Left of the political spectrum and among the Social Democrats in particular. Nevertheless, though always interested in the working-class movement, their main focus was the German elites and how they responded to the perceived threat from the Left. And this is where Eley, Evans and Blackbourn came in to argue that the lower middle class began, from the 1890s onwards, to pose a similar challenge to the Hohenzollern monarchy. Like the industrial working class, these groups were said to be in rebellion against the traditional oligarchical structures of local and national politics.[20] There emerged—Eley continued—a radical, rather than a conservative, Right. It was brought into its own by the advent of modern politics and propaganda, as it learned skilfully to exploit existing civil rights of free assembly and organisation and, at the Reich level, of universal suffrage. As these groups became more vocal and better organised, the established elites found it more and more difficult successfully to control and influence them for their own political purposes.

It will be immediately obvious that this is a different interpretation of Wilhelmine domestic politics than is to be found below, but not as fundamentally so as might appear at first sight. To begin with, it merely extends the notion of socio-political division without refuting it. Eley's radical Right has joined the radical Left as a destabilising force in Wilhelmine politics and society. Beyond this, the debate between him and the 'Bielefelders' goes on, and here are the bones of contention: There is the question of just how destabilising lower middle-class politics and organisations, like the Navy League, actually became. In the introduction of a new edition of his *Reshaping the German Right*, Eley has further elaborated his position by emphasising that, contrary to what some of his critics had perceived, he was less concerned with the sociology and social history of nationalist organisations than with how their leaders, many of whom were retired officers and other notables, addressed the petty bourgeois rank and file ideologically and tried to mobilise the political experiences of ordinary members for radical patriotic causes.[21] This raises the problem of the function of their nationalism which also remains in dispute. According to Eley, right-wing nationalism, after early rumblings since 1903/4, became a centrifugal force of change after 1906/7 and must be differentiated from the conservative nationalism touted by the government and the elites that aimed to integrate the divergent political forces of the Right and the centre on the basis of the constitutional and socio-economic status quo. However, did not all types of nationalism, whether radical or conservative, act as a stabilising force in that they all rallied the lower middle classes against an alleged external enemy and against the 'unpatriotic fellows' of the Left at home? This at least is how the nationalist associations are seen in this book, even if it must be admitted—and has in fact always been argued in this study and elsewhere—that they became increasingly difficult to handle. Indeed, Tirpitz was the first to discover this. No less important, the self-assertion of the nationalist associations was an element in the progressive general deterioration of the monarchy's domestic position in the years prior to 1914—a central theme of this study. What is at issue therefore is the janus-faced character of modern nationalism and the question of how the scales between integration and disintegration were tilted at various points in time. In one respect, however, the 'British' critique of power relations must be fully accepted. The first edition of this book, in line with the 'Bielefelders'' view of Wilhelmine politics, placed too much emphasis on the power and influence of Germany's pre-industrial elites. A large part of Chapter 1 has been revamped in response to this criticism.

In a volume first published in Germany as *Myths of German Historical Writing*, Eley, in a wide-ranging and provocative essay, followed by a more cautious piece by Blackbourn, went beyond the earlier critique of the Junker-centred view.[22] No less unhappy with the implied notion that, compared with Western Europe, Germany had taken a 'special path' (*Sonderweg*) into the twentieth century that finally culminated in the Third Reich, Eley argued that Germany had undergone a bourgeois revolution like France and Britain. In presenting his case, he highlighted the modern industrial-capitalist features of Wilhelmine Germany and down-sized the importance of the agrarian elites and of the agricultural sector. Not the failure of the liberal bourgeoisie to assert itself against the Prussian conservatives, he added, had pushed Germany towards catastrophe, but the pathology of bourgeois modernity in general, of which the German development was an integral part. This hypothesis has led to further lively debate in which the 'Bielefelders' vigorously argued against abandoning the *Sonderweg* as an analytical framework. After this, it appears, Eley himself came to feel that his notion of a successful German 'bourgeois revolution', treated on a par with what had occurred in France and Britain in the eighteenth and nineteenth centuries, may have overstretched the evidence. Rather, he now argues, the shifts in the balance of power between the traditional agrarian elites and a capitalist-industrial bourgeoisie that took place in Germany at this time are more comparable to those which Japan experienced during the Meiji Restoration.[23]

These developments have left me to wonder if there really has been a paradigm shift; I began to ask myself if the often bitter polemics had not obscured the fact that the two sides in the debate were merely looking at the same problem from opposite angles. And that problem was not really, as Evans put it, the 'final curtain of the Third Reich' (although this question will also always loom on the horizon and has done so not only in the work of the 'Bielefelders', but also in Eley's); the task is rather to explain the state of German society in 1914 and why this society ended up in a catastrophic world war. The 'new' social historians never expressed much sympathy with the interpretations of Hildebrand and Schöllgen, and in fact operate in the same territory as the 'Bielefelders' in their quest to understand why German society evidently found it so difficult to cope with its problems of modernity at the level of politics. There-after the crucial point was this: if as much change had occurred, especially in the 1890s, as the 'new' social historians have found and if the country's society, economy and culture had become as varied and complex as their research had demonstrated, it would appear perfectly logical to raise the question of whether similar changes had occurred in the constitutional and political framework within which this bustling society existed; and it would appear to be legitimate to ask whether this framework was flexible and adaptable enough to deal with the manifold and mounting pressures that those well-organised groups and special interests were exerting upon it.

Certainly, with a wealth of information now available on the organisational life and ideological positions of these groups, it is no longer sufficient simply to state the discovery of a pluralist Wilhelmine society. The next step is to inquire into the changing balances of power and influence among this plurality of forces and into what the final balance-sheet looks like. History is not just about structures and processes, experiences and mentalities; it is also about winners and losers in the contest for power and influence. What, moreover, were the alliances that were forged between different social and political forces with the aim of winning and how durable and effective were they? In the face of a tangible political crisis and a growing inability of the political system adequately to respond to the pressures upon it, it suddenly becomes clear that the pluralisation of societal and organisational life and the ever more hectic manoeuvres to form powerful political and ideological blocs, portrayed in this book, are in fact the two sides of the same coin. The attempts to forge these blocs which, to achieve greater cohesion, tended to divide the world into friends and foes were successful enough to destroy what little prospect there still was of a national consensus over basic questions of Germany's future development; they were also powerful enough to accelerate the breakdown of the legislative process and produce a paralysis of the political system as a whole.[24]

In grappling with a manifest political crisis in the last years before 1914, the historian is bound to ask what direction the Prusso-German monarchy was then moving into. As to the 1890s, there may be enough evidence to support the position of John Röhl, who has never wavered from arguing that the crown emerged strengthened from the turmoil of the early post-Bismarckian period and that a system of 'Personal Rule' by the Kaiser was eventually put in place. Yet the trouble was that William II never lived up to his charismatic role and that the turn of the century saw the erosion of his prestige and his power.[25] Observing this decline, some have taken the view that Germany was slowly and imperceptibly sliding into a constitutional monarchy, with the Reichstag as the new power centre. In the 1970s, Manfred Rauh, building on the work of a number of constitutional historians,[26] became the foremost advocate of this parliamentarisation thesis.[27] It is significant and reassuring that Eley and the 'new' social historians never fell for Rauh, even if they have tilted towards Stanley Suval's notion that a surprisingly stable electoral and political culture can be discerned.[28] Now, if it is correct that parliamentarisation was a chimera and if the veto powers and the resistance of the Kaiser and the forces still loyal to him therefore ruled out any attempt to create a political order more viable and responsive to socio-economic change around it, then whither Germany? If the answer to this question is related to the fact that the country found itself in a major war in 1914, this book is trying to provide such an answer. And so, the more I immersed myself in the findings of the 'new' social history, the more I began to wonder how far it has actually corroborated rather than changed the basic framework of *Germany and the Approach of War in 1914*. This is a book that portrays a rapidly diversifying society whose political system found it progressively more difficult to solve the problems that were coming to the surface under the impact of social, economic, and cultural change. By 1913/14 that system had reached an impasse. The modernity and richness of the country's organisational and cultural life notwithstanding and, indeed, perhaps because of it, in the end Wilhelmine politics was marked by bloc-formation and paralysis at home and abroad and finally by a *Flucht nach vorn* (flight forward) on the part of the political leadership that was fast losing control, but still had enough constitutional powers to take the step into a major war. It is the evolution of this outcome and the political culture that made it possible that still requires further study.

There now remain two smaller, though significant themes, broached in Chapters 9 and 10, on which discussion has also continued. The first relates to the War Council of December 1912. Fischer and his supporters have never stopped being convinced that the decision to go to war in the summer of 1914 was made at that meeting.[29] With other historians, I continue to hold in Chapter 9 that Fischer's is not the most plausible interpretation and that it was only the setbacks to German foreign and domestic policies in 1913 and 1914 that tipped the scales in favour of a pre-emptive war in July

1914. It is more difficult to deal with the second debate. It grew out of the discovery by Bernd Sösemann that the entries in the Riezler Diaries for July 1914 were separate from the scrapbooks that Kurt Riezler, Reich Chancellor Bethmann Hollweg's private secretary and adviser, had been using since 1911 to record his daily experiences and thoughts.[30] Since Karl Dietrich Erdmann, the editor of the Riezler Papers, had not indicated this in his footnotes in 1972,[31] I therefore took the quotations used in Chapter 11 to be unproblematical. It is now clear that the entries for July 1914 are loose-leaf notes (*'Blockblätter'*) attached to one of the scrapbooks for the war period, after the scrapbooks for the period up to June 1914 were destroyed by Riezler's brother after 1955. Further detective work led Sösemann to the conclusion that the *Blockblätter* were not the originals. Rather, he added, they probably represented a revised version which Riezler had produced on the basis of the originals some time after 1918, possibly under the impression of the bitter war-guilt debate.

Fischer subsequently seized upon Sösemann's cautious conclusions by publishing a paperback in which he argued quite bluntly that the original version had contained details about Bethmann Hollweg's policy in July 1914 so compromising that Riezler had decided to rework the evidence after the war.[32] He felt that the now missing originals would have confirmed his view of Bethmann Hollweg as the man who coolly planned an aggressive world war from the start and that nothing less than this objective had been behind the issuing of the 'blank cheque' to Austria-Hungary on 5 July 1914. Fischer supported his hypothesis with further circumstantial evidence from the private papers of fellow historians who had learned about the content of the July entries from colleagues or from Riezler himself. He also alleged that senior historians, hoping to undermine his arguments on the origins of the First World War, had conspired to prevent the full truth of the Riezler Diaries from ever being revealed. Erdmann has angrily defended himself against these attacks on his integrity as the editor of the Riezler Papers. He and his pupils have maintained, and tried their utmost to prove beyond reasonable doubt, that the *Blockblätter* were the originals and that no other version had ever existed.[33]

The controversy raises intriguing questions about how this source is now to be treated. To be sure, these are not fabrications like the hoax about the 'Hitler Diaries'. All agree that the *Blockblätter* were written by Riezler himself. The problem is when they were recorded and consequently whether what we now have is a 'cleansed' version. The separation of the entries from the scrapbooks is clearly suspect. On the other hand, if Riezler tried to expurgate his records in the 1920s or even after the Second World War, his redrafting was rather poor. The content of the (supposedly revised) *Blockblätter* as finally published in 1972 is, after all, disturbing enough to have scandalised a German public that after 1918 was convinced of Germany's innocence. After careful re-reading of the arguments presented by the two sides, it seemed to me unjustified to discard the surviving version of the Riezler Diaries altogether. Rather I would continue to use this source as before, that is in conjunction with other material that has been recovered. This material points overwhelmingly in the direction of Bethmann Hollweg having opted, at the beginning of July 1914, for a localised war strategy. He envisaged a limited conflict between Austria-Hungary and Serbia in the Balkans, although he took a conscious risk that war might escalate into a major conflagration. There were, it is true, the military who even at this early point leaned towards a *va banque*. But it seems advisable to separate them, during the early stages of the crisis, from the civilians in Berlin who, on July 5–6, were given the green light by the Kaiser to pursue their localisation policy. The evidence for this interpretation seems to me to be stronger than for Fischer's more radical view.

Bethmann Hollweg's calculations of early July 1914 also make better sense on psychological grounds. From the perspective of later generations who know that the July Crisis ended in a catastrophic world war, the Reich Chancellor may have taken an unacceptably high risk. But it is important to remember that the risk-takers in Berlin did not know that future at that point. Only as the crisis unfolded, did it become clearer just how risky the limited war strategy had been. Small wonder, therefore, that a week or so after the 'blank cheque' had been issued he and his advisers had become noticeably more nervous, irritated not least by the long delay in the delivery of Vienna's ultimatum to Belgrade. By this time things were clearly no longer going according to the original calculations so that it is vital to take account of the evolving crisis also in terms of its effect on the decision-makers' state of mind.

Sam Williamson's most recent study of the July Crisis from an Austro-Hungarian perspective adds further force to this line of argument.[34] Overall, his book is designed as a reminder that the

Fischer Controversy has tended to minimise the question of Vienna's share. He does not shift the balance of responsibility completely, but enough to make us realise once again how recklessly Austria-Hungary pursued its war against Serbia, even though 'the risks of a wider war were clear'.[35] Williamson continues: 'In Vienna in July 1914 a set of leaders experienced in statecraft, power and crisis management consciously risked a general war to fight a local war.' And yet they also 'made every effort to keep the war localized and to deny Russia any pretext for intervention', while suffering from a kind of 'cognitive dissonance' (L. Festinger) when it came to St Petersburg's response:

> For whatever reason, [Chief of the General Staff] Conrad paid less and less attention to the Russian problem in the later stages of the July Crisis. At the same time he urged the militarized civilians to reject every opportunity to negotiate a way out of the crisis or to accept a German cover for a retreat. Despite the evidence reaching him, Conrad kept his attention riveted on Serbia and Plan B. Possibly surprised by the extent of Russia's military preparations and the activism of St Petersburg, the general reacted in an almost classical fashion by ignoring the information that contradicted what he most wanted—war with Serbia.

The notion that there existed in Berlin, as in Vienna, a hawkish military faction next to a more moderate civilian group also helps to explain most plausibly why the generals gained the upper hand at the end of July; for when they returned to Berlin from their vacations (which they had either never interrupted at the time of the 'blank cheque' or taken immediately thereafter) and found that the localised war strategy had begun to come apart at the seams, they went for a major war—some because this had been their preferred solution all along and others because the alternative of keeping the crisis confined to the Balkans was now rapidly crumbling. In the absence of new material, I therefore did not feel compelled to change my earlier argument on the July Crisis in favour of Fischer's, and the reader is again invited to disagree.

To repeat, this is a history of how Wilhelmine foreign and domestic politics became more and more polarised and not a history of society and culture whose hallmark was its growing diversity. The element of deterioration to the point of impasse and ungovernability is important here. Subsequent chapters pay special attention to what became progressively one of the major bones of political contention and one of the main reasons for the gradual unravelling of the Prusso-German monarchical order, that is armaments. I hope I have succeeded in showing fairly convincingly that this aspect is of crucial importance for understanding the background to the July Crisis. Neither the development of German domestic affairs, above all the decisive questions of taxation and internal reform, nor the course of Wilhelmine diplomacy can be adequately explained without reference to the all-pervasive influence of armaments. It is true that other powers were also vexed by social problems resulting from industrialisation. They, too, adopted imperialistic policies. But it is the special function of armaments which places German domestic and foreign policy into a category of its own.

This means at the same time that military men play a prominent part in this study. This is not in order to revive Gerhard Ritter's rather too narrow concept of militarism and to blame everything on a few generals.[36] Clearly the military establishment of the Prusso-German monarchy cannot be separated from the rest of society. Yet there is equally little doubt that the powerful officer corps was most intimately connected and interwoven with a small minority that wielded political and social powers incommensurately larger than their numbers. It is not surprising that this elite should try to preserve its privileged position against the pressure for greater popular participation and that, in view of the major political weight of the officer corps within the power structure, military values should tend to influence the formulation of basic policies. Nothing is more characteristic of this tendency than the fact that *armaments* came to be seen as the panacea for the monarchy's increasing internal and external difficulties and that the flexibility of political compromise was replaced by a rigid all-or-nothing military dogmatism.

Another peculiarity of this book, related to the previous point, is that it is concerned at some length with problems of political perception. Analysing individual or group perceptions of the world has, of course, meanwhile become a major preoccupation also of social and cultural history and the history of mentalities in particular. There is also no doubt that perceptions shape individual lives just as they shape larger historical processes and developments. Here the focus is mainly on elite groups and top decision-makers, as Wilhelmine Germany apears to offer a good example of a country in which the realities of a particular situation counted for abnormally less than what those elites thought reality to be. As will be seen, the leaders considered the Reich to be in a more favourable position at the turn of the century, and later in a much more precarious one, than was actually the case. It was this gap between reality and the warped perception of it which resulted time and again in serious political miscalculations and in what appears in retrospect to be an amazing lack of wisdom and far-sightedness. Thus the structural crisis of Prusso-German monarchy which resulted from inexorable socio-economic and political change was compounded by its exaggerated perception on the part of those who were determined to defend the *status quo* to the hilt and to whom gradual reform was not an option.

1 The Crisis of the Prusso-German Political System

When, on 4 August 1914, the German Empire entered the First World War it had at its disposal two formidable military instruments, the Army and the Navy. The country was united, or so at least it appeared, and both the Reich Government and the population expected a quick victory. Most people hoped that the soldiers would be back home again by Christmas.[1] As it turned out, this hope was soon disappointed and over the next four years Germany found herself involved in a devastating and protracted war which she finally lost. At the beginning of November 1918 revolutionary uprisings led to the final collapse of the Hohenzollern Monarchy. A republic was proclaimed. The Kaiser fled to Holland and an armistice was signed. After several months of confusion and turmoil, elections were held for a National Assembly which eventually ratified the Versailles Peace Treaty and adopted the so-called Weimar Constitution.[2] In short, the defeat of 1918 brought about a new political order based on the principles of parliamentary government.

The emergence of this new political system in Germany was one of the most significant results of the First World War. The Monarchy, whose policies—as will be seen—had decisively contributed to the outbreak of war in 1914 had at last been dismantled, even if the 1918 German Revolution had not brought a major shift in the distribution of social and economic power. No less important in trying to understand the country's pre-1914 history is the fact that the German Empire had fought the war against the Triple Entente and its allies almost exclusively with its land forces. Apart from extensive, but ultimately futile submarine warfare and the odd sortie of the battle fleet, the Imperial Navy spent the entire war bottled up in Kiel and Wihelmshaven, and when at the end of October 1918 the Navy High Command ordered a do-or-die battle against the Royal Navy, the German fleet did not get very far. Suspecting that they were about to become pawns in a reckless gamble by their officers to save the prestige of the Navy and to secure its political future in the post-war world, the sailors simply refused to embark upon this suicidal mission.[3]

The minor role played by the Navy in the First World War would not appear to be worth emphasising to someone who is accustomed to seeing the German Empire as a continental power. The fact that the Hohenzollern Monarchy, during the First World, War, acted almost solely as a land power gains significance only if it is related to the Reich's armaments policy in the two decades preceding the war. One would expect a nation which, by virtue of its geographical position alone, is constantly confronted with the possibility of a war on land to neglect the Navy. But a glance at German armaments expenditure will show the opposite to be true. From the mid-1890s onwards, naval expenditure increased enormously while, at the same time, the expansion of the Army came to a virtual standstill. The last significant increase of the Army took place in 1893. There followed two decades of stagnation until, rather suddenly and hastily, two major Army bills were introduced and approved in 1912 and 1913.[4] General Karl von Einem, the War Minister from 1903 to 1909, wrote in his memoirs that the Reich Government and, above all, the Reich Chancellor and the State Secretary of the Reich Treasury, should be held responsible for the Army budget being frozen at the 1893 level.[5] It is true that financial considerations and the explosive nature of the tax issue did play a part in this development.[6] Nevertheless, what the former War Minister wrote in 1933 was at best a half-truth. The documents, published from the files of his own Ministry, show that it was the leadership of the Army itself that had called a halt to expansion.[7] Just before the turn of the century, Einem himself, then still a departmental head in the War Ministry, had voiced his opposition to the 'rage de nombre' which, he thought, obsessed the Chief of the General Staff, Alfred von Schlieffen,[8] and this continued to be his view after he was appointed Minister.

In 1904 there was an opportunity for additions to the establishment to be made when the quinquennial appropriations law expired. But Einem remained passive and agreed to extending the law without change until the end of March 1905. When Schlieffen, permanently worried about the balance of armed forces on the European continent, reminded the War Ministry of this deadline and of the need for Army increases, Einem responded by sending him a lengthy 'Clarification of My Views on the Future Development of the Army'.[9] Writing that the Kaiser and the Chief of the Military Cabinet had approved its views, he stated:

> Both from the point of view of the formation of new units and the establishment of new troops, the development of the Army can, at the present time, be regarded as being by and large complete. The question of whether the number of cadres is sufficient to meet the case of war can, in my view, on the whole be answered in the affirmative. This also applies to the further question of whether the number of soldiers is large enough to secure the adequate strength of the existing cadres as well as the training of sufficient recruits so that the required reserve and *Landwehr* units may be formed in the case of war.

Four years later, the War Minister was still opposing those 'people who never cease wanting to expand the Army'.[10] The 'further development of the Army', Einem maintained unwaveringly, 'can, in a certain sense, be regarded as having reached its limits'. If there were anything left to be done, it would be 'to fill the gaps'. This was also the view of Einem's successor, Josias von Heeringen, who told Reich Chancellor Bethmann Hollweg in 1910:[11] 'The last occasion when the Army establishment was fixed was through the Law ... of 25.3.1899.' He did not intend to enlarge or reduce that establishment. 'I do not', he wrote, 'have to explain to Your Excellency the reasons for this which, military considerations apart, belong to the realm of politics and are connected [also] with the international reputation of the Reich.'

It is worth examining more closely the reasons which were so self-evident to Bethmann Hollweg and Heeringen that they did not have to be spelt out. The nature of these unspoken assumptions emerges most clearly from the above-mentioned memorandum which Einem wrote to the Chief of the General Staff. It could not be said, the War Minister admitted, that the Army was without 'weaknesses and gaps'. The infantry, especially, suffered from 'a not inconsiderable shortage of officers'. The only way to change this, Einem continued, would be 'to lower the standards regarding family background etc. of officer aspirants' But he would find it impossible to accept such a policy 'because we can then no longer prevent the acceptance, on an increased scale, of democratic and other elements which are not suited to the officer class'. For the same reason the Army as a whole could also not be enlarged. Any increase in the intake of conscripts, Einem concluded, which was not accompanied by a parallel growth in the number of officers would not 'strengthen, but weaken the Army'.

In other words, the Army leadership feared that an influx of 'undesirable' elements would destroy the homogeneity of the officer corps. But the War Ministry and the Military Cabinet preferred stagnation in the size of the Army to the acceptance of officers with 'inferior' background which any Army increases would have necessitated. What this implied becomes clear when one looks at the social composition of the officer corps. There can be little doubt that it was dominated, at least socially, by the aristocracy,[12] and if the total percentage of nobles in the officer corps had declined since the founding of the Empire in 1871, it was only because too few suitable aristocratic candidates were presenting themselves. This shortage forced the Army to take in sons from middle-class families; but it did so with great reluctance, fearing that too many of them would destroy the exclusive character of the officer corps and lead to the 'bourgeoisification' of the Army. If, on the other hand, the intake could be carefully controlled, the elaborate system of integrating the aspirants from non-aristocratic stock would continue to be operative. Being an officer was to remain a privilege, carrying high social prestige, but also guaranteeing absolute loyalty to the existing order and its supreme military commander, the monarch.

It was because it feared a dilution of these principles that the Army leadership became so worried about the homogeneity of the officer corps and the position of the nobility in it, whose dominance was secured not only by restrictive policies of selection, but also of promotion. Thus it was no secret that the Chief of the Military Cabinet, Count Dietrich von Hülsen-Haeseler, 'an ultra-conservative politically, had done much to improve promotion prospects in the Army, but only by favouring the nobility and the Guard regiments to an outrageous extent.'[13] The result of this practice was that 'the bourgeois elements in the Army became profoundly disillusioned' and that there was 'an alarming decline in the number of applicants'. In 1902, for example, no less than 56 Prussian infantry regiments failed to attract a single officer aspirant.[14] To make things worse, a cleavage developed between those who were posted in the provinces, many of them officers with a middle-class background, and aristocratic officers who were assigned to the prestigious Potsdam and Berlin regiments or to the General Staff. Unwilling to change its promotion policies, the best the Army leadership could think of was to raise the pay and the pensions of the middle ranks.[15] This, to Hülsen at least, seemed a much better way of spending additional funds than increasing the size of the Army. Indeed, Hülsen never regretted the decline in the number of officer aspirants. It provided him with an impeccable argument to freeze the size of the Army as a whole and thus to reduce the 'undesirable' elements also among the recruits and the non-commissioned officers. Who were these? Theoretically all able-bodied young men were eligible for military service. But it was obvious that the chances of selecting recruits increased if the expansion of the Army did not keep pace with Germany's growing population. However, to appreciate fully why a wider choice was welcome to the Army leadership and why universal military service presented problems, it is necessary first to examine the social and political structure of the Second Empire. For it cannot be emphasised too strongly that the constitutional order of pre-1914 Germany was far removed from a parliamentary democracy which, theoretically at least, enabled all Germans fully to participate in politics and to determine their own government and legislative processes.

The founding of the German Empire in 1871 had resulted, inter alia, in the introduction of a Constitution. Modelled on the North German Constitution of 1867, it had been drawn up not by a Constituent Assembly, but by Otto von Bismarck, the Prussian Prime Minister, who under the terms of the new document was appointed Reich Chancellor. There had been some input into the Bismarckian Constitution from various political parties which had come into existence well before 1871, but the document's basic structure had been laid down 'from above'. The Preamble reads rather differently from the beginning of, for example, the U.S. Constitution and thus made these origins clear enough:[16]

His Majesty, the King of Prussia in the name of the North German Federation, His Majesty the King of Bavaria, His Majesty the King of Württemberg, His Royal Highness the Grand Duke of Baden and His Royal Highness the Grand Duke

of Hesse and by Rhine, for those parts of the Grand Duchy of
Hesse which are south of the river Main, conclude an everlasting
Federation for the protection of the territory of the Federation
and the rights thereof, as well as to care for the welfare of the
German people. This Federation will bear the name 'German
Reich', and is to have the following Constitution.

According to the 78 Articles that made up this document, a Federal
Council (*Bundesrat*) was the official government of the new Reich. It
was composed of the princes of the German States. Prussia had
reserved a veto right against the other members by virtue of the
way voting privileges were allocated under Article 6. Being by far
the largest, most populous, and politically most influential State,
Prussia and its hereditary monarch also had de facto dominance of
the Federation.

The hand of the Prussian king in the Reich was further strengthened by a constitutional provision that he would always occupy the
position of German Kaiser. This position invested him with further
powers which his British counterpart had long lost to a representative assembly. Among these was his exclusive privilege to conduct
the foreign affairs of the Reich and—what was perhaps the most
crucial clause—to decide whether or not to declare war. Moreover,
he held the position of supreme commander of the armed forces. He
could nominate and dismiss the Reich Chancellor and shape the
composition of the rest of the Reich Government, even though
officially Reich ministers were state secretaries and hence under the
Chancellor's formal authority. Finally, the Kaiser could dissolve the
Reichstag, the new National Assembly, and call fresh elections, if he
saw fit. Given these truly impressive powers, complemented by
similar executive rights at the level of the Federal States (except, of
course, for the right to conduct Germany's foreign policy), it is clear
that any rights that the Reichstag might have, were already seriously
curtailed by the letter of the 1871 Constitution. Nevertheless, the
National Assembly was not completely unimportant. In fact, with
Article 20 providing for its 'universal and direct election with a secret
ballot', it looked, at least at first glance, like one of the most
democratic institutions in Europe, and in this respect the Reichstag
differed from the diets of the Federal States which were elected
through a variety of restricted suffrage systems, usually based on
property and/or tax qualifications.

However, it would be quite wrong to deduct from the democratic way in which the National Assembly was elected by all male citizens that it had powers comparable to those of the British Parliament or the American Congress. The Monarchy, not the Reichstag, was the power centre of Prusso-German Constitutionalism, as this very special political system came to be called. This meant that the deputies in Berlin were free to debate foreign and domestic issues, but they did not have the right to initiate legislation. Nor did they have the exclusive power to pass it. Proposed bills rather came to the Reichstag, with the approval of the Kaiser, from the Reich executive via the Federal Council of princes. They became law either if voted without change by a majority of the deputies or with whatever amendments the Kaiser and the Federal Council were prepared to accept. Compromise was therefore an essential element of smooth government under these peculiar constitutional procedures. A third alternative would be for the bill to be withdrawn again by the executive, which—it must be remembered—had not emerged, as the national government, from the majority of deputies, but was the unrepresentative creation of the monarch. However, if compromise or withdrawal proved impossible, executive and Reichstag found themselves on a collision course that might quickly escalate into a major political crisis similar to the Prussian Constitutional Conflict of 1862–6.[17] At that time, the king of Prussia, deadlocked with the diet over an Army finance bill he considered vital and advised by a number of hardline conservatives, toyed with the idea of a coup (*Staatsstreich*) designed to abolish the 1850 Constitution. The aim was to re-establish the pre-constitutional conditions that had existed under absolutism in order to forestall a parliamentarisation of the Prussian political system, the dreaded alternative, which appeared to be looming in the face of a progressive left-wing shift in the diet and the electorate. The crown, not the representative assembly, was to remain the power centre.

Bismarck, who was brought in as Minister President in 1862, ultimately found yet another solution to the crisis short of a *Staatsstreich*. He had the king dissolve the diet (as was his constitutional privilege), but not with a view to permanently destroying the Constitution. Instead he relied on a clause which, he argued, allowed him to implement the Army finance bill and to seek retroactive approval by the diet at a later date, once more favourable conditions for the constitutionally prescribed compromise had been created. In short, Bismarck invoked the so-called 'gap theory' and then worked for the subsequent indemnification of his unilateral action. After several years of confrontation and deadlock, during which the Minister President also used the full powers of the executive to harass and weaken the Liberal opposition, this opportunity finally arose in 1866, after the swift Prussian victory over the Austrian army. Bismarck called for fresh elections which, carried forward by a wave of patriotism and elation over the Army's success, produced a conservative majority eager to compromise with the government. It voted to condone the illegalities of the previous years and to provide finance for the military.

As will be seen, the experience and memory of the Prussian Constitutional Conflict and its eventual resolution remained very important to the way politics was practised in the Second Empire, the more so since the provisions governing the relationship between the executive and the Reichstag were basically the same as in Prussia, where three factors—the crown, the upper house dominated by the nobility, and the representative assembly—had to forge legislative compromises or face deadlock and crisis. In the Reich it was an unrepresentative government nominated by the Kaiser, a princely Federal Council and a popularly elected National Assembly that operated under the same sword of Damocles. But what made the situation so volatile in the long run was that the Kaiser felt able only to co-operate with Reichstag majorities that included the agrarian conservatives, whom he regarded as the only reliable support of his government, while these majorities were rapidly shrinking and by 1913 even impossible to bring about.[18] The Kaiser's resulting dilemma was a direct consequence of the growing strength of the Social Democrats who, helped by the universal suffrage, were the beneficiaries of a rapidly expanding industrial working class and its rising frustrations with a political system that evidently proved incapable of reforming itself and of responding to the aspirations of millions of voters.

It is not too difficult to visualise the consequences for the political process of these developments, which must be related to the country's unstoppable industrialisation and urbanisation and the concomitant social and economic change in the late nineteenth century. If conservative majorities prepared to support government bills that were usually designed to buttress the status quo could not be found and the calling of fresh elections did not generate such a majority either, the spectre of a violent *Staatsstreich* once again appeared on the horizon. Indeed, throughout the history of the German Reich, a coup was repeatedly contemplated as a way out of the constitutional dilemma and growing political impasse.[19] And if it was rejected, this was because the risk of finding the monarchy embroiled in a civil war was considered too great. Other solutions had to be found.[20] The era of conflict in the 1860s had been traumatic enough not just for the Liberals, but also for the crown and the political forces most loyal to it. This did not mean that there were no occasions when the threat of a *Staatsstreich* or rumours about one were deployed because they were deemed politically useful for that moment.[21] Bismarck used this device with some success on a few occasions as a way of bringing the deputies into line. After his fall, however, this strategy began to lose its intimidating effect. The deputies came to realise themselves that the government was unlikely to stage a coup and to unleash an era of domestic violence. Accordingly, the Kaiser and the Federal Council preferred to find parliamentary majorities through elaborate pre-arranged compromises and tit-for-tat deals with key parties of the Right and the centre. And when just before the war even the engineering of such compromises became virtually impossible following the resounding successes at the polls of the Social Democrats, who were by then the largest party in the Reichstag, the executive simply sat tight. The trouble was that no complex society like Wilhelmine Germany can be ruled for any length of time by inaction on the part of a government which under the Constitution had the exclusive right of initiating laws. Faced with paralysis and reluctant to resort to a *Staatsstreich*, an 1866-style war came to be seen once again as a way not only of settling accounts with hostile Great Powers and of breaking out of the country's international isolation, but also of overcoming domestic gridlock. Surely, a swift victory would have brought the Hohenzollern Monarchy the kind of conservative majorities in the Reichstag with which it would have been possible to revive conservative government.

However, the peculiarities of Prusso-German Constitutionalism and its legislative dilemmas come into full view only if the analysis of the formal constitutional power structure and its incongruities undertaken so far is complemented by an examination of the networks of informal power and influence that cannot be looked up in the constitutional document. We have to study what the Germans call the *Realverfassung*, as opposed to the formal written Constitution. When Bismarck founded the Reich, socio-economic and political power still lay predominantly in the hands of the Kaiser and his fellow princes and of the pre-industrial elites running the Army and the civilian bureaucracy at the local and national level. Most of its members then still came from the nobility, old as well as new, whose families continued to wield their traditional influence. However, with the expansion of trade and industry and with Central Europe unified under Prussian leadership, old power and old money came to be challenged by a prosperous middle class who demanded a voice in the political system. Such demands had, in the final analysis, also underlain the Prussian Constitutional Conflict with its perceived threat of parliamentarisation. Political parties had come into existence well before 1871 as vehicles for the expression of middle-class demands, and there was even an embryonic labour movement.[22] Initially these parties reflected the informality of a system in which politics was largely defined by aristocratic or bourgeois notables.

The growing organisation of society after 1871 soon also began to affect party politics. Parties solidified into permanent associations of interest articulation, with clearly identifiable ideological positions and programmes. This development was partly promoted by Bismarck's *Kulturkampf* against Catholicism in the 1870s which in turn rallied Catholic voters to the side of the Centre Party and secured for it a stronger representation in the Reichstag and the diets in the Federal States.[23] The growth of an industrial proletariat whose leaders saw an opportunity of gaining a voice in the Reichstag via the universal suffrage, also contributed to the slow decline of the politics of notables and the rise of permanent party 'machines'.[24] These developments forced the agrarian Conservatives into supplementing their traditional channels of informal access to the court and the government with formal organisations. Meanwhile the role of all parties expanded not only as lobbies in government and bureaucracy, but also as rallying and pressure points through the ballot box. This is where trouble loomed for the agrarian Conservatives, as industry expanded and Germany underwent a population explosion. More and more people, who often had voted for them under pressure, left the countryside in the hope of finding a better job in the burgeoning urban and industrial centres of the Reich. Worse for the Conservatives, electoral behaviour became more closely aligned with socio-economic class, except for most Catholic regions where voters of different social background continued to support the Centre Party. Beyond Catholicism, it thus became unthinkable for a non-Catholic industrial worker to vote for the Conservatives, just as a middle-class person would vote overwhelmingly for one of the liberal parties.

In trying to cope with these threats to their political existence on top of the economic challenge they faced from industry and commerce, the agrarians had some success in mobilising the peasantry. But with the demographic shift to the urban centres continuing, this pool of potential supporters was dwindling, while that of the Social Democrats increased. Neither the government's refusal to adjust constituency boundaries to take account of the huge migrations to the cities, nor the practice of local lords to march their land labourers to the polling station on election day and to tell them to vote Conservative was able to reverse the tide. In this way, industrialisation and urbanisation steadily eroded the traditional bastions of the agrarians, however much Bismarck, through legislation and other devices, tried to help maintain them. Economically they had to retreat before the growing strength of the commercial and industrial bourgeoisie, since there was simply no longer as much money to be made in agriculture as in the 1850s and 1860s. The agricultural depression of the 1870s and 1880s exacerbated the situation. However, the traditional political power and influence of the landowners did not immediately experience a corresponding erosion. No less significantly, they were able to exploit their strategic positions within the Prusso-German monarchy to wrest concessions from the government and in this way to prop up their declining economic fortunes. Privileges were thus prolonged; reforms and adjustments to the changing realities were blocked. And in most cases the Conservatives could be sure to have the Kaiser and his aides on their side, all of whom saw a vital interest in preserving, for as long as possible, agrarian influence against the bourgeoisie and even more so the menacing industrial working class. The government was thus reinforced in its traditional role of seeing itself as the protector of the most loyal supporters it was thought to have. More and more, the Prusso-

German political system became what Wilhelm Liebknecht, one of the first Social Democrat leaders, had called it in 1871: a 'princely insurance company against democracy', except that towards 1914 larger parts of the middle classes, worried about the rise of the socialists, also began to take out cover and to pay their premiums to this 'company'. They now became part of a political bloc-building process which has been noted before[25] and which, accompanied by pessimistic perceptions of the future, occurred, at first glance paradoxically, in a bustling and culturally diversifying society. However, it becomes all much less of a paradox, if, in focusing on the evolution of politics, one studies the peculiarities of the Prusso-German monarchy and its power structures.

Another reason why it was important to include this discussion is that it helps us to understand the background to the Reich's peculiar armaments policies, as described at the beginning of this chapter, and ultimately also of the decision by the Kaiser and his advisers to embark upon war in 1914. For even if a violent *Staatsstreich* 'from above' became less and less a realistic option to stabilise the monarchy, the Army had to remain firmly in the hands of the crown also in order to rebuff the challenge of liberalism and Social Democracy. Should it prove impossible to contain these challenges within the existing Constitution by 'peaceful' means, the Army would become the last bastion of the status quo; for it must not be forgotten that in this age armies had a dual function. They were instruments of defence against 'external enemies', but also had an internal role as a weapon against opponents of the monarchy. Although Army personnel policies, as described above, indicate that in the view of the leadership middle-class elements were also suspect and considered 'unreliable', the working class and its movement were seen as the real threat. The determination with which the Social Democrats resisted the anti-Socialist laws and the period of Bismarckian repression during the 1880s, gave rise to considerable concern after the lapse of these laws. Conservatives in the military and elsewhere were haunted by the nightmare of a socialist revolutionary uprising and of the 'subversive' elements that the universal service drew into the Army.

It is indicative of these fears soon after the lapse of the anti-Socialist laws in 1890 that the Prussian War Minister, with Bismarck's approval, sent a directive to the local military commanders reminding them of the measures available to the Army under the State of Siege Act of 1851. There are probably few laws which betray more clearly the basic character of the Prusso-German political system than this one. It provided for a complete take-over by the local military commanders not only in the case of an external emergency, but also in the case of internal disorders. What is more, it was left to them and their superiors to decide if and when the time for intervention had come. Once the state of siege had been proclaimed, the military had the power to abolish basic civil liberties. They were allowed to censor newspapers and to ban publications which, in their view, constituted a threat to public safety. They could, moreover, arrest alleged ring-leaders and other suspected 'trouble-makers'. In short, with the proclamation of the state of siege, the old Prussian *Militärstaat* re-emerged, squashing whatever constitutional rights there were in its way. As Frederick William IV of Prussia remarked in the margin of the revised Constitution of 1850: 'In periods of acute danger the king assumes the dictatorship.'[26] In other words, he claimed the right to invoke an extra-constitutional law of emergency in order to rescue the existing order from destruction. This law, to quote Hermann Bischof (1860), was to save the state not only from 'external dangers', but also from 'internal anarchy, civil wars, from the devastations of Communism and the boundless despotism of bestial passions'. It applied in particular 'when the uprising of the plebeian masses threatens to annihilate Church and State' and when 'the passions unleashed by it' lead to a disregard for 'inherited custom and the inviolability of private property'.[27]

There can be no doubt that the monarchy was aware of the far-reaching possibilities which the Act of 1851 offered. This emerges from the above-mentioned directive of the Prussian War Minister and the studies on 'fighting in insurgent towns' which the General Staff completed in 1907. Some local commanders even went so far as to make detailed preparations for an internal crisis, envisaging the arrest of Reichstag deputies and merciless operations against all signs of public resistance. And, on a minor scale, the Zabern Affair which will be discussed later can be regarded as an object lesson in Prussian military rule.[28] Indeed, the Army was the *rocher de bronce* of the Prusso-German political system. 'The Army', Philipp zu Eulenburg wrote in 1903, 'has become the castle-guard and has to do sentry-go because we have not even yet contrived to win the hearts of the people.'[29] Repeatedly the Kaiser pointed to the fact that it was 'the main support of My country, the main pillar of the Prussian throne'.[30] 'We shall know how to defend the authority of the State, the majesty of the Law, the security of the country and the stability of the Monarchy', Reich Chancellor Bülow hinted darkly in a speech in 1904.[31] In the final analysis the Army existed, as Alfred von Tirpitz observed in 1896, 'to suppress internal revolutions'.[32]

No one, of course, was more conscious of the Army's role in the preservation of the internal status quo than those against whom it was to be used: the Social Democrats. To them this institution represented the hard core of the monarchical class-state. It became the object of their most scathing criticism, and the irritated reaction of the government to it merely demonstrated how right they were. Bülow admitted openly that the left-wing attacks on the Army touched the 'most sensitive spot' of the Prusso-Germany monarchy.[33] This explains also why the Army leadership was always very concerned about the effect which the S.P.D.'s agitation might have on the public and in particular on the conscripts. The question was whether an Army could still be regarded as a reliable instrument of the crown against internal unrest if those against whom it was to be used served in its own ranks. As long as the majority of the recruits came from rural areas, the leadership could be fairly confident that the soldiers, politically uneducated and accustomed to the patriarchical conditions of the countryside, would obey orders when it came to shooting on demonstrators or insurgents. But in the meantime the industrialisation of Germany had led to large-scale population movements from the countryside to the cities. This meant that an increasing number of industrial workers were drafted into the Army who, if they did not whole-heartedly agree with it, were at least familiar with Social Democrat criticism of the monarchy and its military arm.

In these circumstances it was no longer certain that the troops could be relied upon when ordered to crush fellow-workers on the other side of the barricades. Was it not just as possible that they would fraternise with the strikers or rebels? The officer corps was terrified by the spectre of a mass army consisting of Social Democrats who would disobey orders and turn their weapons against the existing state. Worried about the revolution which was to be avoided at all costs, Einem, writing in December 1905, warned of 'the constantly rising number of socialist-infested elements' among the rank and file and the propaganda against the Army which undermined its effectiveness 'in war and peace'.[34] One way of solving the contradiction between conscription and the conservative function of the Army was to isolate the recruits from the rest of society. If the Army was to remain a 'sharp [and] reliable weapon in the hands of its kings',[35] its leadership had to take 'special care' to keep 'other influences' away from it.[36] The result was that the War Ministry soon launched a 'struggle against the spreading of the Social Democrat movement inside the Army'[37] which was to absorb a good deal of its energies until 1918. Nothing was left untried to preserve the reliability of the armed forces. Membership of the S.P.D. or one of its branches was prohibited; recruits were not allowed to subscribe to left-wing newspapers; 'soldiers' homes' were established to 'remove, where possible, N.C.O.s and soldiers from the danger of social intercourse with Social Democrats'.[38] To bar the entry of socialists as volunteers, the local commanders were instructed in 1894 to inform themselves about the political views of the applicant. Conversely, the Army sought to imbue the conscripts with monarchical ideas. Conservative newspapers were put on display in the 'soldiers' homes' and the recruits were subjected to 'lectures of patriotic content' in order 'to create and reinforce a sense of national identity'.[39]

As far as is known, few recruits were won over by this sort of indoctrination and the question of reliability continued to worry the Army leadership. It is this concern which offers a first key to an understanding of the Reich's peculiar armaments policy in the two decades before 1914. If the size of the Army was not increased, it was because the War Ministry and the Military Cabinet tried to preserve a homogeneous officer corps and because it was never quite certain how the soldiers would react to a repression of the Left. Possessing a small and coherent officer corps and a manageable number of conscripts was preferable to training all available men—at least as long as foreign political considerations remained less important than internal ones. For in Germany armaments policy directly reflected the tensions within the country's social and political structure. These tensions were caused by the growing rift between a quasi-absolutist monarchical system and a society which, under the impact of industrialisation, was undergoing a process of rapid change. The rift could have been bridged only if the conservative elites in charge of the system had permitted its gradual transformation into a parliamentary type of government. But it was precisely this development which they wanted to prevent, believing that they could survive only by rigidly adhering to, and defending, the existing state of affairs. Practically from the moment of its birth the German Empire was afflicted by a latent internal crisis, which Bismarck and his successors tried repeatedly to master. Although the first Reich Chancellor did not think it possible to stop industrialisation which in the last analysis was causing this dangerous dichotomy, he did hope to emasculate the liberal and socialist movements, the social products of the industrial revolution, which had begun to challenge the Prusso-German monarchy in its pre-industrial shape and form.

It is undeniable that Bismarck was at times astonishingly successful in his attempt to stabilise the existing order. And yet he was unable to silence the demand for greater political parti-cipation. On the contrary, the more Germany developed a modern industrial economy, the more menacing became the potential of those groups of the population which were profoundly dissatisfied with the class barriers and social injustices of the entire system. The working classes especially, raised their voices to advocate basic change. Shortly before his dismissal, Bismarck became convinced that the end of the road to a 'peaceful' solution of the consti-tutional dilemma had been reached and, quite consistently, he began to contemplate a *Staatsstreich*.[40] This time violence was avoided because the old Chancellor was dismissed. But tensions continued to build up under the surface of German society and it became clear that his policies had done no more than postpone a conflict. In view of this, any future crisis was likely to be all the more dangerous and hence required all the more powerful antidotes.

The pressure which was building up within German society was exposed for a brief moment when Bismarck's successor, Chancellor Leo von Caprivi, reduced agricultural tariffs and supported further industrial growth by negotiating favourable commercial treaties with Russia, Austria-Hungary, Italy and a number of smaller nations.[41] Caprivi's trade policy did no more than take account of the fact that industry had gradually overtaken the agricultural sector of the economy. With the period of retarded economic growth slowly coming to an end, it was now pushing beyond the frontiers of the Reich into the world market, and new economic energies were being unleashed. But the price which the country had to pay for this was the bitter resistance of the agrarians. It was directed not only against the economic consequence of reduced tariffs, but also, and perhaps even more importantly, against the social and domestic repercussions of industrialisation and the resulting demand for a colonial policy. This policy was rejected, because it merely furthered the growth of an industrial proletariat and undermined the basis of the existing order. The Secretary of the Treasury, Arthur von Posadowsky-Wehner, for example, complained in January 1896

> that Germany is becoming more and more an industrial state. Thereby that part of the population is strengthened upon which the crown cannot depend—the population of the great towns and industrial districts, whereas the agricultural population provided the real support of the monarchy. If things went on as at present, then the monarchy would either pass over to a republican system or, as in England, become a sort of sham monarchy.[42]

There is an even more illuminating statement by Otto von Völderndorff, a close friend of Reich Chancellor Prince Clodwig zu Hohenlohe-Schillingsfürst.[43] 'We must', he wrote in November 1897,

> keep away from international rivalries (*Welthändel*); we must confine ourselves to securing our country against the two neighbours [i.e. France and Russia]. Greatest parsimony (except for the Army) and a rebuilding of the Reich on the only reliable estate, the rural population. Our industry is not worth much anyway. It is in the hands of the Jews; its products are...'cheap and bad'; it is a seedbed of Socialism....Moreover, we are coming too late; all valuable overseas possessions are in the hands of others who hold on to them. We are also not wealthy enough to carry on the great power policies we have embarked upon in 1870.

This, as a matter of fact, had also been Bismarck's attitude towards imperialism. Accustomed to thinking in continental categories, he had for a long time resisted pressures to acquire colonies. 'There are', he said in 1879, 'no new lands to be discovered anymore; the planet has been circumnavigated and we are unable to find moneyed nations of in any way sizeable dimensions to which we could send our exports.'[44] If, in the 1880s, the Reich Chancellor nevertheless lent his support to the colonial enthusiasts, he did so in the hope of strengthening his domestic support. Imperialism was to him a useful device to influence Reichstag elections in a patriotic direction and to gain, in return for promises of government help in the colonial field, the support of certain commercial and industrial circles for his conservative policies at home.[45]

The reluctant, though typical, attitude of Bismarck to overseas expansion had implications for the future of the Reich which turned out to be most unfortunate: led by a pre-capitalist Junker class, Germany failed to gain colonial territories of any significance at a time when the 'scramble for Africa' was in full swing. Countries like England and France whose parliamentary systems responded more quickly and with less resistance to the demands of an expanding capitalist economy pocketed the lion's share of the blank areas on the map. By the beginning of the 1890s it was clear that the Reich had come too late almost everywhere. Soon some people came to believe that the failure to acquire a solid bloc of colonies spelt disaster for Germany's future. For without an empire of its own, German industry would always be dependent on other great powers. No difficulties were to be expected as long as these powers kept their own empires open to German goods. But Free Trade appeared to be on the decline and, like Germany, other nations had adopted protectionist policies. Even if they were not excluded outright, German industrialists and exporters began to fear that they might be subjected to discriminations. Some even thought in Social Darwinist terms and anticipated the formation of huge empires surrounded by high protective tariff walls, competing against one another for the domination of the globe with its markets and raw materials. This doctrine gained widespread popularity when, by the mid-1890s, the Reich was seized by an economic boom. There was an upsurge in production, inducing fresh optimism, but at the same time making the entrepreneurs painfully aware of their dependence on markets which were politically controlled by other nations. There were, it is true, no immediate difficulties. But what about the future, especially if German goods became more and more competitive?

Faced with this threat, various pressure groups now began to call on the state to protect what they considered to be the vital economic base of the Reich. They tended to agree with Professor Gustav Schmoller who wrote just before the turn of the century: 'In the last resort our merchants will have to be backed up by the *ultima ratio regum*. This is how the world is made.'[46] It was obvious, however, that the German Army was not suited for this task. All it could do was to exert a pressure on countries which were accessible by land. Against the then most important colonial power, Great Britain, on the other hand, nothing could be gained from threatening to mobilise the Army. And if war broke out, a British blockade would cut the jugular vein of industrialised Germany. As long as the Reich had only continental aspirations, a powerful Army had been sufficient. In the twentieth century, however, which everybody anticipated to be an era of colonial empire-building and *Weltpolitik*, navies would assume a crucial role. They alone would be able to protect overseas interests.

What is more: to many Germans a strong navy appeared to offer the means of making up for Bismarck's failure to acquire large colonies in the 1870s and 1880s. If used as a political lever against other nations, warships might even help the Reich to extract territorial concessions. The building of a navy was therefore seen as being both a safeguard for existing possessions and as a shortcut to obtaining new ones. However, these were the prospects for a more distant future. The important point is that, for the present, the Prusso-German political system was faced with latent domestic and foreign problems, to which must be added that, after the lapse of the Russo-German Reinsurance Treaty,* the Tsarist Empire had moved closer towards France, the Reich's enemy, and, in January 1894, had actually concluded a formal alliance with her. It depended on the successful solution of these manifold problems whether the monarchical system would survive in the twentieth century.

By the mid-1890s the dilemma of the monarchy had become so acute that the Kaiser and his advisers were growing increasingly

---

*This treaty had been secretly concluded by Bismarck in 1887. It contained, in essence, a promise of neutrality in war unless Russia attacked Germany's ally, Austria-Hungary, or Germany attacked France. It lapsed when it came up for renewal in 1890 and its main effect was to delay the Franco-Russian alliance.

nervous. In the Reichstag the parties of the centre and the Left made it more and more difficult for the government to get legislation passed. The agrarians were rabidly opposed to the Caprivi tariffs and were not prepared to accept anything short of a basic revision. Realising that he could not do without the support of the Conservatives, William II immediately considered the possibility of ruling without the Reichstag, i.e., of implementing the violent solution. Towards the mid-1890s he began to think of replacing Reich Chancellor Hohenlohe by Bernhard von Bülow whom he expected, mistakenly perhaps, to take a tough 'Prussian' line. 'Bülow', he confessed to his friend Philipp zu Eulenburg, 'shall be my Bismarck, and just as *he* and grandpa forged Germany together through external war [in the 1860s], we two will clean up the mess of parliamentarism and the party system at home.'[47] The aim was to strengthen the Emperor's position or to establish, as Gustav von Senden-Bibran, the Chief of the Naval Cabinet, put it, an *'absolute monarchy'*.[48] Senden, too, pleaded for 'a strong government which can manage without the Reichstag'.[49]

But the time was not yet ripe for such a policy of repression, and men like Hohenlohe and the Navy Secretary Friedrich von Hollmann strongly advised the Kaiser against it. Nevertheless the memories of the setbacks which he had suffered over the past years and which seemed to point to an increasing parliamentary influence caused him to worry about what looked like a gradual erosion of his powers by the Reichstag. To him it was quite inconceivable that he should ever come to occupy a constitutional position like that of Queen Victoria, his grandmother. William II found it impossible 'to get used to the thought that the [mere] existence of the Reichstag restricted his powers'.[50] Consequently, as Friedrich von Holstein put it, 'the idea of ruling without the Reichstag is constantly on his mind and is also being encouraged by one sector of his entourage'. Yet how could a dissolution of Parliament followed by a purge of the Opposition be engineered? Could a demand for an exorbitant naval building programme, which the deputies were bound to reject, perhaps be used to initiate a *Staatsstreich*? By the winter of 1896–7 these discussions had reached a point at which General Alfred von Waldersee felt encouraged to draft a plan for action.[51] 'In view of the tremendous growth of the Social Democrat movement,' he argued in a memorandum to the Kaiser, it appears to me to be inevitable that we are approaching the moment when the state's instruments of power must measure themselves with those of the working masses....But if the struggle is inevitable... the state cannot gain anything from postponing it....I feel that it is in the state's interest not to leave it to the Social Democrat leaders to decide when the great reckoning is to begin; rather it should do everything possible to force an early decision. For the moment the state is, with certainty, still strong enough to suppress any rising.

Heinrich von Goßler, the War Minister, was also attracted by this solution. Early in 1897, fear of the 'revolution' had reached such proportions in the Army circles that he decided to raise the subject in the Prussian State Ministry. The 'subversion' of the armed forces, Goßler explained to his colleagues on 26 January 1897, had become a source of serious concern.[52] It would be difficult to keep the Army intact. The meeting then entered into a discussion of the pros and cons of a new anti-Socialist law and its chances of ratification by the Reichstag. The result of these deliberations was negative, and against the advice of his ministers the Kaiser could not bring himself to take, as Waldersee put it, 'a really decisive step'.[53] Nor was it feasible to solve the problem of Army reliability by abolishing conscription and re-introducing 'small professional well-paid armies to be deployed in the first place against internal enemies'.[54] Although it is indicative of the critical predicament in which the monarchy found itself that such ideas were even ventilated, in the end the risks of a violent solution appeared to be too great.

Later, of course, court circles made Hohenlohe and his govern-ment responsible for this retreat. It was allegedly due to the latters' 'weak-kneed attitude, meanness and lack of interest' that the preliminary steps to a 'giant fleet programme'—such as 'Reichsstreich, revision of the Constitution etc.'—were not taken.[55] Nevertheless those who had been trying to persuade William II that 'he could initiate a great era of conflict, change the Reich Constitution, abolish universal suffrage and build innumerable cruisers'[56] had once again been effectively defeated. When he received Hohenlohe at the beginning of March 1897 for a discussion of the political situation, the Kaiser merely fought a rearguard action. Referring to his grandfather's conflict with the

Prussian Diet, William II said on this occasion that it would be his duty to create a navy which was strong enough to fulfil its mission. If the Reichstag refused to approve the money required for this purpose, 'he would go on building and send the bill to the Reichstag later. Public opinion would not bother him'.[57] When the Chancellor reminded him that, unlike in Prussia, he had only such powers in the Reich as the Constitution gave him, the Kaiser turned round completely and muttered that, apparently, he was powerless. But it was precisely this feeling of suffering a loss of power which again aroused his determination to defend his rights, if necessary by force. He did not care, he now informed the flabbergasted Chancellor, what rights the Constitution gave him. 'The democratic South German states would not trouble him. He had eighteen army corps and would be able to cope with the South Germans.'

These strong words indicate quite clearly that the monarch was all too conscious of the critical state in which the existing political order found itself in the late 1890s. Hohenlohe's refusal to support any of the wild schemes of the military, on the other hand, demonstrates that although he shared the fears of an erosion of monarchical support and the rise of the industrial proletariat,[58] he had not yet abandoned hope of a 'peaceful' solution to the constitutional dilemma. As early as September 1895 the Chancellor had outlined his own favourite strategy to the Baden Ambassador. This strategy, so the Ambassador reported to his government in Karlsruhe,[59] presupposed a 'calming of public opinion as regards the fears of a reactionary policy'. Once 'the population is again more fearful of the Social Democrats than of a reactionary policy which, it is thought, will lead to a curtailment of civil liberties', it would be possible to turn the tide. The government would then be able to obtain a conservative majority in Parliament and 'an improvement of the overall political situation would set in'.

This concept was finally adopted in the summer of 1897 and Hohenlohe's hand was strengthened by the appointment to key executive positions of Bülow, Tirpitz and Johannes von Miquel who were advocating a rallying (*Sammlung*) of all conservative forces in Germany against the Left. There were, it is true, differences of opinion between these three politicians about whether this front should include the Catholics. Still, the catalyst which was supposed to facilitate a *Sammlung* was the Navy which, only a few months earlier, the hard-liners around the Kaiser had been wanting to use as a pretext for a *Staatssreich*. For this reason it will be necessary to analyse, in the next chapter, the function which Tirpitz's battle fleet was to fulfil in Wilhelmine politics at the turn of the century. Without this analysis the origins of the First World War cannot be understood.

2 Tirpitz's Grand Design

In the previous chapter it has been indicated that the German Empire, far from being a stable country, was vexed by potentially very dangerous internal and external problems. There were some people who proposed to cut the Gordian knot by means of a preventive strike against the popular assembly and the 'revolutionary' working-class movement and then to concentrate upon achieving continental hegemony. Hohenlohe's 'peaceful' policy, they believed, would merely destroy the Prusso-German Constitutionalism as well as its agrarian beneficiaries. Other advisers of the Kaiser, like Bülow, warned against a violent solution. In this case, he wrote in December 1896, 'the dilemma which is now a more latent one between parliamentarism ... and a Bismarckian policy ... would come to the surface and the crown would have to choose.'[1] In Bülow's view there was a third path which he defined as 'royalism *sans phrase*', and Hohenlohe, in September 1895, had named its components: the popular fear that the clock would be put back by means of a *Staatsstreich* must be redirected against the Social Democrats. Fear of the Left, it was hoped, would persuade the middle classes to collaborate once again with the agrarians and thus secure conservative majorities in the Reichstag. The government would then find it easy to initiate legislation stabilising the existing order. Instead of creating difficulties, a majority of satisfied deputies would flock around a popular Kaiser who, unimpeded by party haggles and public pressures, could steer the Reich towards a better and safer future. A good deal has been written about William's 'Personal Rule'[2] and there can be little doubt that his strong desire to decide everything himself represented an important element in his character. Even more important was the fact that, with the monarchy beset by manifold problems, a focal point was needed. If the existing power structure was to be saved from the impact of a changing industrial society, William II had to be turned into a people's Kaiser whose charisma would help to reduce internal tensions and secure Germany's position as an admired and respected world power.

At the same time men like Bülow, Eulenburg or Tirpitz who recognised these necessities quite clearly were intelligent enough to realise that 'caesarism' alone would not suffice. What was needed in addition to the integrating power of the crown was a 'social interest aggregate', as G. W. F. Hallgarten has called it.[3] The question was how one could offer, in a sort of package-deal, economic and political benefits to those groups in German society which were destined to form the basis of the conservative *Sammlung*. How in particular could the bourgeoisie be induced to support an anti-Socialist status quo policy and how could the militants among the conservatives be persuaded to abandon the idea of a *Staatsstreich*? In order to understand the calculations of Hohenlohe, Bülow, Tirpitz and Miquel, it is now necessary to move into a sphere which is of crucial relevance to an understanding of the interaction between state and society. For while it is correct that it was the government which, by introducing the naval bills of 1898 and 1900, activated the integrating potential contained in the building of a large battle fleet, there existed at the same time strong forces in German society which demanded a naval armaments programme.

This demand sprang from the special interests of certain social groups which, although they were articulated politically, were in the final analysis rooted in the economic sphere. Lacking a secure position overseas, many industrialists began to view a strong navy as an insurance against future setbacks. Yet their desire for a navy did not only stem from the fear that, in the twentieth century, huge empires would emerge with high protective tariff walls around them to exclude foreign competition. The experience of the 'Great Depression' was another contributing factor. This period of retarded growth, lasting from the mid-1870s to the mid-1890s, had a traumatic effect on the German business community. Although it is important to emphasise that the industrialisation of the country did continue, the experience of an 'extended period of economic bad weather'[4] shook the confidence of the early 1870s. And as, in this pre-Keynesian age, one had not yet learned to manipulate the economy, much of the optimism of the so-called *Gründerzeit* disappeared. It is true that with the beginning of the renewed boom in 1895–6, the moaning about slack business, unfair competition and low profits gradually came to an end. But the business community continued to be haunted by the 'fear of a relapse'[5] similar to the one the economy had seen after the ephemeral recovery between 1879 and 1882. A close observer of this atmosphere of uncertainty was the director of the Imperial Shipyards at Kiel, Hunold von Ahlefeld. As late as 1899 he wrote to Tirpitz that 'the capitalists [were still lacking] courage'.[6] Would the Navy Secretary, he added, perhaps be able to help? In fact, Ahlefeld himself had discovered long ago how industry could be encouraged and given a special 'injection' against possible setbacks. He did not think it feasible to give direct 'confidential assurances' that the Navy would 'become much bigger still' and that the industrialists would 'get a share'. But he insisted quite bluntly that 'the iron ore tariffs must be reduced'. This was, of course, what industry had been demanding all along.[7]

A reinforcement of the Reich's naval armaments hence not only raised German hopes that, once the fleet was ready, the Reich would be strong enough to conduct a 'great overseas policy', which Tirpitz held out to the Kaiser in September 1899;[8] it also helped the business community to gain fresh confidence. The government was promising increased orders to the shipyards and their suppliers, and the temptation to accept the bait became irresistible when Tirpitz introduced a bill which provided for a long-term regular building tempo of a defined number of ships. Its regularity made the future more predictable and production more independent of the ups and downs of the international market. Understandably the industrialists were keen to give the expansion of the mid-1890s an extra boost. But they were also interested in implanting a stabilising element into a national economy which had just overcome a long period of retarded growth. 'Capitalists and industrialists', Ahlefeld concluded his report to Tirpitz, felt a 'strong desire to exploit every opportunity'. However, they would require encouragement and assistance.[9] Tirpitz was the man to provide both.

Above all the ship-building industry could hope to benefit directly from a naval programme which guaranteed regular orders. The volume of business could be expected to expand. At the same time, and more important perhaps, the shipyards found 'steady employment, independent of economic cycles and so desirable for them'.[10] Considerable advantages could, in the age of steel-plated ships, be expected to accrue to the iron industry, and indeed its output increased 'enormously' within the few years before the turn of the century. Other beneficiaries were the supply industries whose order books also could be expected to become fatter through stepped-up naval armaments. Shipping and the export trade were involved more indirectly, with Hamburg and Bremen occupying a leading position. By the late 1890s, the Hanseatic merchants had cast off the last remnants of their former Free Trade ideology and began to see the benefits of a state-financed fleet programme. Most of the chambers of commerce in the other parts of the Reich followed suit.[11] The bankers were also certain to be in favour of Tirpitz's plans, the more so as the government proposed to finance a certain proportion of the programme through loans.

The most striking evidence of how much German business circles appreciated naval legislation is contained in a letter which Tirpitz received from the president of the Navy League, an industry-financed propaganda organisation founded by Krupp.[12] 'Gentlemen of different party orientations', so Prince Otto zu Salm wrote in December 1901 when the ship-building industry was affected by an ephemeral recession, had approached him with regard to the present economic troubles and the consequent 're-dundancy of many thousands of workers'. They had asked him to agitate for an acceleration of the current building tempo. If such an acceleration were achieved, an improvement of the situation could be expected and the workers would again find employment. One of the most important reasons, however, which his business friends had mentioned was, Salm added, 'that the ordering of new warships would stimulate trade and industry. This, in turn, would push stock-market prices up, save many assets and bring about a consolidation of the economy.'

This brief sketch of the interconnection between German in-dustry and naval armaments ought to show that there was a poten-tially very powerful front of economic pressure groups which could be mobilised quickly. This front was reinforced by the educated bourgeoisie to whom 'ships were floating ... manifestations of German *Kultur*'.[13] In turning their eyes towards a glamorous naval policy they discovered a new sense of purpose and were distracted from the harsh realities of the domestic power structure in which the crucial decisions were taken by a small unrepresentative elite. In particular, many teachers and university professors were not only receptive to naval propaganda, but developed into ardent propagandists themselves They made innumerable speeches and gave their publications a scientific flavour by dressing their arguments up with impressive statistics. Invariably these arguments revolved around the future development of the Reich and there was widespread agreement with Bülow's dictum that the decisive question was whether Germany would become the 'hammer or the anvil' of world politics.[14] 'Unless Germany owns a strong fleet,' *Nauticus* proclaimed in 1900, 'she will be without colonies by the end of the twentieth century.'[15] And 'without colonial possessions she will suffocate in her small territory or else will be crushed by the great world powers...' Professor Ernst Francke even visualised the consequences of such a development. 'The rising number of hungry stomachs and empty hands,' he wrote, 'pushes us into industrialism which is accompanied, like a shadow, by a [growing] proletarian workers' movement.'[16] It was for this reason, Francke concluded, that Germany was 'forced to adopt a global economic policy and to move out into the world market'. This was no more than a variation on the idea propounded by Cecil Rhodes in 1895 that in order to avoid civil war, it was necessary to resort to imperialism.[17]

Men like Tirpitz and Bülow were among the first to recognise the usefulness of naval armaments as an instrument of distraction and social integration. As early as 1895 the later State Secretary of the Reich Navy Office had been demanding an expansion of the fleet. 'In my view', he wrote, 'Germany will, in the coming century, rapidly drop from her position as a great power unless we begin to develop our maritime interests energetically, systematically and without delay.'[18] He added that an expansion had become a necessity 'to no small degree also because the great patriotic task and the economic benefits to be derived from it will offer a strong palliative against educated and uneducated Social Democrats'. In other words, Tirpitz's naval policy was nothing less than an ambitious plan to stabilise the Prusso-German political system and to paralyse the pressure for change. The Navy was to act as a focus for divergent social forces which the government hoped to bribe into a conservative *Sammlung* against the 'Revolution'. Promises of a great political and economic future were made with the aim of maintaining big landowners, the military and the bureaucracy in their key positions within the power structure.

There is some evidence that the monarchy's social imperialism had even more far-reaching goals and aimed at winning over the working-class. The Navy was, as a friend of Tirpitz put it in August 1895, 'called upon to play a substantial role in the solution of the social question'.[19] And there was indeed an alternative to the repressive policy which Waldersee proposed: although genuine reforms and changes in the distribution of wealth and power were just as unthinkable to the 'moderates' as they were to the 'radicals' around the Army, the former nevertheless thought it possible to arouse the materialism of the workers. As Eulenburg said in 1900, a far-sighted policy was required if the masses were to be kept at bay.[20] It was not only that, in his view, they were lacking an ideal, but also that they were greedy and wanted to acquire material wealth. The implication of this was, of course, that the monarchy should do something to satisfy the emotional and material needs of the workers. Francke was more specific in this respect. He believed that naval armaments were particularly suited to 'elevate the masses to higher levels of moral conduct and wealth'.[21] To him 'the promotion of power' was identical with the 'promotion of prosperity'.[22] The working-classes, he stated, would benefit from the economic fruits of German world policy. On the other hand, they would be the ones to suffer most from Germany's exclusion from the world market.

Bülow was a particularly eager propagandist of this idea. Time and again he pointed to the favourable economic and political repercussions which he expected from the building of battleships. 'A courageous and generous policy which succeeds in maintaining a positive attitude towards our national life in its present shape and form', he said, would offer the best medicine against the Social Democrats.[23] What was required was a 'policy which mobilises the best patriotic forces ... a policy which appeals to the highest national emotions'. In his view, 'the patriotic aspect must be propagated relentlessly through [the creation of] national tasks so that the idea of nationality will never cease to move the political parties, to bind them together and to divide them'. Such a 'national policy under the firm leadership of a purposeful and gallant government', he thought, was particularly important to combat the S.P.D.:[24] 'We must unswervingly wrestle for the souls of our workers; [we] must try to regain the sympathies of the Social Democrat workers for the state and the monarchy [and] to keep the non-Socialist workers away from Social Democracy.' Then the S.P.D. would become more and more isolated and the Reich would move towards a new era of peace and unity. 'We do not wage our struggle against Social Democracy in order to hit the worker', he concluded, 'but in order to pull him away from the ensnarements of the Socialists and to accustom him to the monarchical order.'

It appears from such statements that William II and his advisers were hoping to rally not only the middle classes but also the industrial proletariat behind a successful naval and world policy. At least they expected to make 'moral and political conquests' among the working-classes and 'to convince a considerable proportion of those who had not yet gained a real understanding of their predicament of the equity of the conservative-monarchical system'.[25] The idea of a big navy, it was thought, had the power 'to revive the patriotism of the classes and to fill them again with loyalty to, and love for, the Emperor and the Reich'.[26] This would, in turn, lead to a strengthening of the right-wing parties in the Reichstag and enable the government to introduce conservative legislation. The danger of a genuine parliamentary system or even a collapse of the monarchy under the impact of a revolutionary upheaval would disappear once and for all.

There was yet another dimension to Bülow's and Tirpitz's naval programme which, like the concept of a conservative *Sammlung* had, if implemented, considerable implications for the maintenance of the autocratic power structure. As has already been mentioned, the Reich Constitution of 1871 had put the supreme command over the Navy into the hands of the Kaiser. It was his decision how the fleet was to be organised and used in time of peace and war. But because of the involvement of the Reichstag in the approval of the Budget, his powers with regard to the Navy were limited in one important and, as it turned out, ever more irritating respect: the deputies could influence the organisation and the size of the fleet by querying the need for the particular type or quantity of ships which the crown deemed essential. It is not surprising that the monarch, always worried about the growth of parliamentary interference, was keen to mend this hole in the fence of absolutist prerogatives. Some thirty years earlier the Army had demonstrated how this might be done. By fixing the peace-time strength of the Army at one per cent of the total population and by introducing a system of long-term appropriations, the budgetary rights of the Reichstag had been effectively reduced to a septennial (later quinquennial) review of such demands as the Army was asking for above the established level.[27] Otherwise the Kaiser was subject to no controls and was free to use the Army for internal and foreign political purposes as he thought fit.

This successful attempt to assert the rights of the crown over the popular assembly is interesting not only because it must be seen in connection with the repressive function of the Army, but also because it served as a model for the Navy. Just as the principle of the 'king's army'[28] had been maintained in the Bismarckian era, William II aspired to remove the threat of a 'parliamentary fleet'[29] when, in the 1890s, the Navy began to assume a crucial part in the struggle for the preservation of the monarchy. For the Navy, just as for the Army, 'the guiding hand of the monarch' was to be 'the starting point of its development and the *terminus ad quem* of its unfolding power'.[30] Once more the right of command (*Kommandogewalt*) became a decisive factor in the power struggle between the monarch and the popular assembly as representing that part of the supreme command 'which the crown wished to exert without the impediments of constitutional responsibility'.[31] It is only against the background of these considerations that we can understand why Tirpitz assured the Kaiser in February 1898 that it was one of his primary aims 'to eliminate the disturbing influence of the Reichstag on Your Majesty's plans concerning the development of the Navy'.[32]

The best way to reach this aim was to try and establish an 'Iron Budget', i.e. to persuade the Reichstag to ratify a bill which provided for a fixed number of warships as well as their automatic replacement after a certain period. Only if Tirpitz obtained a so-called *Marineaeternat* could he be certain that Parliament would be barred from exercising its budgetary powers. According to the Reich Constitution changes of laws could be effected only with the approval of the Prussian-dominated Bundesrat, a great difference from British constitutional practice of one parliament being free to revise the decisions of its predecessors. The decision hence rested ultimately with the monarch who was very unlikely to abrogate the rights which a *Marineaeternat* would give him.

The great constitutional significance of the navy bills which Tirpitz submitted in 1898 and 1900 emerges from a basic policy statement which he wrote in November 1905. Referring to the

Reichs-Militär-Gesetz of 1874 he argued:[33]

> Once the Reichstag has approved the money for the formation
> of new cadres, they are in practice eternalised (*äternisiert*). The
> Reichstag cannot, on its own initiative, reduce the number of
> cadres.... For the Navy, however, the ratification of a [fixed]
> organisational structure would, as such, not yet represent a gain.
> By refusing to replace ships, the Reichstag can in fact immob-
> ilise the Navy (*aufs Trockene setzen*). Only through a legally-
> binding clause fixing the replacement of ships can the Navy gain
> a similar stability as the Army possesses. As the earlier [pre-
> 1898] period has shown, the Reichstag disposed over great
> powers vis-à-vis the Reich government [because of its] annual
> appropriation of ships.

The idea of the *Marineaeternat* was to wrest these 'great powers'
from the popular assembly and to place the Navy under the exclusive control of the crown. This is why not only the German business
community, hoping for steady armament orders, but also the
Kaiser and his advisers were so eager to get the navy bills of 1898
and 1900 passed. For them the idea of fixing the tempo of ship-
building and of securing the automatic replacement of the naval
establishment after a certain number of years had a crucial political significance since they did not fail to recognise that 'in this
modern era the connection between politics and economics' had
become 'more intimate than it had been in the past'.[34] It was
obvious that 'all important economic interests' transformed themselves 'in one way or another' into political pressures.[35] Both domestic and foreign policy were becoming more and more sensitive
'to the oscillations and changes of a highly-developed industrial
economy'. But it was precisely this trend which aroused the concern
of the monarch. If 'the preponderance of economic interests' did
indeed turn all 'politics into economic and commercial politics' [36]
and if, in the twentieth century, diplomacy was 'basically nothing
but commercial policy',[37] then industry could be expected to
emerge as a rival to the crown and the conservative elites in charge
of the German State. It was generally accepted that the Navy
would be the most important instrument of future German
Weltpolitik so that one rightly anticipated attempts by the business
community to influence the shape and use of the fleet. Only the

establishment of an 'Iron Budget' could block such dangerous anti-monarchical influences. Just as the survival of Prusso-German Constitutionalism necessitated exclusive control over the Army as an instrument of internal repression, the power-political problems raised by the need to build up a Navy directed William II towards an *absolute monarchy*.[38] Without interference from the Reichstag, the presumed focus of economic pressure group activities, he wanted to 'decide how big the Navy' should be and to define the direction of Germany's 'great overseas policy'.[39] In promoting naval armaments, the Kaiser intended to facilitate Germany's rise to world power status within 'the shell of a conservative authoritarian state'. The Reichstag and the industrial pressure groups behind it were to be confined to the 'vestibule of political power'.[40] As Eugen Richter, the leader of the Progressives, observed in December 1897, the bill was directed 'against the popular assembly, against the nation as a whole'.[41]

It was of course unwise to reveal these more far-reaching calculations to the public. Tirpitz did not want to provide those who were opposed to the naval programme with further ammunition. This explains why he decided to proceed in stages, rather than to admit openly that he aspired to a *Marineaeternat*. One of his first steps was to put a clause into the 1898 navy bill to the effect that all battleships and heavy cruisers be replaced every 25 years. If he now succeeded in gradually filling the gap between 1898 and the beginning of the automatic replacement of ships in 1923 with a regular building programme of three ships per annum, the replacement clause would secure an 'Iron Budget'. If, moreover, the Reichstag could be persuaded to reduce the replacement period from 25 to 20 years, Tirpitz's *Marineaeternat* would be reached in 1918. The sources show that the Reich Navy Office proceeded in accordance with this strategy from 1898–9 onwards.[42] The Navy Law of 1898 fixed the replacement period and laid down the building of ships sufficient to maintain a tempo of three ships until 1900. This was the point when Tirpitz introduced a second bill which provided for a continuation of the *Dreiertempo* up to 1906. That year saw the beginning of the next stage extending the regular tempo to 1912 and bringing the Navy very close to the 'Iron Budget', the target pursued ever since the turn of the century.

Domestic considerations apart, there was yet another reason which induced Tirpitz to resort to a step-by-step expansion of the

Navy rather than to reveal his entire concept from the beginning. This reason was rooted in the growing awareness of Germany's potentially precarious foreign political position which has been discussed above and must be seen against the background of a mushrooming Social Darwinism of the 1890s. 'The "struggle for survival"' Ahlefeld wrote in February 1898,[43] 'is raging between individuals, provinces, parties, states. The latter are engaged in it either with the force of arms or with economic means; there is nothing we can do about this, except to join in. He who doesn't will perish.' However, this kind of crude Social Darwinism developed a somewhat more sophisticated variant which gained considerable popularity in naval and commercial circles and which might best be circumscribed as 'mahanism'. This term is derived from the name of the American naval officer Alfred T. Mahan whose books became international best-sellers in the late nineteenth century.[44] Mahan was, on the one hand, a famous strategist who influenced the thinking of a whole generation of naval officers all over the world; at the same time he formulated a 'philosophy of naval warfare'[45] which was bound to comfort all Germans who were worried about their country's failure to acquire a large colonial empire.

Using historical examples, Mahan provided them with arguments to show that, throughout human history, naval power had always been the decisive factor in international relations and that the hierarchy of nations had never been permanent. Especially the thesis that constant international competition led to the decline of some states and the rise of others found a warm reception in the Reich. It is certain that the naval officer corps as well as William II and his advisers were fascinated by Mahan's theories which they believed to apply not only to the past but also to the future. 'The globe is constantly being redistributed', Senden remarked in 1899, 'and it can be said that another redistribution has just begun.'[46] Bülow advanced the same argument in November 1899, but added, for tactical reasons perhaps, a cautious question mark:[47] 'It has been said, gentlemen, that in every century there will be a great conflict, a major liquidation [of some empire] in order to re-allocate influence, power and territorial possessions on the globe. Are we just about to witness another redistribution of the earth...?' He did not believe, he added, that the moment had quite come yet. Only a few weeks earlier, the Kaiser, speaking at a dinner in the City of Hamburg, had been urging his audience to survey the world and its rapidly changing face:[48] 'Old empires are fading away and new ones are about to be formed.' There was no doubt in William's and in Tirpitz's mind that Germany was to be counted among the 'young' nations of the world and that she could look forward to a future of wealth and prestige, provided she possessed a power-political instrument to make her claims heard. 'In view of the changes in the balance of power in Asia and America', Tirpitz explained in February 1899, 'the Navy will, in the coming century, become increasingly important for our defence policy, indeed for our entire foreign policy.'[49] The growing strength of the Reich, he wrote as early as 1879, 'evoked feelings among the civilised nations of Europe and particularly in England' which reminded him of 'Society's responses to a social climber'.[50] They were 'in this case perhaps mixed with a feeling of uncertainty as to what this new [power] factor might still hold in store for the future,' he added.

From then on England, the first sea power, began to occupy an ever more central place in Tirpitz's political calculations. To him the British Empire became the stumbling block which threatened the expansionist aspirations of the Germans. He knew that the collapse of other colonial empires (Portugal's, for example) would not bring Germany territorial gains as a matter of course. Ultimately any colonial acquisition was dependent on the tacit or explicit approval of the British. Germany's industrial power and wealth appeared to be built on sand as long as they were at liberty to block her drive into the world market. The building of a navy was seen to be a prerequisite to a future German world empire. Only when the fleet was complete could Germany, as Tirpitz put it in 1909, 'expect "fair play" from England'.[51] The notion of a power-political instrument to be used by the Reich against Britain implied, of course, the idea of a future conflict. Such a conflict seemed all the more likely because British trade and industry would become increasingly exposed to competition from the Germans. Economic rivalry would, many Germans believed, lead inevitably to a political confrontation.

Now it was quite obvious that the Reich stood to be defeated unless the Imperial Navy was strong enough to pose a genuine military threat to Britain. As long as this condition was not fulfilled, the Royal Navy could always be used to force Germany to abandon her political demands or to face defeat in a war. There was only one logical conclusion to be drawn from this: a German Navy which was to be employed as a political lever against England had to be capable of actually defeating the Royal Navy. Tirpitz was among the first to appreciate this. Although it was impossible to say this in public, there are a number of private statements by him and other naval officers to the effect that, if it came to a showdown, England could and would be beaten. Their calculations were based on the assumption that the British Empire was most vulnerable in the North Sea. In their view, the first task was, therefore, to build a battle fleet to be stationed right on England's doorstep. But how strong would this force have to be?[52]

Naval strategists of the time were agreed that a navy whose strength was two-thirds of its more powerful opponent had a chance of winning if it came to an all-out battle. It was this 2:3 ratio which was to play a crucial role in the planning for the step-by-step expansion of the Imperial Navy. If Tirpitz succeeded in building three capital ships per annum over a period of twenty years, from which date they would be replaced automatically, he would gain not only an 'Iron Budget', ridding the Navy of Reichstag interference, but also a battle-fleet of no less than 60 ships. Under the 2:3 ratio this meant that Britain would have to build and replace 90 ships over the same period. To this figure had to be added such ships as were needed for the protection of Britain's overseas interests. Her imperial commitments, so Tirpitz argued, would force her to keep these ships stationed abroad. The European balance of naval power would thus remain unaffected. The Reich Navy Office reckoned it to be possible for England to maintain a force of this size, but no more. Ninety ships plus a cruiser force for the protection of the Empire would stretch British resources to their limit so that from about 1918–20 onwards an equilibrium would develop in the North Sea.

Above all, it was thought, the British would be unable to find the manpower to man their battle-fleet. For, unlike Germany, they could not draw on an almost inexhaustible pool of conscripts. In short, England's professional navy would, according to German calculations at the turn of the century, restrict her ability to survive the kind of *quantitative* naval arms race on which Tirpitz embarked when he introduced his bills of 1898 and 1900.

In a file note of February 1900,[53] the Reich Navy Office maintained

that the enlargement of the British fleet cannot proceed at the same rate as ours because the size of their fleet requires a con-

siderably larger number of replacements. The [attached] table
... demonstrates that England ... will have to construct and replace a fleet almost three times as large as the German one as
envisaged by the Navy Law [of 1900] if she expects to have an
efficient fleet ... in 1920. The inferiority in tonnage which our
battle-fleet will continue to have vis-à-vis Britain's in 1920, shall
be compensated for by a particularly good training of our personnel and better tactical manoeuvrability of large battle formations
(*in der taktischen Schulung im grossen Verbande*).... The [enclosed]
figures ... on the tonnage which both battle-fleets keep in service
amount to a superiority of Germany. In view of the notorious
difficulties in England to recruit enough personnel, it is unlikely
that this favourable position will change.

Tirpitz was more direct, when he told the Kaiser in September
1899 that 'thanks to our geographical position, our system of military service, mobilisation, torpedo-boats, tactical training, systematic organisational structure [and] our uniform leadership by the
Monarch we shall no doubt have [a] good chance against England'.[54] But the bluntest were the comments which the State
Secretary scribbled into the margin of two secret documents.[55] The
Germans, he wrote, should concentrate all their 'efforts on the
creation of a battle-fleet against England which alone will give us a
maritime influence vis-à-vis England'. Furthermore 'the battle
must first have taken place and have been won before one can
think of exploiting it'. It would be impossible, in a war with
England, to keep the sea lanes to the Atlantic open 'without a
victorious battle'. '"Victorious" is the decisive word. Hence let us
concentrate our resources on this victory.' It would not make sense
to cut up 'the bear skin before the bear has been killed'.

These statements seem to indicate that Tirpitz did, in fact, hope
to build a fleet which, once completed, would pose a genuine military challenge to Britain. However, it does not follow from this that
the Imperial Navy actually intended to launch an *offensive* against
the British forces in the North Sea. There was an important
qualification attached to the 2:3 ratio which Germany was planning
to reach: only in a battle in which the numerically *stronger* navy
acted offensively did the inferior opponent gain a chance of victory.
Tirpitz's idea of constructing a navy against England was therefore
not overtly aggressive in a military sense. It was to be used as a

military lever only if the Royal Navy tried to destroy it. Their ability to respond quickly would, in this case, have gained the Germans an opportunity of defeating the Royal Navy and thereby to shift the balance of power at one stroke. But deep down in his heart Tirpitz preferred to rely on the deterrent value of his battle-fleet rather than to become involved in a risky war with Great Britain. Yet it would be wrong to deduce from this preference that the Imperial Navy was designed to be no more than a deterrent in the narrow sense of the word; in fact, it was to be used for a policy of diplomatic bullying. The sheer size of a fleet of 60 battle ships in the North Sea, Tirpitz hoped, would force Britain to concede "'fair play'" to Germany. Then, perhaps, even a partnership based on equality would be possible, with the Reich's new ally tolerating or even actively supporting German colonial aspirations. Obviously this was a very dangerous strategy which was bound to have far-reaching consequences on the shape of German policy.

The historian Ludwig Dehio was among the first to analyse in some detail the true nature of Wilhelmine imperialism.[56] Germany, he wrote, was hoping to push her way into a 'global balance of power system' and was speculating on achieving equal partnership in a condominium of world powers. However much the German government, Dehio continues, might profess its 'peaceful' intentions, objectively Wilhelmine foreign policy and 'its centrepiece, the naval programme', pursued the offensive aim of displacing other powers, and England in particular. The Reich started a Cold War and a dangerous arms race. Tirpitz accepted the risk of a shooting war, always hoping that the Reich could realise its ambitious aims without one. 'For the opponent the risk of war was to be made so costly that he would not dare to turn the cold war which had been forced upon him into a hot one and would rather abandon his position peacefully,' Dehio concluded.

Any account of German naval armaments policy before the First World War which puts Tirpitz's programme merely into a domestic context is thus bound to be incomplete. It is true that the navy bills of 1898 and 1900 were intended to serve as a basis for a conservative *Sammlung* against the forces of change. Moreover, by establishing a *Marineaeternat*, it was hoped to liberate the crown from all parliamentary restrictions. But in the emerging era of heightened commercial and maritime rivalries the Imperial Navy was supposed to fulfil yet another mission. Presuming that it would retain its deterrent effect on the Royal Navy and would not have to be employed in war, Tirpitz wanted to bully the other powers into recognising Germany's need for a colonial empire. 'If one disregards the military position', he informed the Kaiser in September 1899, 'which is by no means hopeless, England will [after the completion of the German fleet] have lost, for general political reasons and because she will view the situation from the purely sober standpoint of a businessman, all inclination to attack us.'[57] Instead, 'she will concede to Your Majesty such a measure of maritime influence which will make it possible for Your Majesty to conduct a great overseas policy'.

It was at this point that the domestic and the foreign political aims of the naval programme merged into a single all-embracing consideration : the stabilisation of the Prusso-German political system. The more direct and immediate consolidation was to come from the unifying effect of the naval armaments programme at home. More indirect and more long-range were the stabilising benefits which the government hoped to derive from the Navy as an instrument of foreign policy and German imperialism in the twentieth century. But it is not difficult to see that, in the final analysis, the result would be the same. It is in this sense that the decision to build a large battle-fleet represented an 'inner-political crisis strategy'[58] designed to contribute to the survival of the Prusso-German political system : with the help of the Navy, the monarchy wanted to overthrow the *status quo* internationally in order to preserve it at home.

This was also the promise which could be held out to the agrarians, without whose support the navy laws could not have been passed. Their basic attitude towards *Weltpolitik* was one of hostility because they realised that the new impulses it gave to the industrialisation of Germany tended to undermine their privileged position. As Eulenburg said in June 1896, there existed such a dichotomy between the monarchical principle and 'the pre-dominance of liberal-progressive or liberal-Catholic (Centre Party) ideas that this is one of the main reasons for the apparent unsteadiness [of the political system] which everybody in Germany deplores'.[59] It was this unhealthy state of affairs which Tirpitz's plan was supposed to resolve. The expansion of the Reich, to be executed under the guns of a powerful Navy, would, it was hoped, strengthen the position of the crown and would, at the same time, support the economic existence of the agrarian elites. William's 'great overseas policy' was to help maintain their tax and other privileges. This, together with the assurance that the industrialisation of the country would take place within the framework of an autocratic monarchy, was expected to persuade them that acquiescence in economic change was preferable to blind opposition.

There were also immediate advantages to be gained by the agrarians which they owed to their strategic position both in Parliament and in the bureaucracy. As we have seen, the big landowners had been struggling against the Caprivi tariffs ever since their introduction in 1892. The proposed expansion of the Navy now presented the landed aristocracy with an opportunity to demand a return to pre-Caprivi levels of agricultural tariffs. They threatened to vote against 'the ugly and horrible fleet'[60] unless the bourgeois parties and the government complied. And they got their way. In the end, the Reich Treasury issued a statement to the effect that higher tariffs would be reintroduced in due course.[61] There is hence a link between the naval legislation of 1898 and 1900 and the increases in agricultural tariffs which the Reichstag finally sanctioned against the furious opposition of the Left in 1902. The alliance between the conservatives and the middle classes, based upon an economic as well as a political understanding, was complete; the subsequent history of the Wilhelmine Empire cannot be understood without it.

For although this alliance constituted an impressive feat, it bode ill for the future of Germany. Born from the fear of parliamentarisation, it was not the beginning of a progressive policy 'which, in a statesmanlike fashion, tried to come to grips with the inevitability of the industrialisation of the Reich and to solve the problems of the feeding and of the political participation of the industrial masses'.[62] Instead it merely 'stabilised' and balanced anew a social structure which had been legalised by Bismarck's founding of the Reich and which, in the meantime, had begun to crumble.' As a result, 'the whole problem of the social basis on which German foreign policy would be conducted' remained unresolved.[63] The question was not only how a modern industrial economy with its rapidly changing social structure could be reconciled with a monarchical political structure, but also how the Prusso-German *Militärstaat*, whose elites were steeped in a feudal value system, could evolve a calculating, 'businesslike' foreign policy. Was there not always the danger that the policy of integration and distraction would not work and that the internal tensions of German society would lead to an explosion? And, equally, was there not always the possibility that the few men who held in their hands the decision to go to war would, in an international crisis, find it difficult to arrive at a rational and sober assessment of the situation and thus to preserve peace?

The domestic alliance of 1898–1902 almost guaranteed that such crises would come : the decision to build a fleet against the first sea power was bound to alienate the British, whereas the agricultural tariffs offended Russia whose main export commodity to Germany was grain. France had been the Reich's irreconcilable enemy ever since the defeat of 1870–1. It was therefore not difficult to foresee considerable tensions accumulating on the western and eastern frontiers of the monarchy which might well lead to an alignment of these three great powers. The Kaiser's *Weltpolitik* and *Sammlungspolitik* had antagonised them, or at least made them suspicious of the aims of the unstable and restless nation in the centre of Europe. The seeds for the subsequent 'encirclement' of Germany by England, France and Russia were sown when the country's political leaders decided to solve the problems of the Prusso-German constitutional order, i.e. their own problems, with the help of an ambitious and long-range naval armaments programme.

3 The Anglo-German Naval Arms Race

The inauguration of Tirpitz's naval and world policy inspired the leadership of the Reich with new hope. It appeared to offer a panacea for all of Germany's domestic and foreign political problems, and it was a policy which looked far ahead into the future. The Kaiser and his advisers initiated a programme which would bear fruit in the 1920s and 1930s. But it was precisely the long time-span over which their naval armaments policy was conceived which spelled grave dangers for the Reich's future. For the time being at least, these dangers lay less in the field of domestic politics. As long as the Navy retained its catalytic function and united agrarians and middle classes, the left-wing opponents and victims of the alliance could do no more than to voice their disgust. The foreign powers against whom the expansionist aims of the Empire were directed were in a much better position to organise resistance than the Social Democrats at home. There could be little doubt that Britain in particular would feel challenged by Tirpitz's plans and would react sharply to his proposed destruction of the existing balance of power.

Inevitably, the British reaction would in turn influence the domestic development of the Reich. The more persistently England tried to upset the aspirations of Germany's armaments policy, the more violent the criticism of this policy would become inside Germany. Instead of acting as an integrating focus, the Navy would turn into a divisive force. The cracks which had merely been papered over by the *Sammlung* threatened to re-emerge and bring the Prusso-German political system close to disaster and paralysis. Although these alternatives continued to loom on the horizon, the immediate fear of revolution and the pessimism of the mid-1890s began to subside after the turn of the century. Tirpitz's naval armaments, it was felt, would facilitate Germany's breakthrough to world power status and secure the survival of the monarchy. And while everything seemed to be going smoothly, the vistas of a great future time and again exerted their intoxicating effect on William II. 'Just as My Grandfather reorganised his Army', the Kaiser proclaimed on the first day of the new century, 'I shall unswervingly complete the task of reorganising My Navy so that ... it shall be in a position, internationally, to win for the German Reich that place which we have yet to achieve.'[1] Both the Army and the Navy, he continued, would help him 'to realise the dictum of Frederik William I: if one wants to participate in the decisions of this world, "the pen will be useless unless it is supported by the sword".'

In the first years after the turn of the century it was indeed easy to be optimistic and to overlook that the crisis of the 1890s continued to smoulder. Following the Fashoda incident* France and England were on very bad terms and tensions existed also between Russia and Britain. There was even some justification for assuming that rivalry between those three powers would grow. Although England was undoubtedly the leading world power, many Germans believed that she had overstretched her commitments and dissipated her resources. Moreover it was a popular view that Britain was an ageing power whose sprawling empire and the resulting colonial conflicts would push her increasingly into complete isolation. Surrounded by enemies, she would be unable to maintain her strength in the long run. One element in this low estimate of British capabilities was the aversion of the conservative groups to parliamentarism. London to them was a swamp of corruption dominated by degenerate aristocrats and greedy businessmen. They thanked God that Germany did not have a parliamentary government and was led by a monarch who knew where the country should be going. They were convinced that ultimately this young German Empire, which was bursting with energy, would overtake the British. All the Germans had to do was to wait patiently until History had run its course and until they possessed a navy strong enough to be used as a political lever against other nations.

Waiting for the fruits to ripen also implied that the Reich had to keep aloof from the colonial squabbles of other powers and that the

*In the autumn of 1898, French troops which had moved across Africa from Brazzaville encountered British contingents under General Horatio Kitchener at Fashoda, a small town on the Upper Nile. The French claimed the region for themselves to which the British objected fearing that France might interfere with the irrigation of the British-dominated Lower Nile. London took a tough line and made preparations for war whereupon Paris abandoned its claims and accepted a severe diplomatic defeat.

anti-British aims of Tirpitz's naval programme would have to be kept secret. As long as the fleet had not yet attained its intended deterrent value, Germany's international position would be precarious. German diplomacy was therefore faced with the dual task of keeping Britain, France and Russia divided and of avoiding, at the same time, formal alliance commitments which might, directly or indirectly, involve the Reich in conflicts with Britain. 'We must operate so carefully,' Bülow wrote in July 1899, 'like a caterpillar before it has grown into a butterfly.'[2] William II had to try and maintain friendly relations with all powers without committing himself to one of them. The only exceptions were the existing alliances with Austria–Hungary and Italy. Otherwise Germany had to maintain a 'free hand'[3] and to adopt a wait-and-see attitude.[4] Dynastic connections proved to be an invaluable asset in the German attempt to please everyone. The Kaiser's frequent exchanges of hospitality with the House of Windsor and the Romanovs betrayed a superficial cordiality which appeared to make treaty relations unnecessary. It is thus a somewhat futile exercise to examine the alliance opportunities which the Reich government is said to have missed in the early years of this century. Other obstacles apart, the British Foreign Secretary's famous offer of 1901 for close and formal co-operation was bound to fail simply because neither the Kaiser nor Bülow desired an alliance with Britain.[5]

The trouble was that Germany's 'free hand' policy contained a number of serious miscalculations. Obviously it was most dangerous to assume that England could never overcome her isolation, and yet to Bülow an Anglo-French *rapprochement* was unthinkable. At the end of November 1900 he stated firmly that it 'would be against the logic of politics' if Britain were to move closer to the Franco-Russian bloc, at any rate 'in the near future'.[6] When, in the spring of 1903, Hermann von Eckardstein reported from London that such a combination could no longer be ruled out completely, the Reich Chancellor refused to believe him.[7] As none of the other diplomatic missions were able to confirm Eckardstein's assertion and as the Ambassador to London himself advised his government to remain calm and wait, Bülow happily reassured the Kaiser on 20 May 1903 that prospects of changes in the existing alliance pattern were negligible.[8] As late as January 1904, Friedrich von Holstein, the grey eminence of the German Foreign Office, recommended that Germany should take a reserved attitude towards Russian feelers for closer cooperation because Great Britain would react angrily;[9] and then, three months later, the Entente Cordiale was formed. England and France had settled their colonial disputes, and there was now a real danger that they might also co-ordinate their policies on the European continent.

The forming of the Entente Cordiale threw the German Foreign Office into a mood of 'deep depression' and was widely considered to be 'one of the worst defeats for German policy' since the conclusion of the Franco-Russian Alliance.[10] Holstein now would not even exclude the emergence of a Triple Entente.[11] It was for this reason that he became convinced the Reich government must try to obtain an alliance with Russia.[12] Bülow agreed that 'the situation was no longer intact',[13] and shortly after the Dogger Bank Incident* which provoked a serious crisis of Anglo-Russian relations,[14] he even went so far as to draft a treaty of alliance with Russia. But these hectic plans came to nothing. Two years later, little, if anything, was left of the once seemingly so favourable position of the Reich. Friendly relations with England or Russia could hardly be said to exist. The clash between France and Germany following the Kaiser's visit to Tangiers on 31 March 1905 and his declaration of support for the Moroccans only strengthened the Entente Cordiale.[15] Although the British government acceded to the international conference proposed by Bülow, they openly backed the French, thus flouting Germany's intention of humiliating France and of exposing the uselessness of the Entente. And sixteen months after the end of the Morocco Conference, in August 1907, Britain at last obtained what she had been working for ever since 1903: a settlement of her disputes with Russia in Central Asia. The Triple Entente had become a reality and it was now Germany, not Britain, which found herself in an isolated position. The diplomatic premises of Tirpitz's naval plan had been severely shaken.

There can be little doubt that this development was, in the first place, due to the activities of British diplomacy. Nevertheless the search for the deeper causes of the new departure in Britain's foreign policy must start in Central Europe. In fact, the Empire

---

*En route to the Far East at the time of the Russo-Japanese War, the Russian Baltic Fleet, on 21 October 1904, mistook British trawlers, fishing off the Dogger Bank, for Japanese torpedo boats and opened fire, sinking one of them. The incident provoked great indignation in Britain and almost led to war between the two countries.

merely responded to a German policy which amounted to nothing less than a deliberate, though veiled challenge of its dominant position in the world. On the German side, to be sure, this causal chain was quickly forgotten. Yet what the Reich government henceforth perceived as the 'encirclement' of Germany is more aptly described as a reactive policy of containment; in effect Germany had 'circled herself out' of the great power concert.[16] To put it differently: although the Kaiser and his advisers had pinned great hopes on their naval armaments policy and had always played down the risks of Tirpitz's grand design, these risks were now for the first time beginning to show up their true proportions. Tirpitz's detailed calculations notwithstanding, it was by no means certain and probably even highly unlikely that he would be able to win his Cold War against England. But at least this leads us away from the diplomatic actions and reactions of the European powers to the underlying power conflict between England, the *status quo* power, and the 'unsatiated' German Empire which, by embarking upon a naval and world policy, had begun to challenge the existing international system. Although Anglo-German rivalry must be seen within the broader context of the phenomenon of Western imperialism, it assumed its explosive character as a result of the different bases from which the two countries set out. Whereas Britain could call a huge colonial empire her own, the Germans were hoping to gain a permanent place among the first-rank world powers. This difference also accounts for the different functions which the Royal and the Imperial Navies had within the framework of their country's foreign policy. England maintained her large fleet to defend existing interests; Germany, on the other hand, wanted to use her Navy as a political lever against British hegemony.

The fact that Tirpitz thought this lever could be applied most effectively in the North Sea directed British policy almost automatically back to the European continent.[17] Because the Reich immediately threatened the European balance of power, England ultimately had no other choice but to settle her colonial disputes so that her back would be free for the organisation of an anti-German alliance system. However, to contain Germany by diplomatic means in conjunction with Russia and France was in itself hardly an adequate response to the German challenge. After all, this challenge did not take the shape of a diplomatic strategy, but was based on a long-term naval armaments programme. In view of this the British Foreign Office could offer an indispensable political support by creating ententes which shifted the military balance of power in England's favour. But no amount of diplomacy could compensate for the fact that the balance depended ultimately on the outcome of the arms race which the Reich had initiated in 1898. Britain had to reply in kind unless she wanted to abdicate her leading role and to let the Germans have their way.

As early as January 1898, soon after the publication of Tirpitz's First Navy Law, voices could be heard in London arguing that the German programme, if executed, would 'altogether upset the present balance of naval power'.[18] The Admiralty reacted promptly. The Bill of 1898 had hardly been ratified when the First Lord gave assurances 'that if any great naval power took action as regards ship-building which would materially disturb the existing balance of naval power, this country would have to reconsider its naval programme'.[19] From this time onwards, Germany figured prominently in Britain's naval armaments policy,[20] and after the turn of the century, following the passage of the Second Navy Law, the Reich became the focus of the Admiralty's attention.[21] 'The Germans' aim', Sir Francis Bertie suspected, 'is to push us into the water and steal our clothes.'[22]

The counter-measures which were now taken were designed to increase the efficiency and the preparedness of the Royal Navy for war. At the same time the Admiralty tried to uphold Britain's numerical superiority, and by the spring of 1904 it was obvious that it was above all the German challenge which was stirring it into action. The distribution of the fleet was changed in favour of a greater concentration in the European waters. Steps were taken to improve the training of personnel as well as battle tactics. Army and Navy began to discuss the co-ordination of their operations, and it is no accident that for the first time detailed plans were drawn up for operations against the Reich.[23] These reforms were greatly aided by the promotion of Sir John Fisher to the position of First Sea Lord on 21 October 1904. Fisher, full of creative energy and ruthless determination, was to become Tirpitz's great opponent at a moment when the Anglo-German arms race entered into a crucial phase. It was due to his activities that the Royal Navy was able to overcome its personnel shortages on which the Reich Navy Office had based the German calculations in 1900. Moreover he introduced further changes in the distribution of the fleet. When in

March 1905 the German Naval Attaché in London forwarded a booklet on British recruitment methods to Berlin, he added that, in his view, the publication was 'another proof of how sensibly and with how much common sense the Admiralty proceeds in all its policies at the moment'.[24]

Fisher's most important decision, however, concerned the size of big capital ships. Largely on his initiative, the Royal Navy laid down the *Dreadnought,* which was considerably more powerful than any of the German battleships. Although it is not certain how far Fisher was influenced in his decision by what he saw happening in Germany and how far he merely anticipated an inevitable international development, the importance of this measure for the future course of the Anglo-German arms race can hardly be overestimated.[25] So far this arms race had been a quantitative one. Tirpitz believed that he could catch up with Britain and reduce her numerical superiority sufficiently to obtain a political lever against her. But by building the *Dreadnought,* Fisher had added to the Anglo-German arms race a *qualitative* dimension which caught Tirpitz unprepared. The crucial question was now whether Tirpitz would follow suit. If he introduced another numerical increase in 1906 which he had been preparing for since the turn of the century and simultaneously joined the qualitative arms race, the anti-British ambitions of the Imperial Navy would be clear to everyone. In this case London could only try to undermine Germany's aims by engaging her in a fully-fledged quantitative *and* qualitative arms race and by strengthening links with France and Russia; the Reich, on the other hand, was faced with the choice of defying England's counter-measures and of holding out at the risk of overstretching her economic, social and political resources. Alternatively Germany had the choice of curtailing her far-reaching plans in order to reach an understanding with Britain. The Kaiser and his advisers had come to the cross-roads when they discussed the country's future armaments policy in the autumn of 1905.

As we know, the programme of the turn of the century was not abandoned. In 1906, Tirpitz put another naval bill before the Reichstag which provided for further increases in the basic number of capital ships and secured a continuation of the *Dreiertempo* until 1912. Furthermore the deputies were asked to approve considerable rises in construction costs—which was a more diplomatic way of saying that the Navy was planning to emulate Fisher and build

German dreadnoughts.[26] But in order to appreciate the significance of this step fully, we shall have to examine again the peculiar relationship between Germany's armaments policy and her diplomacy in this period. As will be remembered, Tirpitz's programme was intended to solve the manifold problems of the Wilhelmine Empire and had assumed a strategic place in government planning, including foreign policy. Diplomacy's main task was to shield and veil the plans by which William II hoped to establish the Reich as a world power with all the advantages this was supposed to bring for the stability of the Prusso-German political system. In fact, Bülow's 'free hand' policy, however inconsistent it may occasionally appear to have been, can only be understood in conjunction with Tirpitz's conviction that the Reich needed peace and quiet during the twenty years in which the Navy would be built up to its projected strength. Tirpitz's attitude emerges most clearly from a letter which he wrote to the German Foreign Office on 1 November 1904 and in which he voiced his opposition to Bülow's and Holstein's demand for an alliance with Russia.[27] Such an alliance, he said, would be of little strategic or political value to Germany. It would be better to wait and not to depart from the foreign policy maxims of the previous years. Basically, so the State Secretary summed up his argument, 'our most important political task is to gain time and to expand our Navy'.

This letter is interesting for two reasons. One is that it contains a reminder of the essentials of Wilhelmine policy which Bülow and Holstein, intensely worried by the Entente Cordiale and the Dogger Bank Incident, appeared to be losing track of. Tirpitz therefore did not feel any regrets when Bülow's attempts to conclude a Russo-German alliance ended in failure. German diplomacy continued to be subordinated to armaments policy which limited its scope. This state of affairs was bad enough. But to make things worse, the impact of German armaments on the other powers had meanwhile turned Bülow's policy of voluntary abstention into a policy of enforced isolation and as a result Tirpitz's armaments began to exert an even greater weight on the decisions of the Foreign Office than before. The effect of this peculiar dependence of diplomacy on armaments was that German foreign policy became increasingly militarised.

An early deployment in battle of the arms which the Reich had been producing all these years appeared to be quite logical, especially to those who were professionally concerned with the preparation of war. And in times of crisis, the idea of escaping a diplomatic setback by declaring war became particularly tempting. Although Tirpitz, as his letter of November 1904 shows, was opposed to such a solution and preferred to keep peace until the deterrent effect of the Navy would come into operation, he could not prevent others from propounding their 'militaristic' views.[28] We have noted the existence of such 'radicals' or 'militarists' in the German leadership before. They had kept in the background as long as the Kaiser's *Weltpolitik* appeared to be successful. But now, with the dangers of the 'peaceful' solution becoming clear, they began to raise their voice again.

The Dogger Bank Incident and its aftermath is a good case in point. In connection with this incident, the Kaiser ordered that a commission be constituted under the chairmanship of August von Heeringen. It was to make proposals on how 'our readiness for war might be increased'. Heeringen began his final report of December 1904 by stating that 'the expansion of our fleet has so far been based on the assumption that peace could be preserved until its completion'.[29] Yet since the outbreak of the Russo-Japanese conflict war had become a distinct possibility. In view of this, Germany had no choice but to put her 'preparedness for war ... above all other considerations'. Henceforward the question of what would happen in the more distant future would have to be subordinated to the consideration of how a genuine gain in naval strength could be achieved 'in the period immediately before us'. It was, Heeringen continued, ten times more preferable 'to burden oneself with unnecessary difficulties in peace-time' than 'to be surprised by war in a state of insufficient readiness'. If the Navy were defeated under such circumstances, 'History and the Nation will make the *military* authorities responsible for the deficiencies in military preparedness' and neither the argument that German diplomacy had shown a lack of foresight nor the excuse that the naval programme had not yet been completed would find acceptability.

In his report, Heeringen challenged not only, as will be seen later,[30] Tirpitz's concept of a systematic, long-term expansion of German naval power, but he also stimulated further discussions on the possibility of an early war. One of the fruits of these deliberations in naval and court circles was a memorandum by the Chief of the Admiralty Staff, completed in February 1905, 'concerning operations against England'.[31] A war with Britain, so Wilhelm von Büchsel argued, would lead to a blockade of the Reich which would cause considerable damage to the German economy. There might be 'a financial and social crisis [!] with incalculable consequences'. In order to prevent this it would be necessary, he said, to confront France with the choice between supporting the Reich or siding with England. The advantage of the latter alternative would be that Germany would be given an opportunity of using her land forces. 'Our large working population which a blockade will have made jobless and breadless' would be offered 'employment' and, hopefully, could be fed 'on the enemy's soil and at his expense'. This remarkable idea of solving the social question by waging a war of expansion will re-emerge in 1914, as will the realisation that in any future war, even one against the first sea power, England, the Reich would have to rely on the Army.

This was most decidedly also the view of the General Staff which early in 1905 began to occupy itself seriously with the possibility of a war against France and England.[32] Schlieffen in particular became very concerned about the growing isolation of Germany and advocated an immediate attack in the West. He wanted to use the temporary weakness of Russia after her defeat in the Far East to crush France. 'The outcome of the war', he told the Saxon Military Attaché, 'would depend on the French campaign and not upon the Navy.'[33] But the Chief of the General Staff was uncertain how the Kaiser would react to these plans. As it turned out, William's reaction was negative, at least for the time being. Nevertheless the discussions of the military throw an interesting light on the effect which the primacy of armaments policy was having on German policy planning as a whole: it reinforced the above-named 'militaristic' element in the basic orientation of the Reich's foreign policy. With Germany's position deteriorating year after year, a victorious war came to be seen by the 'radicals' as a cure for the country's internal and external problems. The temptations of this kind of thinking manifested themselves clearly enough in Büchsel's memorandum; but they emerge most uninhibitedly from a letter by Admiral Georg Alexander von Müller.[34] What, he asked Tirpitz in February 1905, should be done if Germany's naval armaments policy and a diplomatic crisis led to a war with England? 'I feel we ought to be clear about this question even before it is asked; for, our present policies will be defined by the way in which we propose to answer it. And our answer must be: then [we shall wage] a world war which will lead our armies into India and Egypt.' The 'militarists' in the Army could not have put it more candidly.

The infusion into German diplomacy of a fresh dose of military policy is also reflected in the government's handling of the Moroccan crisis. French research has shown that the Kaiser's visit to Tangiers was not the direct result of economic pressure group activities.[35] The decision to intervene was based rather on considerations resulting from the changes which had taken place in the *European* balance of power since 1904. Holstein, who was in close touch with Schlieffen, apparently hoped to use the Moroccan crisis as a pretext for either a preventive war against France or, at least, the destruction of the as yet untested Entente Cordiale. His plan misfired when France refused to react in the expected fashion. Théophile Delcassé, the French Foreign Minister, resigned and it appeared as if Germany had won a great diplomatic success. But it was a Pyrrhic victory. The humiliation of France so worried the British government that it decided to give Paris diplomatic support.[36] In the end Germany was not only left empty-handed, but the crisis also reinforced her isolation.

Yet this defeat at least offered another advantage: it could be exploited domestically. To understand the interconnection between foreign and internal policy it is important to remember again that the monarchy had staked its future on a long-term naval programme which was to have a stabilising effect on the entire political system. One vital aspect of Tirpitz's plan was that it provided for a step-by-step expansion of the Navy. According to the calculations of the Reich Navy Office the next naval bill was due in 1905–6 when the building tempo of three ships per annum came to an end. To maintain this tempo and thus to enable the completion of the following stage, new ships had to be approved. Definite preparations for this bill had begun as early as 1903. At the same time the Reich government began to become concerned about the public reception of the bill and tried to create favourable parliamentary conditions for it. Tirpitz's naval armaments policy thus cast its long shadow not only over Bülow's foreign policy, but also over the country's domestic development.

In practice the preparation of the public was most difficult because, Bülow's optimistic prognostications and beaming face notwithstanding, the crisis of the monarchical system continued to spread. Whereas the parties and social groups which had supported the government's naval and tariff legislation of 1898–1902 did not as yet show any marked centrifugal tendencies away from the idea of a conservative *Sammlung*, the working classes refused to become reconciled to the existing order and to be deluded by the mirage of *Weltpolitik*. The increase in agricultural tariffs, introduced for the benefit of the ailing landed gentry, had further disillusioned those groups whose income was largely swallowed up by the weekly food bill. The dissatisfaction with the monarchy came to the surface in the 1903 Reichstag elections in which the socialist vote rose from 2,108,000 (1898) to 3,008,000. In spite of various handicaps imposed on the S.P.D. by the electoral system, a total of 81 Social Democrat deputies took up their seats in the popular assembly. The strike movement of January 1905 gave further evidence of the continued existence of dangerous latent tensions in German society. That the support for William's policy was still small was driven home to him when he visited Kiel, one of the bases of his proud fleet, in June 1904. One might have expected all citizens, not just the bourgeoisie of Kiel, to have been particularly grateful for all that the Kaiser had done for the city by expanding the Navy. But when he appeared in the Imperial Shipyards, the assembled workers did not burst into jubilant cheers; they greeted their ruler with icy silence.[37]

The first years of Germany's diplomatic isolation were thus accompanied by very definite evidence that the idea of a monarchy, based on the prestige of a popular Kaiser and a powerful fleet, had failed to capture the imagination of a majority of Germans. Under the glittering surface of Wilhelmine optimism and rising prosperity, there emerged anew the old fear of 'Revolution'. Waldersee's diaries are probably extreme examples of the deep pessimism prevalent among the conservative elite.[38] But it is also a recurrent theme in other contemporary sources,[39] while Bülow's speeches, especially after the Russian Revolution of 1905, displayed an increasingly aggressive tone.[40] Shortly before the 1903 elections, the Kaiser had been in an extremely boastful mood and even predicted the gradual decline of parliamentarism in the Reich.[41] But as if to prove just how thin the layer of optimism was, he would no less quickly fall into the other extreme. One such occasion was witnessed by Eulenburg in August 1903. In the course of a private dinner, the Kaiser was suddenly overcome by fears of the working-class and began to talk of 'the coming revolution and its defeat' by the Army.[42] 'I shall have to take *revenge* for [18]48', he thundered, '*revenge*.' Similiarly the Conservative leader Count Udo Stolberg warned the Reich Chancellor in December 1903 not to minimise the Social Democrat danger. 'It is not enough', he wrote, 'to continue social reforms if the threat of a social revolution is to be averted.' [43] As far as the middle-class parties were concerned, the main task would be to convince them of the need for a united front and for 'energetic counter-measures', lest 'we drift into one of the most pernicious revolutions'.

Even Tirpitz, who had been hoping that the socialist danger could be removed by 'peaceful' means via his naval armaments programme and the benefits to be derived from it, was overcome by first doubts. At a meeting of the Prussian State Ministry in January 1904 he took the view that he would not consider it 'a misfortune' if the S.P.D. continued to develop its 'anti-national tendencies'.[44] This would, he explained, 'hasten the necessity of resorting to repression'. It is no accident therefore that the abolition of the universal suffrage was once more discussed in government circles. But as Posadowsky-Wehner, the State Secretary for the Interior, pointed out, universal suffrage could not be abolished or modified 'without a monstrous catastrophe for which nobody would be prepared to take responsibility'.[45] This was also the conclusion which the Prussian State Ministry came to when it discussed the idea of a new anti-Socialist law in January 1904.[46] The Prussian Minister of the Interior held on this occasion that the time to 'initiate repressive measures against Social Democracy had not yet come'. Neither the other federal governments 'nor the bourgeois parties would give such a move the necessary backing', he said. In view of this, there was no choice but to try and win the support of the masses. As before, the *Staatsstreich* was to be used only as the very last resort.

It is symptomatic of the crisis in which Germany found herself by the middle of the decade that the approach of an 'era of conflict' similar to that of the 1860s was rumoured in military and court circles. Some advocated an early dissolution of the Reichstag and, should the subsequent elections not result in a swing towards the Right, they wanted to stage a *Staatsstreich*. Such a solution appeared all the more desirable since the Catholic Centre Party which occupied a key position in the *Sammlung* coalition of 1898–1902 was beginning to make difficulties.[47] The advantage of embarking upon a violent course of action was, moreover, that the introduction of dictatorial rule based on the emergency regulations of 1851 would have freed the Army from internal restrictions to waging a war against France. It was impossible to contemplate an invasion of France without either the backing of the entire nation or a prior silencing of domestic opposition. This, at any rate, was the basic message of a letter which William II sent to the Reich Chancellor on the last day of that troubled year 1905. An immediate foreign war as envisaged by the 'radicals', he argued, would be out of the question. To send 'a single man abroad' would, 'because of our Socialists', spell 'extreme danger to the life and property of the citizens'.[48] The first task would be to get rid of the Socialists, 'if necessary by means of a bloodbath, and then a foreign war, but not beforehand and not *à tempo*'.[49]

If we now ask ourselves how the 'era of conflict', as outlined by the Kaiser, was to be initiated, we have to return to German foreign policy and its interrelationship with Tirpitz's armaments policy in order to find an answer. For, in view of the growing complications in the domestic field, the setback of the First Moroccan Crisis was not so disastrous, after all. Although the international position of the Reich had been weakened by the outcome of the Algeciras Conference, the diplomatic events of 1905 offered an ideal opportunity for agitation at home. Was not the Crisis a clear proof that Germany was 'encircled' by her enemies and that further armaments were the only adequate response? Those who were most worried by the monarchy's internal predicament and external isolation now began to agitate for a massive navy bill, not so much because they were hoping that this would lead to an immediate improvement of the country's military posture, but rather because the Reichstag's refusal to approve such increases would present William II with a pretext for dissolving the popular assembly. Then the *Staatstreich* programme could go ahead as scheduled.

It is against the background of these calculations that we can understand why the Conservative deputy Karl von Richthofen-Damsdorf chose a Reichstag debate on *naval armaments* in December 1905 to launch a fierce attack on the Social Democrats. Pointing to the outcome of the Moroccan Crisis, he demanded better preparations both against the external and the internal enemy.[50] Similar demands appeared in the conservative *Kreuz-Zeitung* on the following day; a few weeks later Tirpitz was put under direct pressure at a social gathering to which the Prussian Finance Minister Georg von Rheinbaben had invited a number of colleagues and deputies.[51] The Conservatives and 'radical representatives of the Agrarian League', Tirpitz noted, repeatedly talked to him about 'the inadequacy' of the new naval bill which the State Secretary had just introduced. The fact that such approaches coincided with moves to cut the taxation programme by 'about 100 mill marks' seemed to indicate to Tirpitz that the dissolution of the Reichstag was in the offing and that the naval issue was to be made a topic of nationalist agitation to defeat the left and to strengthen the conservatives. The Navy was to be the 'battering ram'[52] to effect a renewed *Sammlung* or, failing that, to inaugurate the 'era of conflict' followed by external war. Tirpitz was most unenthusiastic.

Bülow, on the other hand, not only found it more difficult to elude these pressures of court and military circles than Tirpitz, but also took a more positive attitude towards them. Clearly his reputation at home and abroad was no longer what it had been at the turn of the century, and to strengthen the position of the monarchy, as well as his own, he became increasingly tempted to pull off in 1905 the feat which he managed to execute so successfully a year later when he used a Reichstag controversy over German South-West Africa to dissolve Parliament and, with the help of intensely nationalistic propaganda, inflicted a heavy defeat on the Social Democrats.[53] Explaining his attitude in October 1911, Bülow had this to say about his strategy in the period prior to the 'Hottentot Elections' of January 1907:[54]

Our present monarchical and conservative system (including world political status of the Reich and of Prussia) will fall only if Socialism and Liberalism, if workers and petty bourgeoisie unite. This is how the Revolution was won in 1789, 1830, 1848, [and] this is what the British aristocracy has always known how to prevent. Between 1903 and 1906 I therefore pursued the aim of discrediting Social Democracy in the eyes of the educated bourgeoisie.... After I had thus prepared for the battle (and there can be no victory without slow and long preparation!) I moved forward in December 1906.

If the Reich Chancellor did not move in 1905, it was in the final analysis because Tirpitz was opposed to making the Navy the

'battering-ram'. It is not that the Navy Secretary was averse to
continuing the Reich's risky naval armaments policy. On the
contrary, under his programme of expansion by stages another step
was due to be taken in 1905. But after very careful examination of
the external and internal problems facing his fleet bill, he had
come to the conclusion that it was better to keep the numerical
increase of the Navy down to six new battle-cruisers. Any more far-
reaching proposals, as put forward by the German Navy League,
would, he believed, inevitably alarm England.[55] For it was not only
the stepping-up of the building tempo from three to four ships per
annum, as suggested by the agitators, which worried him, but also
the fact that his more modest bill provided for the construction of
German dreadnoughts. The combined effect of the Navy League's
numerical increases over and above the *Dreiertempo* and his own
qualitative improvements of the individual ship implied, he felt,
'such a shift [in the balance] of the *real power factors* that even a
calm and rational British government *must* arrive at the conclusion
[that it is better] to crush such an opponent before he has acquired
the military strength which will be dangerous to England's position
as a world power'.

At the same time, the State Secretary was concerned about the
domestic repercussions of a vast building programme. Such a programme would lead people to think—'and not without justification'—that the Reich government was 'aiming for a fleet which is
equal to the British one'. For this, Tirpitz continued, 'no majority
will be found *in the present Reichstag*' so that Parliament would have
to be dissolved. As it was unlikely that premature elections would
lead to 'better Reichstag', the consequences of a dissolution would
be incalculable. The deficit in the Reich budget and the need for
tax increases, 'the general inflation of prices (shortage of meat and
effect of the commercial treaties [i.e. of the higher agricultural
tariffs]', Tirpitz warned, would quite possibly turn the elections
into a fiasco and weaken the internal and external prestige of the
monarchy. The naval bill, he added, 'which requires huge expenditures and will, no doubt, entail great political risks' as well as 'the
events inside Russia and Austria with their effects on German
Social Democracy' would also have to be considered. It was because
Tirpitz appreciated the very high stakes for which the Prusso-
German monarchy was playing that he counselled caution and
relative modesty. He was convinced that his naval bill represented
the maximum of what, in view of the precarious diplomatic and

domestic situation, could be achieved. Any acceleration of his armaments programme would place the stability of the existing order in jeopardy. For Tirpitz was doubtful that the Reich in its present predicament 'possesses the inner strength' necessary 'to master a "period of conflict"'.

These arguments demonstrate that Tirpitz was a man of considerable political acumen, perspicacity and vision. He was not prepared to exploit a momentarily favourable situation which, if things went wrong, might well lead to foreign war or to chaos at home. He had always predicted that, with the Anglo-German arms race gaining momentum, the Reich would have to weather a number of storms. Consequently he was also opposed to solutions like the ones proposed by Schlieffen or by William II. Steadiness was required, rather than rash and hectic decisions which, he feared, would push the monarchy to the brink of disaster. The decisive point is that the Navy Secretary, one of the most powerful men in Wilhelmine Germany, got his way. War did not break out in 1906; nor was the naval bill the beginning of a new 'era of conflict'. In May 1906, the Reichstag ratified a naval armaments programme which provided for the construction of six additional ships and increases in the displacement of battleships to 18,000 tons.

There can be no doubt that Tirpitz's stubbornness prevented a major domestic and international crisis from breaking out in 1906. But this, of course, did not remove the causes of Germany's internal problems; nor were the advocates of a radical solution to the dilemmas of the monarchy overruled for good. On the contrary, the above-mentioned 'militarisation' of German policy continued. To make things worse for Tirpitz, the implications of the 1906 Naval Law were not lost on the British government. Although in 1905 the Liberals had come to power with the plan to reduce armaments expenditure so as to invest more money in social reforms, more and more people in England were becoming aware of the German challenge. The Reichstag had now passed a bill which envisaged not only more capital ships but also stronger ones. The test question which Fisher had put to Tirpitz when improving the quality of capital ships had received a positive answer. The Admiralty had to react. On 1 January 1907 Sir Eyre Crowe completed a Foreign Office memorandum which is of basic importance to an understanding of how the British Empire assessed the German threat:[56]

If it be considered necessary to formulate and accept a theory that will fit all the ascertained facts of German foreign policy, the choice must lie between the two hypotheses here presented: Either Germany is definitely aiming at a general hegemony and maritime ascendancy, threatening the independence of her neighbours and ultimately the existence of England. Or Germany, free from any such clear-cut ambition and thinking for the present merely of using her legitimate position and influence as one of the leading powers in the council of nations, is seeking to promote her foreign commerce, spread the benefits of German culture, extend the scope of her national energies and create fresh German interests all over the world wherever and whenever a peaceful opportunity offers, leaving it to an uncertain future to decide whether the occurrences of great changes in the world may not some day assign to Germany a larger share of direct political action over regions not now part of her dominions without that violation of the established rights of other countries which would be involved in any such action under existing political conditions. In either case Germany would clearly be wise to build as powerful a navy as she can afford. The above alternatives seem to exhaust the possibilities of explaining the given facts. The choice offered is a narrow one, nor easy to make with any close approach to certainty. It will, however, be seen on reflection that there is no actual necessity for a British Government to determine definitely which of the two theories of German policy it will accept. For it is clear that the second scheme (of semi-independent evolution, not entirely unaided by statecraft) may at any rate merge into the first, or conscious-design scheme. Moreover, if the evolution scheme should come to be realised, the position thereby accruing to Germany would obviously constitute as formidable a menace to the rest of the world as would be presented by any deliberate conquest of a similar position by 'malice aforethought'. It appears, then, that the element of danger present as a visible factor in one case, also enters, though under some disguise, into the second; and against such danger, whether actual or contingent, the same general line of conduct seems prescribed.

The Reich government was soon to feel the effects of such recommendations. While the British policy of diplomatic containment was perfected with the conclusion of the Triple Entente of August 1907, the Admiralty concentrated on the arms race with Germany. And by deciding further to improve the fighting-power of the individual vessel, Fisher hit Tirpitz's programme where it was most vulnerable. Unwilling to abandon his original aim of making the Imperial Navy so strong that it could be used as a political lever against Britain, Tirpitz was compelled to increase the displacement of the German dreadnoughts; otherwise the superior firing-power and speed of the British capital ships would have condemned the Germans to accepting the international *status quo*. What made matters so difficult for Tirpitz was that in 1906 the Reichstag had approved financial estimates of the Reich Navy Office which, the deputies had been assured, would last for a good many years. But the pressure to follow the pace of the British Admiralty and to spend more money per ship than had been calculated in 1905, meant that the funds would be used up much sooner than expected. Towards the end of 1906 it became clear that Tirpitz would have to ask Parliament for an additional allocation to cover the increased costs of the qualitative arms race. This was particularly unfortunate in view of his plan to introduce yet another navy bill in 1911–12. This bill was to provide for an increase in the number of ships as well as a reduction of the replacement period from 25 to 20 years and would thus have established the 'Iron Budget' which the State Secretary had been working towards ever since the turn of the century.[57]

With a major success of his entire programme seemingly just around the corner, Tirpitz began to look for ways and means to circumvent the difficulties created by Fisher's policies. To introduce a fleet bill in 1908 and another one in 1911 was more than the deputies could be expected to approve. Tirpitz had to try to combine the two bills and put them before the Reichstag in 1908. This appeared all the more urgent after Bülow's premature dissolution of Parliament in December 1906 and his successful creation of the Bülow Bloc, which, by replacing the Centre Party with the Left Liberals, had put the *Sammlung* of 1898 on a new footing.[58] The Bloc secured a patriotic majority in the Reichstag. But it was an uneasy alliance which, many people predicted, would not survive for very long. Tirpitz decided to act before it was too late. In the early summer of 1907, the Reich Navy Office forwarded, with the Kaiser and Bülow's approval, the draft of a fleet bill to the Reich

Treasury. It requested additional funds for qualitative improvements on capital ships and a reduction of the replacement period
from 25 to 20 years.[59]

Ordinarily this latter proposal would have resulted in so many
ships coming up for immediate replacement that the previous
building tempo of three ships per annum would have gone up to
four. In order to avoid this and to enable a continuation of the
traditional *Dreiertempo*, the Reich Navy Office had postponed the
scheduled replacement of a number of ships until after 1911. In a
memorandum of February 1907, one of Tirpitz's closest advisers
argued that the continuation of the *Dreiertempo* was imperative for
foreign policy reasons.[60] 'Should Germany,' he wrote, 'introduce a
temporary building tempo of four ships per annum over the next
few years and for no recognisable reason, the stigma of having
caused a fruitless arms race will be impressed on us and the
German Empire will encounter even greater animosities than at
present when our reputation as a troublemaker is bad enough.' Far
more disastrous, he felt, would be another result of a stepped-up
German building tempo: 'The Liberal Cabinet in Britain will be
thrown out of office and be replaced by a Conservative one which,
even if one hopes for the best, will, by making huge investments in
the Navy, completely obliterate all our chances of catching up with
Britain's maritime power within a measurable space of time.'

These words demonstrate the undiminished ability of Tirpitz and
his collaborators to calculate the choices and necessities of the
Anglo-German arms race fairly rationally. The same could not be
said of the Kaiser and parts of German public opinion. The year
1905 had seen the appearance of forces which wanted to utilise the
precarious predicament of the country for the unleashing of a victorious war or, alternatively, of a *Staatsstreich* followed by an attempt
to break up the 'ring' of the Triple Entente. The result of these
tendencies and the increasing fear of 'encirclement' was that
German policy became riddled with irrationalism. Up to 1904 the
Reich government had more or less succeeded in keeping wild
agitators at bay. But under the impression of growing internal and
external difficulties even government circles and ultimately the
Reich Navy Office found it increasingly difficult to estimate the
realities of the developing international conflict correctly. Dieter
Senghaas has analysed this phenomenon with reference to the
Soviet–American arms race and defined it as 'autism'.[61] The

autistic actor, he argues, moves in a vicious circle from which he cannot escape The result of his wrong and invariably exaggerated perception of the conflict is an overreaction leading to what has been called 'overdesign'. At the same time, Senghaas continues, pent-up aggressions become projected on to the outside enemy. It seems useful to apply the analytical tools of social psychology and sociology to a society like that of pre-1914 Germany in which the outside threat was built up out of all proportion and led to the psychic militarisation of large parts of the population. The ruling elites in particular developed pathological fears and could no longer judge their environment accurately. The Kaiser's marginal annotations in this period are particularly interesting examples of this loss of control over the environment which was accompanied by an increasing political dogmatism.

At first, the Kaiser and his advisers began to blame Germany's difficulties on the Entente powers. Later they added practically everybody else—Socialists, Liberals, Jews, etc.—to their list of enemies. We shall have ample opportunity to observe this search for scapegoats in subsequent chapters—an obsession on the part of the decision-makers without which it is impossible to understand why they went to war in July 1914. For the purposes of this chapter the autistic tendencies in German policy are significant in so far as they help to explain why, in the autumn of 1907, all reason was cast aside and Tirpitz was forced to introduce a navy bill which provided for a building tempo of four ships per annum.[62] Agitation for a bigger navy, regardless of international reactions, had by 1907 become so powerful and so impervious to rational considerations that the entire fleet plan of 1898–1900 took a most dangerous turn. This digression from the original programme was bound to accelerate the arms race even further. But the agitators and the Kaiser cared little about the warnings of heightened danger. The isolation of the Reich had helped to foster a fortress mentality inside the country which, in turn, had a useful integrating effect on a society whose political system was, as we shall see, once more beginning to show very dangerous cracks.

4 From Bülow to Bethmann Hollweg

The fact that in 1907 Tirpitz was forced to introduce prematurely another navy bill and on top of it all to adopt a stepped-up building tempo was a direct result of the government's refusal, or inability, to abandon the armaments policy on which the future of the monarchy was so largely dependent. The decision to enter into a fully-fledged arms race with England strengthened the hands of those who were interested in exploiting the alleged foreign threat for domestic purposes. There can be little doubt that Tirpitz did not wish to let things go that far. In 1905–6 he had still been successful in blocking the rise of the 'radicals' who were advocating a violent solution, i.e. an immediate foreign war or the establishment of military rule as a prerequisite of external expansion. The State Secretary did not expect anything good to come from such policies. They would, he feared, throw the country into chaos at home and worsen its international position. With the ratification of the 1908 Navy Law, the fourth since 1898, the 'radicals' had scored a first victory. However, this revised law offered one advantage which made it easier for the Reich Navy Office to cast all inhibitions overboard: the immediate replacement of ships under the 20-year clause, resulting in a building tempo of four capital ships per annum, came to an end in 1911. As from 1912 the tempo dropped sharply to two ships per year until 1918 when the building cycle which had started in 1898 pushed the tempo up again to three ships. There existed, in other words, a gap from 1912 to 1917, and it was this gap which, Tirpitz hoped, could be filled by means of yet another navy bill. His hopes were based, to some extent, on the expectation that a reduction of ship-building by half would be unacceptable to industry. If for no other reason than to prevent a recession in important sectors of the economy, more than two capital ships per annum were required, and it was to be expected that the industrialists would not spare any effort to persuade the Reichstag of the need for additional ships.

But a further increase in the size of the fleet was desirable also for political reasons. If Tirpitz obtained approval for only two extra ships, he would have reached the magic number of 60 to be replaced every 20 years. The all-important *Marineaeternat* would at last have been achieved.[1] On the other hand, the 1908 Navy Law was bound to create appalling difficulties for the Reich's diplomacy. Not only was Germany now building improved dreadnoughts, but doing so at an accelerated rate of four per annum.

The British Admiralty could not possibly ignore such a challenge. The question was, however, how England would react. The most extreme reaction which the Reich government could never exclude entirely, was a preventive strike by the Royal Navy against the unfinished German fleet. The fear of this possibility had been particularly strong at the time of the Dogger Bank Incident.[2] But in view of the accelerated tempo it is not surprising that the leadership of the Reich, and especially the Fleet Commands and the Admiralty Staff, should be haunted by the nightmare of a 'Copenhagen'.

No less dangerous was the reaction which had formed the basis of British policy since about 1904: the qualitative and quantitative arms race. Fisher's measures had caused Tirpitz considerable headache even before 1908. Would the British, now that the German challenge was obvious to everyone, make the 'huge investments in the Navy' which, the Reich Navy Office feared, would 'completely obliterate all our chances of catching up with Britain's maritime power within a measurable space of time'?[3] Tirpitz realised that it would be impossible to prevent British naval increases altogether, as the British government were themselves not particularly keen on excessive arms expenditures. The best way to reinforce their inhibitions and to distract British public opinion from the Anglo-German arms race was to start a diplomatic 'peace' offensive. Once again German diplomacy became the hand-maid of the country's armaments policy, and the Reich's relationship with England assumed a central place in European politics up to 1912.

The 'peace' offensive was launched during the Kaiser's visit to England in the middle of November 1907, only a few days after he had given his approval to the stepped-up 1908 navy bill.[4] Bülow decided to stay at home to preserve the private character of the tour which had one main aim: to mollify British suspicions of Germany. It is very questionable whether the visit served its purpose in the first place. But what little goodwill the Kaiser may have generated, it was soon destroyed again. William II had hardly returned to Berlin when the British press was seized by a 'strong unrest' caused by the fierce naval agitation in Germany preceding the publication of Tirpitz's bill.[5] Even the Liberal press warned that England would have to be on her guard and there was widespread agreement that two British ships should be built for every German one.[6] Sir Edward Grey, the Foreign Secretary, came out in favour of naval increases and King Edward VII cancelled his projected spring trip to Germany. The reports of the German Ambassador to London were regularly full of alarming news about the irritated state of British public opinion.

In this situation, William II took an unprecedented step which can only be interpreted as an attempt to appease the British government. On 16 February 1908 he wrote a personal letter in English to the First Lord of the Admiralty in which he tried to play down the significance of the 1908 navy bill.[7] 'It is absolutely nonsensical and untrue', the Kaiser lied, 'that the German Navy Bill is to provide a Navy meant as a "Challenge to British Naval Supremacy". The German Fleet is built against nobody at all. It is solely built for Germany's needs in relation with that country's rapidly growing trade.' Without going into the details of the letter in which he strongly protested that the Imperial Navy should be used for agitation purposes in England, its contents and language virtually guaranteed that it had the opposite effect. It is perhaps because he realised that William II had completely missed the target that Bülow contacted the German Ambassador to London shortly afterwards.[8] Metternich was directed to emphasise whenever he had an opportunity to do so that British fears of Germany were totally unjustified.

Yet these diplomatic manoeuvres were of little help. Writing before William's visit to Windsor in the autumn of 1907, Grey had outlined the framework in which friendly Anglo-German relations could be established.[9] They could only be so, he wrote,

on the distinct understanding that our friendship with Germany is not at the expense of our friendship with France. And just at this time when the political situation is such as to make France not unnaturally nervous, I am particularly anxious that nothing should occur which would lend any colour to the idea that we are wavering by a hair's breadth from our loyalty to the Entente and are contemplating a new departure in policy.

In fact, German policy since the autumn of 1907 had made it certain that Britain would under no circumstances contemplate a different entente policy.[10] At the same time, the Liberal Cabinet was now reluctantly determined to increase the naval armaments. In the summer of 1908 London made an all-out attempt, the last one until 1912, to reach an understanding with the Reich on the naval problem. The ground had been prepared by two businessmen, Albert Ballin and Sir Ernest Cassel, and in August 1908 Sir Charles Hardinge conducted a series of longer talks with William II at Kronberg.[11] It soon turned out that the Kaiser was not seriously interested in a mutual limitation of naval armaments. Of course, he did not put it so bluntly when he met Hardinge, but merely tried to convince his listener that the expansion of the Imperial Navy was not directed against anyone and that its size was defined by Germany's needs alone. However, his real convictions can be gleaned from his comments on a report by his Ambassador in London. When Metternich mentioned hints in the Liberal press about the desirability of a naval agreement, William wrote into the margin:[12] 'By no means!' He refused to attach any significance to such offers, 'because they all envisage a reduction of our fleet to be a prerequisite of their friendship'.

These attitudes on the part of the Reich government also explain why the attempts of the new Chancellor of the Exchequer, David Lloyd George, to see Bülow about the possibility of a reduced building tempo came to naught. The Reich Chancellor was not even prepared to receive him.[13] On 21 August 1908 Bülow finally issued a directive to stop all press treatments of an Anglo-German naval understanding.[14] It appears that he was nevertheless somewhat uneasy about the abrupt manner in which the British approaches had been rejected. He agreed that this was not the time to change the armaments policy which had occupied a central place in his political plans ever since he came to Berlin in the summer of 1897. He would, he assured the Kaiser on 26 August 1908, always do his best to help complete the fleet programme, the monarch's life task.[15] This task, he added, was endangered above all by a new 'colossal programme' of the British government. In order not to jeopardise future plans he therefore considered it his duty to guide German policy 'through the next few years'.[16] The best way to do this, he concluded, was to refuse official negotiations, but not to decline private discussions of the topic. In short, Bülow's means were more flexible than those of William who had treated Hardinge in rather a high-handed manner.

This was also the view of Tirpitz, who took the opportunity of an audience with the Kaiser to tell him, as politely as possible, that it was unwise to reject all conversations on the naval issue. It is possible that these reminders by senior advisers induced William to give his approval to the publication of his private conversations with Colonel Stuart Wortley which appeared in the *Daily Telegraph* on 27 October 1908 and in which he assured the British of his amicable feelings towards them.[17] The gesture misfired completely. It aroused a storm of indignation both in England and at home and it could not prevent the Liberals from abandoning all hope of a naval agreement. At the beginning of November, the Prime Minister announced a fleet programme which, he said, would demonstrate that the Liberals were determined to uphold Britain's position in the world. Three days later, he proclaimed the maintenance of the two-power standard, i.e. of the principle that the Royal Navy should always at least be as strong as the navies of the next two sea powers combined. As Metternich reported, there could now be no doubt that tensions between the two countries would rise and that, because of Germany's armaments policy, no improvement of the situation could be expected for some time to come.[18] It was at this point and apparently under the impact of the *Daily Telegraph* disaster that a serious conflict broke out between Tirpitz and Bülow.

Both statesmen were agreed that major crises had to be avoided and that all efforts had to be geared to getting 'through the next few years'. But faced with the prospect of a further deterioration of Anglo-German relations, Bülow began to wonder if the arms race might not mean war in 1909. At the end of November he wrote a letter to Tirpitz to ask if, as far as the Navy was concerned, the Reich 'could look forward to a British offensive with composure and confidence'.[19] He must have expected the answer to be no. For on Christmas Day he drafted a second letter in which he proposed 'to give serious consideration to a slowing-down' of the current naval programme.[20] Bülow's arguments in support of this idea seem to indicate that he was not really worried about a war with England, for at the end of his letter he alluded to the existence of financial and technical objections to the present building tempo, and, as will be seen, it seems indeed more likely that he was influenced by these factors and had made himself spokesman of a growing internal opposition to Tirpitz's concept.[21] Tirpitz, of course, was totally opposed to the proposal which, he remarked, required a change of the Navy Law.[22] This law, he told Prince Henry of Prussia on 20 December 1908, is 'at this moment our *only* firm basis'.[23] He would have to submit his resignation if the Law were revised less than one year after the ratification of the 1908 bill. What he did not say openly was that a revision would also destroy all chances of introducing yet another bill in 1911. Far from wanting to reduce the programme, he insisted on its continuation so that the way would be kept open for later increases to fill the gap of 1912–17.

Tirpitz's threat of resignation deterred Bülow from pursuing the matter any further. On 5 January 1909 he expressed agreement with the State Secretary's views and ordered the correspondence to be kept strictly secret.[24] Metternich was instructed not to broach the topic of a slowing-down in his conversations with British politicians.[25] On the other hand, Bülow did not intend to sever all contacts with London. The maxim of German foreign policy was, after all, to keep England waiting, not to estrange her completely.[26] Tirpitz agreed and, asked what might be a suitable topic for long-drawn-out discussions, he put forward the idea of fixing a numerical ratio for the two fleets. He thought that a 3:4 formula might be a good basis for negotiations.[27] It is possible that he proposed this ratio because, after his experiences with Bülow in December 1908, he wished to delay all soundings in London and the best way to do this was to start an interdepartmental debate about the appropriate ratio. The German Foreign Office, at any rate, believed that to mention a formula which was higher that the old 2:3 ratio of the turn of the century would be disastrous. Tirpitz was strongly advised not even to hint at this higher ratio when Edward VII visited Berlin in February 1909.[28] Realising that there was very little room for manoeuvre in the field of naval armaments, Bülow began to look for non-military subjects which might be of interest to the British government.[29] A neutrality agreement seems to have been his first choice, but he must have known that the whole subject was unacceptable to the other side.[30]

In the meantime the Navy Scare which the Reich government had been so worried about since the passage of the 1908 bill was in full swing. Anti-German feelings in England reached a high pitch. In the end, Parliament approved a fleet programme which demonstrated to the world at large and to the Germans in particular the impressive economic and financial resources of the British Empire. In the course of the next year no less than eight capital ships were laid down,[31] a feat which could not but leave the Germans gasping and dealt a mortal blow to Tirpitz's hope of gaining a lever against the British Empire. His immediate reaction to the outcome of the Navy Scare is not known. But the letter which he wrote to Bülow on 21 March 1909 seems to prove that he refused to give up.[32] England, he said, would build twice as many ships as the Reich in 1909. But so what? 'We can wait and see what happens next.' What, precisely, he meant by this emerged in the course of a top-level conference between Bülow, Tirpitz, Moltke, Müller, Metternich, Wilhelm von Schoen, the State Secretary in the Foreign Office, and Theobald von Bethmann Hollweg, then State Secretary of the Interior.[33] The actual purpose of the conference was to find a formula for an understanding with Britain. But Tirpitz, as it turned out, was really concerned about something quite different: the gap of 1912–17. Due to the drop in the rate of construction in 1912 from four to two ships per annum, he explained, 1911 would be the most critical year from the German point of view. As the British government were aware of this, an initiative to resume negotiations would be unlikely to come from across the Channel at this stage. No doubt this renewed discouragement of diplomatic activity served an old purpose: to keep the door open for another fleet bill in the critical year of 1911.

There was one awkward obstacle to this course of action which Tirpitz also tried to remove at the conference: on William's instruction, Metternich had informed the British government in the autumn of 1908 that the reduction in the building tempo in 1912 would not result in fresh naval legislation.[34] It appears that this assurance was given informally. But it obviously contradicted Tirpitz's plans, and he felt that now, after the end of the British Navy Scare, the time had come to disavow the German Ambassador. The impression which Tirpitz's devious tactics left on his colleagues can be gathered from a memorandum by Metternich.[35] Writing on the following day, the Ambassador first of all reproached Tirpitz for not having raised any objections to the instruction at the appropriate time. What was now at stake, he argued, was the credibility of the Reich government and the reliability of the Emperor's word. At the same time he wondered whether Tirpitz sincerely wanted a naval agreement, which he always approved in principle without coming forward with concrete proposals. Metternich deduced from this—quite rightly—that the State Secretary had made a 'mental reservation' concerning the whole complex of Anglo-German negotiations. In view of this, Metternich concluded, further initiatives would be downright dangerous because they would only raise false hopes on the British side. Bülow who was now steeped in domestic troubles agreed. The time for negotiations, he informed Metternich on 23 June 1909, had not yet come although the Ambassador should continue to stress Germany's interest in informal contacts.[36]

This was the state of affairs when in July 1909 Bethmann Hollweg succeeded Bülow as Reich Chancellor. Having participated in the top-level conference of 3 June, Bethmann Hollweg knew that Tirpitz would try to push for another navy bill in two years' time and he was determined to oppose it. However, his negative attitude towards naval armaments becomes plausible only after an examination of German domestic politics. Bülow had not only left his successor a depressing foreign political legacy. The internal situation was likewise a complete shambles, and just as German naval armaments policy was responsible for the country's isolation, it was also due to the ambitious naval programme of the turn of the century that confusion reigned at home.

It has been mentioned that Tirpitz was trying to avoid trouble with the Reichstag and with England when he decided to expand the Imperial Navy by stages. A third major consideration was finance. It is obvious that an armaments programme as far-reaching as Tirpitz's would swallow hundreds of millions of marks. But the Reich Navy Office thought it had adjusted its projected expansion to the expected growth of the German economy. This growth, it was hoped, would create increases in revenue sufficient to avoid the introduction of new taxes. There were people who had warned Tirpitz against such optimism. Hermann von Stengel, then Bavaria's delegate to the Bundesrat and later State Secretary of the Reich Treasury, refused to believe in 1899 that it would be possible to bear the cost increases for the Army, social security and colonies as well as the naval programme without exposing the existing tax system to dangerous strains.[37] Subsequently, as we have seen, the expansion of the Army came to a virtual stand-still and costly social security schemes were being slowed down.[38] The monarchy placed all its bets on the success of its naval armaments policy with economic and political benefits that, it was hoped, would eventually stabilise the entire political system. In 1899 the economy was booming and the financial situation seemed healthy enough to justify some risks.

So keen was the Reich government to get its fleet plans approved by the Reichstag that it even agreed to the insertion of a paragraph in the Navy Law to the effect that, should the Navy prove more expensive than projected, the additional costs were not to be covered by tax increases on mass consumption. This promise appeared all the more necessary because the higher agricultural tariffs, which the agrarians had been awarded in return for their approval of the naval bill, were bound to increase the cost of living. Since the 'little man' was hit by this most severely, any further price rises, resulting from taxes on mass consumers' goods, were politically dangerous. They drove the poorer sections of the population into the arms of those who pilloried the unequal tax burdens as a typical feature of the Wilhelmine class state. Now the above-mentioned clause of the Navy Law barred the Reich government from tapping the most profitable source of revenue which it had at its disposal.

If higher indirect taxes were not available for social reasons, the right to tax income and property was reserved for the federal states. But their bureaucracies and parliaments were dominated by the aristocracy and the propertied classes, and it is not surprising that these groups thought their interests to be better protected in the federal assemblies, with their restricted suffrage, than in the Reichstag. The federal governments were consequently under pressure, if any was needed, not only to keep direct taxation down, but also not to abandon any of their taxation rights to the Reich.[39] In short, the Reich's scope to enlarge its income was very narrow indeed.

But what would happen if Reich expenditure surpassed Reich income and new taxes were not available? In this case, the deficit could be covered either by floating a loan or by so-called matricular contributions to be collected from the federal states. The states were legally bound to pay these contributions if required. But just as in the case of indirect taxation, there was a limit to which both matricular contributions and loans could be relied upon. Loans were dependent on a sufficiently large capital market to service the private as well as the public sector. Moreover, they were not a particularly sound means of covering a deficit, since the debts and the interest payable on them were placed on the shoulders of the next generation. An excessive demand on matricular contributions, on the other hand, burdened the budgets of the federal states and forced them in the long run to levy higher taxes themselves. This, in turn, was difficult because of the resistance with which such a policy would meet in the federal parliaments.

The effect of all this and in particular of the division of taxation rights between the Reich and the federal states was very simple: the whole system worked so long as the Reich's revenue of indirect taxation remained higher than its expenditure. In this case the federal states could even profit from the surplus under the so-called Franckenstein Clause.[40] However, the system was threatened by slow paralysis as soon as the Reich accumulated a deficit. To cover it through higher indirect taxes was dangerous because it aroused the dissatisfaction of the working classes; to try and cover it by increasing matricular contributions or by taking direct taxation rights away from the federal states, would provoke the resistance of the federal governments and the propertied classes supporting them. In other words, the financial constitution of Germany contained political dynamite whenever the Reich government ran up a larger deficit. The federal states would then try to evade higher matricular contributions and oppose any move to transfer direct taxation rights to the Reich; the Reich government, on the other hand, would be reluctant to touch indirect taxes because they would estrange the proletariat further. What was worse: it threatened to alienate the Catholic Centre Party without which the *Sammlung* of 1898 could not be maintained. Being a denominational party, the Centre embraced voters from all social classes and had a fairly strong left wing. This is why its leadership could not afford to be too openly anti-labour, and it was in fact on the initiative of the Centre Party that the paragraph prohibiting higher indirect taxation on consumers' goods had been included in the Navy Law.[41] The Reich government's hands were thus completely tied.

The danger that a Reich deficit might lead to a blockage of the entire system of tax levy arose soon after the turn of the century. The optimistic forecasts turned out to be wrong and from 1901 the Reich developed a growing deficit. The expectation that the 1902 tariffs would restore the balance was soon disappointed. Nor did the practice of raising loans for non-recurrent expenditure or of submitting unrealistically high income estimates improve the situ-

ation. With the federal states resisting higher matricular contributions, a fundamental tax reform became less and less avoidable.
Knowing that such a reform would kindle internal conflict, the
Reich government year after year shied away from tackling the
problem. In 1904, a so-called Little Financial Reform was got
through the Bundesrat and the Reichstag. But it hardly deserved
its modest name.[42] By 1905, the hole in the Reich budget had
become so big that new tax revenue had to be created.

One possible source of income which some considered particularly inoffensive as well as lucrative was the introduction of a
death duty. But this view was not shared by the federal states and
the agrarians. They resented not only the idea of transferring taxation rights to the Reich and the 'democratic' Reichstag, but also
claimed that it would have a disastrous effect on the economically
ailing landed elites. On the other hand and for reasons already
mentioned, the Centre Party was opposed to higher direct taxes.
With the different parties blocking a solution one way or the other,
the struggle ended in 1906 in a 'mutilated financial reform'[43] which
barely covered the existing deficit and left bitter feelings all round.
The Conservatives were particularly furious that a death duty for
distant relatives, though not for next-of-kin, had to be conceded in
the end, and that the Catholics had advocated the transfer of direct
taxation rights to the Reich. In their eyes the Centre Party had
again fallen on its 'democratic front paws'.[44] The manoeuvres to
dissolve the Reichstag and to unleash a 'period of conflict' which
the Conservatives advocated in the winter of 1905–6 and which so
worried Tirpitz were therefore motivated also by the desire of the
Right to get rid of the 'unreliable' Catholics. The latter, having
dared to touch the economic and political privileges of the agrarians, were to be ousted from their key position in parliament. The
'patriotic' issue of naval policy appeared to be particularly suited
for this purpose. There can be little doubt that Bülow was attracted
by the idea of forcing the Catholics to toe the line and support his
conservative *Sammlung* policy or else be driven into opposition. Only
Tirpitz's obstinacy forced him to postpone his plan for one year. In
December 1906 he got his way. He dissolved the Reichstag over
another 'patriotic' issue—colonies—which the Centre Party and
the SPD had dared to criticise. The election campaign was waged
mainly against the 'Reich enemies', Catholics and Social Democrats,[45] and demonstrated how little the ambitious *Weltpolitik* had

reconciled large sections of the population to the existing order. On the contrary, the latent gulf running through the nation had now split wide open.

Bülow's appeal to fears of international isolation and internal 'revolution' helped to strengthen the Right and provided him, after the inclusion of the Left Liberals in his Bloc, with a new conservative majority in the Reichstag. This coalition was to be used to fulfil two main tasks: it was to ratify the 1908 navy bill which the course of the Anglo-German arms race had made inevitable; and it was to legislate a 'big' tax reform to plug the Reich deficit once and for all. In view of the heterogeneity of the Bloc the latter was no doubt the more difficult task and the passage of the Navy Law in 1908 had merely worsened the situation. In fact, it is no exaggeration to say that German armaments policy was almost exclusively responsible for the Reich's financial plight. Over the years a relatively constant figure of about 90 per cent of the Reich budget had been spent on the Army and Navy. Between 1896 and 1908 total armaments expenditure had almost doubled.[46] And since the share of the Army had risen only moderately, it was even possible to identify the root of the financial evils. As in the field of foreign policy, it was again the naval armaments which were causing the basic trouble. The prediction that Tirpitz's programme was well adjusted to the growth of the economy and the Reich's revenue proved to be as false as many other premises of Wilhelmine world policy. The decision to construct German dreadnoughts destroyed, as we have seen, the financial calculations of the Reich Navy Office. More money was required not only for continuing the quantitative arms race against England but also to copy Fisher's qualitative improvements. The Anglo–German naval rivalry which had already done much to upset international peace had thus also become a German domestic problem of the first order. The more the arms spiral was set in motion, the more powerful grew the chorus of those who argued that a continuation of the arms race was financially intolerable. Was it not true that Tirpitz's naval programme not only poisoned the international climate and provoked the containment of Germany, but also polarised political opinion at home by unlocking the dynamite contained in the peculiar financial constitution? More and more people came to suspect that the Navy was doing the opposite of what it had been expected to do: rather than integrating German society on the basis of the *status quo* it was a divisive force upsetting that *status quo*.

Inevitably these feelings undermined the position of trust which Tirpitz had established for himself in the early years after the turn of the century. At that time a majority of deputies in the Reichstag was convinced that the State Secretary's figures were accurate and that he was a great and far-sighted statesman.[47] But by the middle of the decade this confidence had faded. By exploiting the Moroccan Crisis for domestic agitation and by mobilising defensive instincts ('counteract the encirclement'), Bülow and Tirpitz succeeded in papering over the cracks that had developed at home. But only a year later, during the 1907 elections, the nation was clearly divided into two large camps. Tirpitz appreciated full well that the financial issue endangered his entire strategy and the benefits to be derived from it. Not only out of fear of Fisher's countermeasures, but also because he wanted to keep the costs of the 1906 navy bill down, he had shown moderation when the Kaiser, the Reich Chancellor and the Conservatives pressed for huge increases. He did not want the Navy to become the pretext for a *Staatsstreich*. For the same reason he had been urging Bülow ever since 1904 to initiate an early financial reform so that money would be available for the long-planned 1906 navy bill. By this he hoped to avoid the connection between the conflict-laden financial issue and his naval programme becoming all too visible. But in the end the 1906 navy bill and Bülow's tax proposals were discussed almost simultaneously. The reins were beginning to slip from Tirpitz's hands. Even more humiliating was his failure to create additional revenue for future needs.[48] The 1906 finance reform did not provide any surpluses on which the Navy could have drawn when the displacement of capital ships continued to grow. It was the financial dilemma which, as we have seen, forced Tirpitz to introduce a naval bill in 1908 and to adopt a building tempo that made a huge expansion of the Royal Navy unavoidable. The arms race went on at an accelerated pace weakening the monarchy at home.

For just as the deterioration of Germany's international situation and above all of Anglo-German relations between 1908 and 1912 were a direct consequence of the 1908 navy bill, the unwanted *Vierertempo* of 1908 had a similar effect on the German domestic scene. The additional financial burdens which the bill imposed made a major tax reform more urgent than ever. If a compromise between direct and indirect taxation could not be found and sufficient funds be created, internal strife would continue and ultimately paralyse all political activity. The fate of the projected 1912 navy bill would be in doubt and with it the great plans of the turn of the century. Ballin, the Hamburg businessman, was among those who, quite early on, tried to arrive at a sober calculation of economic potentials and to draw the only sensible conclusion from the financial difficulties and the divisive effect of armaments on the country. 'We just cannot afford a race in dreadnoughts', he told Bülow in July 1908, 'against the much wealthier British.'[49] Germany's financial resources, he added, were too limited to permit a fleet programme which could seriously threaten England. Quite consistently he therefore became a warm protagonist of an Anglo-German naval agreement. Such an agreement, he believed, would not only lessen tensions with England, but also reduce Germany's financial burdens and defuse the growing domestic crisis.

Reichstag deputies similarly became convinced that it might be inevitable to curtail the Reich's naval armaments programme. The agrarians, in particular, who had never really loved the Navy and supported it only because it had brought them the revision of the hated Caprivi tariffs, became concerned about the cost of the programme. They could not fail to see that it was due to Tirpitz's miscalculations that the Reich now threatened to break into the tax preserves of the federal states. The introduction of a Reich death duty for distant relatives in 1906 had been a first alarm signal. Was the Reich about to arrogate to itself all income and property taxation? In view of such fears, it is not surprising that, as early as December 1907, Tirpitz gained the impression that the agrarians approached 'the fleet with a completely cold heart'.[50] Some nine months later, in September 1908, he thought he had reason to believe, after reading an article in the conservative *Kreuz-Zeitung*, 'that influential forces are at work to limit the development of the fleet'.[51] And on 12 December 1908 he noted that 'the Reichstag was developing a mania for economy which could become dangerous. Instead of blaming the [Reich's] financial plight on the failure to find sufficient financial cover it is said that the squandering of funds is to be made responsible. [And now] the bill is to be paid by making economies.'[52]

Tirpitz, in other words, was not prepared to revise his plans. On the contrary, he did his best to forestall a further escalation of the criticism and his attempts to influence the size of the expected British increases through diplomatic action assume their true significance only when seen in the context of the German domestic situation. Launching a 'peace' offensive and keeping the Admiralty from accelerating the building tempo too sharply was a means of restricting the influence of those forces at home who considered the Anglo-German naval arms race too dangerous or too expensive or both and advocated an understanding at the expense of the Navy.[53] If this opposition became too strong, the all-important 1912 navy bill was threatened.

There were further obstacles which put Tirpitz's entire policy in jeopardy. It has already been mentioned in connection with our discussion of the Moroccan Crisis that Army circles were pressing for a campaign against France. A victorious war, they hoped, would rid the Prusso-German political system of all its internal and external ills. These 'radicals' had been unable to assert themselves in 1905–06. But the foreign political and domestic developments of the intervening years had only helped to strengthen their position. Two events in particular had contributed to this in 1908: the Bosnian Crisis and the *Daily Telegraph* affair. The annexation of Bosnia and Herzegovina by Austria–Hungary in the autumn of 1908 and the angry reaction of Russia to it came at an inopportune moment for the Reich government.[54] The naval talks with England had just been broken off and Germany was not particularly keen to get involved in another diplomatic crisis. If Bülow nevertheless sided with his Austro-Hungarian alliance partner, it was partly because it was practically the only friend that was left. But at the same time he hoped to drive a wedge between the Triple Entente which would relieve the pressure of 'encirclement', or even nullify it.[55] Moltke, the Chief of the General Staff, voiced similar views in a letter to his Austrian colleague, Franz Conrad von Hoetzendorff. 'Your Excellency,' he wrote on 19 March 1909, 'let us look into the future with confidence. As long as Austria and Germany stand shoulder to shoulder ... we shall be strong enough to blast any ring [around us]. Many will break their teeth [trying to crack] this Central European bloc.'[56] However, unlike Bülow, Moltke added a coda to this affirmation of loyalty behind which the 'militaristic' effect of German armaments policy became once again apparent. The Bosnian Crisis, Moltke argued, offered an opportunity of war 'which will not come so soon again under such propitious circumstances'.

The events on the domestic scene in Germany merely served to reinforce Army radicalism. The publication of the Kaiser's interview with Stuart Wortley in the *Daily Telegraph* at the end of

October 1908, had unleashed a storm of indignation at home.[57] There was an acrimonious debate in the Reichstag which dealt the public prestige of William II and the monarchical system a severe blow. Some ten years earlier it looked as if the crown was about to become the focal point of the Reich with a charismatic monarch leading a cheerful nation into a better future. Now the failures of the grandiose fleet programme began to boomerang on the Kaiser and his reputation reached an all-time low. Deputies protested loudly against Personal Rule and there were demands to extend parliamentary control and to introduce responsible government on western European lines. These were the demands of which the crown had been wary all along and which Tirpitz's grand design had intended to silence. Now William's interview had produced the opposite result. The *Daily Telegraph* Affair is thus symbolic of the extent to which the monarchy had been blown off course. The hopes which the Kaiser and his advisers had had at the turn of the century were fading away.

Because, rather than in spite, of these domestic difficulties those who wanted to use the Bosnian Crisis as an opportunity for war against Russia and France held a 'strong position within the leading circles in Germany'.[58] It is unlikely that the German military were unaware of the advantages which a victorious war promised to bring and which the Russian Ambassador described as follows:[59]

> Encouraged by the undoubted preparedness of the Army and other strata of society for the war and offended [by the *Daily Telegraph* debates] in their traditional feelings of loyalty towards their Supreme Leader, the war party regards war as the only means to restore the prestige of monarchical power which has been shaken in the eyes of the masses. The mood of military circles is nourished by the conviction that the present superiority of the Army promises Germany the greatest chance of success. Such convictions could entice the present Kaiser to give his foreign policy a militant character. At the same time a victorious war could, at least for an initial period, repel the radical currents among the people pressing for a change of the Prussian as well as the Reich Constitution in a more liberal direction. These are, in general outline, the symptoms of the German domestic situation, which could help to explain the causes of the [current] military preparations.

Apart from Moltke, there was at least one other very influential general, Moritz von Lyncker, the Chief of the Military Cabinet, who was prepared to resort to war. In a conversation with *Hofmarschall* Robert von Zedlitz-Trützschler at the end of March 1909 he not only took an optimistic view of Germany's chances of victory in a war against France and Russia, but also considered an external conflict desirable 'in order to get [the country] out of the internal and external difficulties'.[60] The Chief of the General Staff, Lyncker continued, would be prepared to act. But the Kaiser would probably not have the nerve to approve this solution.

If war did not come in 1909, it was not so much because of William's weak nerves but rather because of the desire of the political leadership as a whole to steer the Reich clear of international crises until 1911 or at least until the tax reform had passed the Reichstag. Bülow, it is true, had begun to differ from Tirpitz as to the future of naval armaments and in particular of the projected 1912 navy bill. As early as 1907 the Reich Chancellor had asked his State Secretary impatiently:[61] 'When *at last* will your fleet programme be advanced enough so that ... the *intolerable political* situation may be relieved.' But for the moment both of them thought it more important to avoid war and to re-order Reich finances in a manner which did not tear German society to pieces. They were forced to stand together against the advocates of war. Bülow did not desire war because he feared that it 'would have the most depressing consequences politically, economically and socially'.[62] Tirpitz for his part was bound to find a violent solution objectionable because it was implicitly based on the assumption that Germany should give up her naval and world policy and concentrate on the European continent and her Army. Consequently his future programme was being assailed from two sides. On the one hand, there was the opposition which favoured an understanding with Britain over naval matters in order to stabilise the monarchy's position abroad and, through cost-savings, at home; on the other, the 'hawks' in the Army were agitating for a clean sweep to end the isolation and internal disintegration of the political system.

The latter were supported by Tirpitz's opponents inside the Navy. We have had occasion to observe the first distinct signs of this internal opposition in the winter of 1904–5, when Heeringen in his commission report asked to put Germany's 'preparedness for war ... above all other considerations'.[63] With the introduction of bigger and bigger ships and Tirpitz's desire to give shipbuilding an absolute priority, the problem of military readiness had become so acute by the end of 1908 that the Navy Commands at Kiel and Wilhelmshaven, constantly worried about the danger of sudden war, decided to submit reports to the Kaiser.[64] William II learned from these that, as he put it in a Cabinet Order of 9 January 1909, 'doubts exist concerning the correctness' of Tirpitz's plans 'for the further development of the fleet as well as of the general defensive forces of the Reich against an attack from the sea'.[65] The State Secretary found this internal criticism particularly embittering. Nevertheless he refused to budge, believing that 'to "hold out" is still the best. Then [we shall have the] drop in our building tempo to two ships per annum.'[66] He would find it 'just as impossible to digress from the ultimate aim and to abandon the Navy Law as to give my signature to a humiliation [by Britain]'.[67] He decided not to resign his office until the 'assault' on the basis of his naval policy had been repulsed. The domestic 'reaction against the huge expenditure has only just begun', he added, 'and receives strong support by the menacing attitude of England'. Under these circumstances, nothing could be done to improve the readiness of the fleet for war. It was 'only under the inexorable constraints of the tightness of funds', the Kaiser wrote on 9 January 1909, 'and frequently also of the political situation' that 'justified demands of the "front" had to be left unfulfilled'.[68]

This state of affairs made it all the more important to secure a smooth passage of the financial reform as a prerequisite of future arms programmes. The Reich Treasury Office had meanwhile drafted a plan which envisaged the creation of some 500 million marks in additional tax revenue. Appreciating the crucial importance of the tax bill, the Reich Navy Office detached one of its propaganda experts, Professor Ernst von Halle, to help prepare a campaign in conjunction with the Press Office of the Reich Chancellery. In a letter of 3 August 1908 to his press chief, Otto Hammann, Bülow described what was at stake.[69] The political parties, he predicted, would again try to evade the appropriation of new taxes 'unless we convince the German people that, morally and *materially,* this reform is a matter of *life* and *death*' for the Reich. Yet Bülow's 500-million-mark programme for which he began to agitate on a large scale in the autumn of 1908 had one fatal flaw: while four-fifths of the money was to be raised through additional indirect taxation, the remaining sum of 100 million marks was envisaged to come from a death duty on property inherited by children and spouses.[70] The agrarians reacted immediately. At the beginning of September both the Conservative Party and the Agrarian League announced their vigorous opposition to any widening of the inheritance tax. Ernst von Heydebrand und der Lasa, the leader of the Conservatives, proclaimed that direct taxation must not fall 'into the hands of a parliamentary body elected on the basis of equal suffrage'.[71]

The Conservative campaign would conceivably have failed had not the Centre Party recognised that this was an opportunity of defeating Bülow and of regaining the key position from which they had been ousted in 1907. It was only through the co-operation of the Catholics that the agrarians were able to defeat the government's tax reform bill and to destroy the Bülow Bloc. Neither the National Liberals nor the Left Liberals were prepared to support a financial reform, as proposed by the Conservatives, which shifted all tax increases on to indirect taxation. Political reason demanded that the propertied classes should bear an appropriate share of the burden. They always posed as superpatriots when it came to strengthening the Reich's defences. It was a matter of social justice that those who benefited from Germany's armaments policy should also pay a higher share of the costs. The trouble was that, although they had supported the 1908 navy bill, the Conservatives refused to accept such arguments. They did not want 'to hand the purse of the propertied classes over to the Reichstag', as the East Prussian estate owner Elard von Oldenburg-Januschau phrased it.[72] With the help of the Catholics, Bülow's tax programme was replaced by a bundle of indirect taxes which left agrarian interests untouched and alienated the commercial and industrial bourgeoisie.[73] The *Sammlung* policy of 1898 had at last come to an ignominious end. Germany was divided into three large political camps, the Social Democrats, the middle parties and the conservative Right.

The collapse of the Bloc was not only a disaster for Bülow whose political career it ended, but also for Tirpitz who had been hoping that the tax reform would give the Reich finances a sufficiently sound basis for his own future armaments plans. Now the reckless policy of the agrarians had put these plans in jeopardy. This at any rate was the implication of a letter which Tirpitz received from the State Secretary of the Reich Treasury at the end of August 1909.[74]

His colleague, Adolf Wermuth wrote, would have to realise 'that the internal structure of the Reich, its defence capabilities and its external prestige demand not merely a standstill, but an energetic reduction of [our] expenditure'. Otherwise 'the development will end inescapably in the complete collapse of our finances and all national activities stemming from them'. Put more bluntly, Germany was faced with the choice of either abandoning her ambitious armaments policy which swallowed the lion's share of the Reich budget or else of accepting paralysis at home.

5 The Critical Year of 1911

When Bethmann Hollweg assumed office in July 1909, both German foreign and domestic policy were in a very critical state, and little was left of the hopes with which the Reich government had initiated its naval armaments programme only ten years before. The domestic scene especially was in complete disarray. The Bülow Bloc had fallen apart over the financial reform issue. The tax burdens which the Anglo-German arms race imposed had again been put onto the shoulders of those groups who were largely excluded from the decision-making process. Dissatisfaction with the existing order and the excessive influence of the conservative elites within it had reached dangerous proportions. The Reich government no longer commanded the broad conservative majority of the *Sammlung* period. On the contrary its support in the Reichstag had been successively whittled away and there was now a real possibility of a strong swing towards the Left in the next elections. Then the agrarians who had shown themselves incapable of accepting even the most reasonable and moderate reforms would receive a just 'punishment' for their selfishness. It was to be expected that a clear centre-left majority would be returned to the Reichstag. However, since under the given constitutional and political realities no Chancellor could rely on such a majority and govern against the Conservatives, internal politics were threatened by paralysis. Bethmann Hollweg was caught between two fires. If he identified himself with the reckless policies of the agrarians, the alienation of the majority of the people might so weaken the coherence of the monarchy that a pre-revolutionary situation would develop. On the other hand, any attempt by him to modernise the political system was bound to incur the wrath of the Conservatives.

Faced with these dilemmas, the Reich Chancellor had practically only one way open to him: he had to try and rebuild the bridges between the Conservatives and the bourgeoisie which the financial reform of 1909 had destroyed. A 'reforming conservatism'[1] was the only solution which might keep the Conservatives from drifting into more and more reactionary postures and win them over to a cautious policy of appeasement towards the Left. The total polarisation of political life had to end or else the monarchy might find itself embroiled in a civil war whose outcome would at best be a Pyrrhic victory for the Prusso-German political system, and more likely a catastrophe.[2] In an attempt to define his strategy, Bethmann Hollweg once said that he was pursuing a 'policy of the diagonal'. Yet it was rather a curious diagonal, very much like Bülow's who, speaking in the Reichstag in March 1901, had first used this expression.[3] For it is difficult to see how the new Chancellor could have conducted anything but a policy whose balance was heavily tilted towards the Right. Throughout his life he had been a devout monarchist and a loyal servant of the crown.[4] Never would he utter a critical word about the Kaiser or the monarchical order in public; he would come to their defence whenever the Opposition commented upon the incongruity between Germany's modern industrial society and the quasi-absolutism of William II which was exacerbated by the monarch's eccentricity. When, in August 1910 the Kaiser affirmed his conviction that he ruled 'as an instrument of the Lord' independent of the political opinions of the day,[5] he reminded the Germans once again how little Prusso-German Constitutionalism and the parliamentary systems of western Europe had in common and the resulting public protest against this view gave Bethmann Hollweg an opportunity to defend the crown in the Reichstag. The Chancellor did his best, mindful of Bülow's rather meek defence of the crown during the *Daily Telegraph* debates which had contributed to his predecessor's downfall. After all, it had not been the Reichstag, but William II who, as the Kaiser later put it, had 'chased the scoundrel [Bülow] away'.[6]

Bethmann knew that he could not govern without possessing the benevolent support of the monarch. His rejection of the parliamentary system was no more than the logical corollary of his monarchism. He was convinced that 'political culture and political education will not be advanced but will suffer, the more democratic our electoral system becomes'.[7] All 'the democratisation of parliamentarism' had done to other countries, he added, was to help 'to level off and to brutalise political morals'. In these circumstances it was also beyond him to imagine that the monarchical order could ever be transformed into a parliamentary system. In fact, as long as the crown continued to have full control of the Army, it was more likely that it would try to achieve greater stability by means of a *Staatsstreich* or an expansionist war rather than through political reform. Both at home and abroad, the German political system was on the defensive. It did not require the radical slogans of the revolutionary wing in the S.P.D. for the ruling elites of the Reich and Prussia to feel threatened; the moderate 'revisionism' of the more right-wing Social Democrats was quite enough to make them think of repression. Deputy Ludwig Frank's refutation of Bethmann Hollweg's assertion that parliamentary democracy had a demoralising and corrupting effect on society contained all those arguments against which the Conservatives of the Empire were putting up an ever more desperate fight.[8] This antagonism was also reflected in Frank's references to the British Parliament which to him was a centre of high political morality and a training ground of far-sighted statesmanship. There, he said sarcastically, ministers were created not because they knew how to play cards, but because of their intelligence and political talent. These comparisons, in fact, pinpointed another important element of the Anglo-German rivalry: it was not merely that the military and economic potential of the two states clashed in the decade and a half before 1914. The naval arms race between Britain and the Reich ultimately involved the question of which of the two political systems would prove more resistant to the stresses and strains imposed by Tirpitz's Cold War.

When surveying the political scene after Bülow's fall, Bethmann Hollweg could hardly fail to appreciate that Germany had not stood up too well to the self-inflicted external and internal pressures on her political system. The 1898 *Sammlung* of all conservative and middle parties had developed such strong centrifugal tendencies that it finally broke completely apart. Since then the Reich government was faced with two 'little' *Sammlung* movements. The first one was led by those forces which, by wrecking Bülow's introduction of a death duty, had thrown domestic politics into complete disarray. They advocated a relentless struggle against the Social Democrats and demanded government protection. The other 'little' *Sammlung* movement was centred around the two main Liberal parties and a new extra-parliamentary pressure group, the *Hansabund*.[9] They were aiming at a combination of the middle classes against the agrarians and their retrograde constitutional and financial policies.

The question with which the Chancellor was confronted in the pursuit of his policy of the diagonal was how these two camps might be brought together again to form a broad *Sammlung* against the socialists; could the parties of the centre perhaps be tempted with the help of a reform of the Prussian three-class voting system which they had been demanding for some time and which had been announced in William's opening speech before the Prussian Diet in October 1908? The proposals which the Prussian Minister of the Interior had drafted by November 1909 were supposed to represent an 'organic evolution' of the existing provisions.[10] Closer scrutiny of the draft shows what this meant: all the reform attempted to do was to 'eliminate the worst abuses of the existing system, such as indirect balloting and the plutocratic distortions due to the use of tax returns as a basis for the division into three classes of electors'.[11] The basic idea underlying so much modesty was, as Bethmann Hollweg explained in March 1910, 'to bar an excessive influx of Socialists and Poles and to give heavy industry, especially in the Rhineland, a chance to be represented in the Lower House'.[12] Although it was thus clear whom the reform was supposed to win over, it pleased practically no one, and certainly did not achieve its 'chief purpose ... which is to pacify the country and to reach a tolerable conclusion'.[13] The Prussian Conservatives were opposed because they feared the erosion of their dominant position; to the Left the proposals were not far-reaching enough. Unable to govern without the Conservatives because a Liberal-Centre-Free Conservative coalition 'would in fact lead us too far to the left', and unwilling to 'make the law without the support of the Free Conservatives and National Liberals',[14] Bethmann finally withdrew the bill altogether. The result was that, as the Reich Chancellor predicted, 'the chasm between Conservatives and National Liberals will widen and the latter will be pushed further to the Left'.[15] He had failed to move the middle parties towards the Right and, what was perhaps even more disastrous, to persuade the agrarians to accept at least a minimum of political change. For 'with their personal, social, religious and political hubris and intolerance' the Conservatives had not only isolated themselves but had, as Bethmann Hollweg concluded, also focused 'everyone's disgust and dissatisfaction against the three-class suffrage which is generally seen as an expression of Junker predominance',[16] i.e. they had weakened rather than strengthened the entire political system.

'Perhaps', he added, 'they will first have to pass through the hard school of the Reichstag elections' before they saw reason.

Out of the acrimonious debates over the electoral reform there emerged one important fact, namely that the *Sammlung* of the centre was not a monolithic movement. The heavy-industrialists, in particular, who had joined the *Hansabund* in 1909 for what may well have been purely tactical reasons,[17] were far from being firm adherents of the anti-agrarian platform of that organisation. As before, they were more worried by the rise of the Left which challenged with great fervour the patriarchical conditions in the coal and steel industries. These priorities also influenced their attitude towards the Prussian reform bill. They felt that, as the syndicus of the Dortmund Chamber of Commerce put it, changes of an electoral law 'which creates a protective wall against the most dangerous enemy of the state' should be avoided. 'For the upholding of this protective wall is immensely more important than the introduction of this or that reform which as such it may be worth discussing.'[18] Henry Axel Bueck, the Secretary General of the Central Federation of Industrialists, placed the issue in a broader political context when he spoke of the need for a merciless and costly struggle against the Left the result of which 'must be the defeat and the complete destruction of the Social Democrat trade unions'.[19] This is why, he continued, the members of the Federation should stand closely together and be prepared to make sacrifices in support of the anti-Socialist campaign.

Such appeals were accompanied by a cautious dissociation from the mainstream of *Hansabund* and National Liberal opinion as represented by Jakob Riesser, the President of the *Bund*, and Ernst Bassermann, the leader of the National Liberal Party. The hope was apparently that a gradual *rapprochement* between the heavy-industrialist right-wing of the *Hansabund* and the agrarians on the basis of a rabid anti-Socialism might, in the long run, act as a magnet also to other elements of the heterogeneous centre. It is hence no accident that similar right-wing tendencies made themselves felt within the National Liberal Party, with Bassermann becoming the target of attacks from the representatives of heavy industry. One of these, Paul Fuhrmann, conjured up the memory of Bismarck's economic and social policy and exhorted the 'close [and] unshakable friendship between industry and agriculture'.[20] The task was, he urged his readers, to oppose 'democracy' which

was bewitching 'so large a part of our people' with its 'illiberal political ideology (*Staatsauffassung*)' and its popular political slogans.
These developments were not lost on the agrarians. Men like
Richthofen-Damsdorf began to woo the heavy-industrialists.[21] It was
pointed out that they had not been hit too severely by the tax
increases which the Conservatives had imposed after Bülow's fall
and that socialism and liberalism had always been the common
enemies of industry and agriculture. But this in itself was not enough
to forge a firm alliance between the Federation and the agrarians.
Nor was a purely negative and intransigent conservatism the appropriate means to induce other groups within the *Hansabund* to break
away and move towards the Right. In view of this impasse and the
continued existence of two *Sammlung* movements, Bethmann had no
choice but to look for different catalysts to obtain a conservative
majority in the Reichstag. The outcome of the electoral reform
debates had shown that carefully-balanced domestic changes did not
help to bridge the gulf between the Right and the middle parties. On
the contrary, fronts had hardened so much that any legislation which
necessitated a compromise between the two camps was doomed to
failure. If a broad *Sammlung* could not be induced by domestic
policies, could foreign policy perhaps do the trick?

The Reich Chancellor could hardly have failed to recognise that
German commerce and the export industries were very worried
about the critical state of Anglo-German relations. With the fleet
still being much weaker than the Royal Navy, the escalation of the
Anglo-German arms race into a war implied a direct threat to their
existence. A war with England would lead to an immediate blockade of the Reich and cut their links with overseas markets on which
they were dependent. From Bethmann Hollweg's point of view, an
Anglo-German naval agreement promised to offer gains in several
respects. It would lessen international tension and relieve the pressure of isolation; it would reduce armaments expenditure and thus
ease the financial plight of the Reich. Finally, it seems that he
hoped an understanding with Britain and a diplomatic success
could prepare the way for a bridge-building operation at home.

In the autumn of 1909, he picked up the thread which Bülow had
dropped under pressure from Tirpitz some eight months earlier. A
fairly precise procedural concept had been worked out by Alfred
von Kiderlen-Wächter, soon to become State Secretary in the
German Foreign Office. The two basic memoranda which he

submitted to Bethmann Hollweg at the end of September and the beginning of November 1909 argued that negotiations for a limitation of naval armaments should be initiated together with carefully staggered discussions on topics of mutual political interest.[22] The political understanding was to be crowned by a neutrality pact between the two countries. According to Kiderlen, the idea of conducting negotiations in the military and the political sphere had one considerable advantage: he expected the political discussions to proceed more smoothly than the disarmament talks of the technical experts, because 'the political sphere is more elastic than the military one'.[23] And once Germany had 'again established a trustful relationship with England as a result of political arrangements', the Reich government could, Kiderlen thought, afford to be 'generous on the fleet question itself'.

This, however, was precisely the point over which Tirpitz profoundly disagreed with the Reich Chancellor. Any generosity on Germany's part, he felt, was improper because it endangered the prospective naval bill of 1911. He did not desire a naval agreement with Britain, at least not at this stage when it was a matter of filling the gap of 1912–17 and of reaching the Iron Budget. Of course, he could not use this argument, especially not at a time when the British Admiralty issued public statements to the effect that England was still looking for ways and means to reduce the armaments burdens. 'This', Tirpitz commented when receiving the news, 'will generate [strong] pressure that we, on our part, approach the British!'[24] He was correct. By September, the Kaiser had given his approval to a re-opening of negotiations and Tirpitz was asked to submit proposals which might serve as a basis for military discussions.[25] The State Secretary complied, but what he put forward was so complicated and so unlikely to attract the British Admiralty that the preparatory discussions within the Reich government slowly but surely ground to a halt.[26] Bethmann Hollweg was therefore not unhappy when Asquith's Liberal Cabinet decided to hold a national election early in 1910. The two governments agreed to postpone their negotiations. Yet with Tirpitz continuing to take an obstructive attitude towards the whole question of an Anglo-German agreement, the diplomatic discussions after the British elections never got beyond their preliminary stages either.[27] The spring of 1911 approached without

Bethmann Hollweg having achieved any foreign policy successes worth mentioning. Kiderlen's timetable in particular, it turned out, not only underestimated the depth of the Anglo-German estrangement, but also the strength of the internal opposition. It proved most difficult to heed Wermuth's advice of August 1909 to scale German armaments down even though it was clear that the naval programme had had such a disastrous effect on the external and internal position of the monarchy.

One reason for this was given by Wilhelm Stemrich, Under Secretary of State in the Foreign Office. 'One does not lightly abandon', he wrote sarcastically in October 1909, 'the idea of great power status.'[28] However, there was another and perhaps more important reason. Over the years, the German ship-building industry had become more and more dependent on orders from the Imperial Navy. In order to cope with the increased building tempo of the 1908 Law, the yards had been expanded and the steel industry had invested considerable sums in the development of additional capacities. But in 1911 arms orders by the Navy would drop by 50 per cent and Tirpitz knew, as he told the Chief of the Naval Cabinet in July 1909, that sooner or later the shipbuilding industry would find itself in a quandary.[29] The military-industrial complex had developed a dynamic of its own and the economic laws of a capitalist armaments industry began to limit the already narrow scope of German foreign policy even further. As Zedlitz entered in his diary on 9 April 1909:[30]

> Well-known enthusiasts apart, there are quite a few influential people here who are opposed to any limitation of armaments. It would be very interesting to learn something about the various connections which exist between the fleet fanatics and the manufacturers of the fleet. The power of the steel kings weighs heavily, and the worry about their business, the desire to keep the share index high has frequently been served to us as a national concern.

The Reich Navy Office was therefore quite rightly expecting heavy industry to spend large sums on agitation for a return to the *Dreiertempo* in 1912,[31] and Tirpitz wrote as early as September 1909, when he was drafting his proposals for Bethmann Hollweg's negotiations with England, that such a tempo would not be 'as hard and uncomfortable for Krupp etc. economically' as a drop to two ships per annum.[32]

Considering that Tirpitz had such formidable allies, it is not surprising that the Chancellor's foreign policy made so little headway. Nor was he helped at home by the dichotomy between those political groups which, alarmed by the arms race, advocated a rapprochement with England and those which demanded a continuation of ship-building for fear of an economic recession. On the contrary, to some extent the conflict between heavy industry and the *Hansabund* majority was a reflection of divergent attitudes towards the Anglo-German arms race which were exacerbated by the trouble over the Prussian electoral reform. Two years after Bülow's fall, the Reich government's record was unimpressive. The polarisation of society had not been arrested and Kiderlen's peace offensive had failed to get beyond its initial stages. 'Nobody knows', Ballin confessed in November 1910, 'where the journey will lead.'[33] This was all the more depressing because the following winter was bound to bring a worsening of the internal *and* external crises. National elections were due to take place in January 1912 and various by-elections which had been held since 1909 indicated that there would be a landslide towards the Left. At the same time Bethmann Hollweg knew that Tirpitz would try to introduce another navy bill and thus provoke a diplomatic crisis with Great Britain.

It is against the background of Germany's desolate political situation and the even more desperate prospects for the future that the events of the summer of 1911 must be seen. 'In my opinion', Ballin wrote to Francke in July 1910, 'we are in the midst of a revolution today, for the fact that all by-elections to the Reichstag return Social Democrats supports the conclusion that a great change is in the making.'[34] Ballin saw only one solution: 'a powerful campaign slogan, ... a few men who have a strong position among the German people. Perhaps Kiderlen will introduce a livelier tone into the matter; or else I shall take a gloomy view [of the future].' In other words, Ballin suggested an aggressive foreign policy to overcome disunity at home and stagnation abroad. By the spring of 1911, the temptation to conduct 'domestic policy with the steam power of diplomacy'[35] had become so great for Bethmann Hollweg and Kiderlen that they decided to act.

Kiderlen had already worked out a plan to use the French inter-vention in Morocco for demanding territorial concessions in Africa. The hope that foreign successes would have a favourable effect on the domestic situation played a major role in Kiderlen's calcula-tions, as is shown by his memorandum of 3 May 1911 in which he outlined his strategy.[36] Replying to the Kaiser's fear that a German occupation of Agadir might result in a diplomatic defeat rather than a victory, the State Secretary of the Foreign Office declared: 'By seizing a [territorial] pawn, the Imperial Government will be placed in a position to give the Moroccan affair a turn which could cause the earlier setbacks [of 1905] to pass into oblivion.' If it were possible, so Kiderlen continued, 'to obtain tangible advantages for Germany' from the 'liquidation of the Moroccan question', this 'would be important also for the future development of political conditions at home'. Bethmann Hollweg had a similarly high appreciation of the interdependence between diplomacy and domestic politics. It was for this reason that the Chancellor was, as Kiderlen informed Heinrich Claß, the leader of the Pan-German League, 'keen to gain a success and is growing impatient'.[37] A diplomatic victory in Morocco as a catalyst for a broad *Sammlung* and a bitterly needed strengthening of the Reich government—these promises made it relatively easy to surmount the Kaiser's fear of a setback. On 26 June he approved the sending of the gun-boat *Panther* to Agadir.[38]

The reception which the news received in the German press confirmed the view that an intervention in Morocco would act as a valve to release some of the domestic pressure on the Prusso-German political system. 'Hurrah! A deed!', was the first reaction of the *Rheinisch-Westfälische Zeitung* which was close to the Central Federation of Industrialists.[39] The *Kreuz-Zeitung* noted that 'a deep sigh of relief' went through Germany,[40] and it affected not only groups which had always agitated for an aggressive foreign policy, but also those who had previously adhered to the idea of an under-standing with Britain. The upsurge of imperialist enthusiasm was particularly marked in the National Liberal Party; for the first time since 1909 a *rapprochement* between the centre and the Right seemed a possibility. Bassermann took the opportunity of writing to Kiderlen to tell him that he welcomed the new 'active policy' which acted 'like a liberation'.[41] Then he reiterated the old fears of the 1890s that Germany might find it more and more difficult to conclude commercial treaties and might be excluded from the world market. 'The thoughtful circles of the nation', he concluded, could not but avoid the feeling that this development would ultimately drive a country like Germany into the *ultima ratio* of war; for she 'must expand if she does not want to be suffocated by her surplus population'. It was these fears which pushed Bassermann towards the Right and into the arms of the Central Federation of Industrialists and the agrarians who were both labouring for a broadly-based conservative *Sammlung*. 'The events in the field of foreign policy', so Karl Mehnert, the chairman of the Saxon Conservatives, reported to Friedrich Wilhelm von Loebell who in turn informed Bethmann Hollweg, 'will come to our aid to facilitate such a procedure.'[42] In the end, even parts of the Left Liberals were swept away by the general enthusiasm so that the Social Democratic *Leipziger Volkszeitung* was quite justified in feeling they had joined the 'imperialist camp' largely for economic reasons.[43] 'The charge of German imperialism', *Der Vorwärts* added, had had 'the effect of a clarion call'. Now 'the game of the Hottentot elections [of 1907] is to have its second and improved repeat performance.'[44]

When deciding on the Moroccan intervention, Kiderlen had been fairly confident of some sort of territorial gain, whether in Morocco itself or in the Congo Basin. However, the French reacted so slowly to the German demands for compensations that the State Secretary in the German Foreign Office began to suspect that France was playing for time to obtain British support against Germany. At the end of July it became clear that Britain could indeed not be discounted. Lloyd George made his famous Mansion House speech which contained a warning the Reich could hardly fail to hear. The British Foreign Office had quickly realised that the German move could not be treated as a purely local Franco-German affair. If successful, Kiderlen's plan was bound to have repercussions on the balance of power in Europe. As Crowe minuted on 18 July 1911,[45]

Germany is playing for the highest stakes. If her demands are acceded to either on the Congo or in Morocco, or—what she will, I believe, try for—in both regions, it will mean definitely the subjection of France. The conditions demanded are not such as a country having an independent foreign policy can possibly accept. The details of the terms are not so very important now.

It is a trial of strength, if anything. Concession means not loss of interest or loss of prestige. It means defeat with all its inevitable consequences.

Sir Arthur Nicolson, the Permanent Under Secretary of State in the Foreign Office, elaborated the view that if Germany had her way 'our policy since 1904 of preserving the equilibrium and consequently the peace in Europe' would collapse.[46]

Under these circumstances it turned out to have been a grave error that Kiderlen had paid so little attention to the possible reaction of the British Empire when he conceived his Moroccan adventure. British intervention in the crisis in July 1911 triggered off two developments which exposed the fatal weaknesses of Germany's strategy. Due to England's backing for France it had become unlikely that the territorial concessions which the Reich government was hoping to extract would in any sense be commensurate with the effort invested in the Agadir enterprise. Since the expectations of the German public had been raised very high, they were bound to be disappointed by whatever colonial possessions the post-Agadir negotiations might now bring. Moreover, Lloyd George's warnings threatened to unleash a war hysteria which would play into the hands of the military. We have seen how the government had been using an 'active' foreign policy and the appeal to defensive instincts in 1905–6 to achieve an integrating effect at home. Yet although the mobilisation of friend-foe feelings did have a stabilising effect, the agitation was always liable to get out of hand and to become grist to the mills of those who advocated an immediate war as the panacea of all problems. These radical forces were almost certain to be encouraged when rumours reached Germany that the Royal Navy had been mobilised.

By the middle of August, Kiderlen had to admit that he could no longer control the spirits he had raised.[47] The Agadir venture began to backfire on the Reich government much as the First Moroccan Crisis had done. In the meantime the internal problems of the monarchy had multiplied and William's alternative—first suppression of the Social Democrats, then a foreign war—had lost much of its earlier persuasiveness. The deterioration of Germany's international position and the growing tensions at home rather served to strengthen the hand of those who proposed to compress the two steps into one. War, the right-wing *Post* declared on 26

August 1911, would not only clarify 'our precarious [foreign] political position', but also bring a 'curing of many political and social
ills'.[48] Heinrich Claß, writing at this time about the 'influence of
foreign policy on domestic affairs', viewed a war as the 'only remedy for our people'.[49] 'A generous passage at arms', the *Deutsche
Armeeblatt* maintained, 'should be quite beneficial also for our
domestic situation, even if it means tears and grief to individual
families.'[50] This was certainly a widespread conviction in the officer
corps. Having been condemned to witness the decline of the
monarchy without being listened to, Moltke now almost lost his
temper:[51]

> I am beginning to get sick and tired [he wrote to his wife on 19
> August] of this unhappy Moroccan affair.... If we again slip away
> from this affair with our tail between our legs and if we cannot
> bring ourselves to put forward a determined claim which we are
> prepared to force through with the sword, I shall despair of the
> future of the German Empire. I shall then resign. But before
> handing in my resignation I shall move to abolish the Army and
> to place ourselves under Japanese protectorate; we shall then be
> in a position to make money without interference and to develop
> into ninnies.

Müller was not quite so dejected, but also believed that 'war is not
the greatest of all evils.'[52]

By the end of August and the beginning of September 1911 the
press was full of reports that war with England was imminent. The
war-psychosis reached a climax. Yet although there was a marked
increase in the strength of the war party as compared with 1906 or
1909, the 'moderates' once more succeeded in asserting themselves. Among them was Kiderlen who, though prepared to go to
the brink of war, was not really keen to have one.[53] In the final
analysis his reluctance to lead the Reich into a shooting war was
connected with the pessimistic view which he took of the
monarchy's future in the event of war. Even a victorious war, he
thought, would not strengthen the existing order:[54] 'All great
victories', he said to the Roumanian Take Ionescu, 'are the work of
the people and the people must be paid for it. After the victory of
1870 we had to pay with universal suffrage. Another victory will
bring us a parliamentary regime.' Bethmann Hollweg seems to

have shared this view. Moreover he was doubtful if the masses would follow their monarch into war. The war scare of the beginning of September led to a rush on bank savings which showed that the domestic situation was as unstable as ever and the country by no means prepared for a major conflict. The Kaiser, whose throne was after all at stake and who had never been particularly happy about the Moroccan adventure, accepted Bethmann Hollweg's arguments with a sigh of relief.

There was yet another powerful man in the Reich government who was opposed to war: Tirpitz. Knowing that all the Imperial Navy could expect from open conflict was destruction by England or the humiliation of being kept in harbour while the Army won its victories against France, he preferred a continuation of the Cold War against Britain which would help him with his projected naval bill. For several years he had fixed his mind on the gap of 1912–17 which he intended to fill with additional ships. To achieve this aim which would be the final link in his elaborate chain of navy laws he had, he thought, made considerable sacrifices since 1908 and especially after the fiasco of Bülow's tax reform. Thus he had responded to Bethmann Hollweg's request to help him come to an understanding with Britain. He realised, of course, that the agreement could only be reached 'at the expense of the Navy' and therefore did his best subtly to sabotage the diplomatic timetable.[55] Not surprisingly, the German Foreign Office soon began to regard the Navy as the root of all its difficulties.

Wermuth at the Treasury was more successful than the diplomats in keeping the Navy Secretary at bay. True to his declaration of August 1909 that Reich expenditure must either be cut back or else the state machinery would slowly grind to a standstill, he surrounded the Treasury 'with barbed wire', as Tirpitz put it after the war. In the autumn of 1909 even Tirpitz's old trick of bypassing the Reich Treasury by appealing directly to the Kaiser proved unworkable.[56] In the budget as presented by Wermuth for 1910 the Navy had to accept a cut of 7 million marks already appropriated in principle under the 1908 Law.[57] This was all the more serious because the pressure to take account of costly technological advances continued with undiminished force. With other nations and above all England constantly increasing their ships' armour and gun calibres, Tirpitz could not but follow suit, though he hated it. 'Must I come to a decision today?', he asked his experts who were pressing

for bigger guns.[58] At the same time cost inflation continued, stimulated by the decision to build four capital ships per annum. The
Reich Navy Office made a desperate effort to break Krupp's mono-
poly in steel supplies for which Tirpitz's allocation policies of the
previous years were partly responsible.[59] He was, as he admitted to
his comrades in the Reich Navy Office on 25 August 1910, simply
'not in a position to go beyond the projected price for the 1911
constructions'.[60] In short, inflationary developments and technical
innovations caused constant shortages of funds and two years after
the passage of the 1908 navy bill the financial state of the Navy was
no better than it had been in 1907.

As before, the front-line commands suffered most from these
deficiencies. The commands at Kiel and Wilhelmshaven were being
furnished with bigger and bigger ships for which a sufficient number of officers was simply not available. Tirpitz had always argued
that it was more important to build ships; all other problems, he
said, could be tackled once the Iron Budget had been reached. Had
Germany possessed a professional navy like Britain, the problem
would not have been so acute. But the German naval officer corps
had to carry out not only its normal duties which became more
complex from year to year, but in the autumn of each year they
were also confronted with a new generation of recruits who had to
be trained from scratch. The result was that the professional officer
corps was permanently overworked while the incoming recruits
impaired military readiness. For several weeks every autumn, the
battle fleet was simply not ready to fight a naval war. Finally, the
fact that Tirpitz was always trailing behind the Royal Navy in
fighting power and ships' speed had a demoralising effect on the
Navy. At the turn of the century it had been relatively easy to
accept Tirpitz's argument that for a number of years the Imperial
Navy would be inferior, but only until 'equality' with Britain had
been achieved. Now it appeared that the determined response of
the British had prolonged the 'danger zone'.

Doubts were raised as to whether the anti-British aims of the
original plan could ever be realised. Worse still, the Anglo-German
arms race had increased the danger of an early war with the first
sea power which began to influence the fleet's morale more and
more adversely. The front-line commands found it impossible to
live with the fact that they would be nothing but cannon fodder in
the event of war and continued to pester Tirpitz to do something

about military preparedness. Ultimately, it was demanded, the ratio with England would have to be brought up to a level which would give Germany the 'prospect of a victory'. Without this prospect the Navy could not in the long run 'maintain the spirit which is necessary to guarantee its efficiency'. It would thus lose its 'value as a power-political asset'.[61] Clearly the Imperial Navy could not dispense with the hope of victory against England if its 'inner morale' and its 'external prestige' was to be maintained.[62] In 1908 Tirpitz had, for the first time, been confronted with an open rebellion which he could quell only with the help of the Kaiser who reminded the fleet commands of the financial dilemma.[63] But internal criticism never died down and could definitely no longer be kept in bounds when the rumours of British preparations for war led to the war scare of August 1911. For the Admiralty Staff and the front-line commands this scare was a golden opportunity to draw attention to the deficiencies of the Navy.

Tirpitz was now less alarmed by these tendencies than he had been in 1909 or 1910. After all, the time was rapidly approaching when the whole question of the size of the Navy would come up anyway. The new bill which he was aiming for would enable him to satisfy the most urgent demands of the front-line commands, too. But his main objective was to persuade the Reichstag to approve a number of additional ships. As Tirpitz told Müller at the beginning of May 1911, 'a tempo of two ships per annum over a period of six years' would be 'intolerable'.[64] The Reich Navy Office saw no alternative but to regain the *Dreiertempo* before 1918'. Unless new ships were added to the fleet, the aims which the monarchy had pursued ever since the turn of the century could not be attained and, what was even more dangerous, the entire system of navy laws might crumble. Seen from this angle, Kiderlen's Moroccan adventure was almost a godsend for Tirpitz. The Reich Navy Office thought immediately that 'the Agadir enterprise, whatever its outcome, will be very useful to naval propaganda'.[65] The State Secretary agreed and began to bank on the 'tremendous indignation' which the imminent diplomatic defeat of Germany would arouse.[66] Eduard von Capelle, one of his closest advisers, was at first rather more sceptical. He could not detect much popular enthusiasm for another expansion of the Navy. But he felt strongly that, whenever the storm of public indignation did arise, the Imperial Navy should go for a 'continuation of a building tempo of four ships against

England' or nothing.[67] 'This requires strong nerves, however!' Tirpitz, in his reply of 14 August 1911, did not expect Bethmann Hollweg and the Kaiser to have strong nerves.[68] Moreover he thought that a *Dreiertempo* plus qualitative improvements and personnel increases would just about be the limit of what Britain would tolerate without war.

At the end of August, the State Secretary believed that the time had come to inform the Chancellor.[69] 'Growing irritation at home', he argued in his letter of 30 August, as well as the loss of German prestige abroad could only be countered by a 'major navy bill'. A stronger navy, he continued, was also the only means of conducting *Weltpolitik*. This is why he would recommend an increased building rate of three ships per annum from 1912, apart from a number of qualitative improvements. The whole plan would not require more than 350 million marks of which 300 million were to be covered by a loan. The remaining 50 million, he concluded, would have to be floated by introducing new taxation and more specifically a further death duty. To make the proposal more palatable to Bethmann Hollweg he urged him to initiate the bill in 'October of this year *before* the Reichstag elections'. This would take 'the wind out of the sails' of the Social Democrats and the Left Liberals and would 'presumably create a cartel of Conservatives, Centre Party and National Liberals'.

Tirpitz's move can hardly have come as a surprise to the Chancellor. He had observed the Reich Navy Office with a good deal of suspicion for some years and knew how much Germany's naval armaments policy had contributed to the deterioration of her position. When he met Tirpitz on 31 August, he therefore immediately pointed to the serious danger of war with England which another navy bill implied.[70] Tirpitz refused to admit that there was an immediate danger. Commenting on the possibility of war, he said that 'we must either take the risk or abdicate politically'. But the Chancellor remained unconvinced and merely repeated his objections during another conference with the State Secretary on 1 September. A naval bill, he added, would moreover be interpreted as an 'admission that we have suffered a setback'.[71] What Bethmann Hollweg did not mention was that he was hoping to use the gap of 1912–17 as a basis for another round of discussions with England and that he saw very serious internal obstacles to a navy bill. Ever since 1909, the Chancellor had been trying to bring about another conservative *Sammlung* which alone promised to give him an acceptable majority in the Reichstag. It was not until the Moroccan Crisis that any progress had been made in this respect. The upsurge of imperialist sentiment which came in the wake of Kiderlen's intervention in Morocco had begun to sway the National Liberals and even some Left Liberal elements. In his letter of 30 August Tirpitz argued that the new momentum which a navy bill would add to Bassermann's enthusiasm for an 'active' foreign policy would enhance the idea of a broadly-based *Sammlung*. If announced in the Reichstag before the elections the Social Democrats and the Left Liberals might be weakened.

Bethmann Hollweg was more than sceptical that this would be the result. The announcement of a navy bill, he expected, would immediately raise the financial question which had been an explosive issue for so many years. In particular, the death duty which Tirpitz had in mind was bound to meet with resistance from the Conservatives. The National Liberals, on the other hand, would press for its introduction. The gulf between the Right and the centre which had just begun to narrow under the impact of the Moroccan Affair would be torn wide open again. Finally he was afraid that an early publication of the bill would provide the S.P.D. with fresh ammunition. The socialists would merely have to remind the electorate of how the 1908 Navy Law had been financed with indirect taxes. As will be seen, the Reich Chancellor prevailed over his powerful Navy Secretary and thus prevented an immediate collapse of the as yet tenuous links between the Right and the centre. When the Moroccan treaties, which awarded to the Reich unspectacular territorial gains in West Africa, were discussed in the Reichstag in November 1911 the parties of the Right and the centre were united in their criticism of the Franco-German accord. Heydebrand declared that the compensations were practically worthless and Bassermann was convinced that 'this agreement is not in line with German interests and [does not bear any relation to] the power and the means of coercion of the German Empire'.[72] Germany, he said, had struck herself off the list of the great powers.

The Reich government patiently endured this criticism, hoping that the discussion of foreign problems would distract the population from burning domestic issues. The official statement which was put out on the occasion of the January elections was careful not to offend anyone, promising support for industry and agriculture and a continuation of social policy. It contained some vague hints as to the future of Germany's armaments policy and avoided taking sides with the Conservatives and the Centre Party. However, neither the imperialist agitation nor the soft-pedalling of the government at home sufficed to prevent a resounding victory of the S.P.D. – i.e. of the party which fiercely challenged the *status quo* and which, in its election platform of 5 December 1911, reiterated its determination to achieve political power in the Reich. All the bitterness and dissatisfaction which had accumulated since 1909 now came to the surface and resulted in a silent revolution by ballot. To some extent the inflationary development of food prices in the second half of 1911 accounted for the massiveness of the landslide. Bethmann Hollweg had tried to combat this development by suggesting changes in agricultural tariffs, but he met with instant opposition from the agrarians. For the S.P.D., this outcome was just another piece of evidence exposing the class-ridden character of the Prusso-German monarchy.[73]

The Social Democrats obtained 34.8 per cent of the votes and were thenceforth represented in the Reichstag with 110 deputies; all other parties suffered more or less heavy losses. The situation which Bethmann Hollweg had been dreading ever since 1909 had come about. To the Chancellor this must have been all the more disillusioning since he had tried so hard to stop a major domestic crisis from breaking out before the elections. The threat of such a crisis originated in Tirpitz's naval programme and involved a basic decision which had to be made about the future of Germany's armaments policy. The following chapter will therefore have to examine why the Chancellor went to such lengths to dismantle the projected navy bill.

6 The Reorientation of German Armaments Policy

When deciding to go ahead with another navy bill, Tirpitz was no doubt aware of the formidable obstacles which he would have to overcome. If he wanted to get his plan of six additional ships as well as the qualitative improvements and personnel increases adopted against the opposition of both Bethmann Hollweg and the Reichstag, he had to employ cunning and toughness. Capelle was the first to appreciate these problems once his Moroccan euphoria had subsided. When he wrote to Tirpitz on 17 August 1911, he no longer mentioned the possibility of a *Vierertempo*. He was not even certain any longer whether a navy bill was advisable or, if it was, how large it should be.[1] 'At the present moment', he feared, 'we shall meet with opposition all round.' This is why the Reich Navy Office, he continued, should 'build on the [long-term] after-effect of the [Moroccan] events among thoughtful people rather than the blustering of the Pan-Germans'. In view of this, the 1913 Budget would be 'the right moment' for the introduction of the navy bill.

At the end of September 1911 Tirpitz was due to see the Kaiser about his plans at Rominten and in the two weeks preceding this visit Capelle's advice was even more candid than before. He agreed with the State Secretary that 'the *attempt* must be made to restore a building tempo of three ships per annum'.[2] But he believed that this attempt would fail. The admission, implied in a new navy bill, 'that we have suffered a setback in Morocco, the fear of new severe frictions with England, the claim of the Opposition that the Reich tax reform [of 1909] had been a splendid failure' represented 'extraordinarily strong counter-arguments'. Capelle expected 'that the Reich Chancellor, Kiderlen, Wermuth, Delbrück [the State Secretary of the Interior] and the Prussian Ministry of State will all stand like one man against Your Excellency'. Moreover 'the south German federal states will be mobilised'. The utmost Tirpitz might be able to obtain 'is a postponement of the question until the next budget (1913)'. If the Kaiser sided with Bethmann Hollweg, Tirpitz

should try to get a decision from the monarch which left all options
open for 1913 and approved an immediate increase of personnel by
4000 men.

Tirpitz thought the Reich Navy Office could not afford to be as
modest as that.[3] Although he saw the advantages of a postponement until 1913, he anticipated that the personnel increases, as
suggested by Capelle, would almost certainly unleash a public
discussion on the question of another numerical increase in ships.
He also asked Capelle to consider that 'due to new inventions (air
ship), Reichstag debates on the future displacement of ships,
increases of crews, [and the whole] domestic situation' would make
it more and more difficult to get another navy bill passed. What
alarmed Tirpitz most, however, was that people might become
accustomed to a building tempo of two ships per annum at the end
of the six-year period. 'The *bonne mine* of England etc. and our
Foreign Office', he continued, would contribute to the eventual
emergence of a permanent tempo of two ships per annum to be
replaced automatically every twenty years. Although he could not
prove that 'the [German] Foreign Office wants [to reduce the fleet
to] 40 capital ships', it was this possibility which worried the State
Secretary most. Some time ago he had tried to discuss this danger
with the Kaiser. But William II had merely referred Tirpitz to the
Navy Law which provided for a return to the *Dreiertempo* in 1918.
The financial problem, the Kaiser had added naïvely, would be
immaterial. Yet it was precisely the financial question which made
the State Secretary take such a gloomy view of what would happen
in 1918. It was true that the Reichstag could not unilaterally
change the Navy Law. But what if the Bundesrat, in collusion with
the Reichstag, changed it in order to rid themselves of the explosive tax issue which, owing to the spiralling costs of the Anglo-
German naval arms race, was menacing the stability of the entire
political system? When devising his ambitious plan at the turn of
the century, Tirpitz had considered such a revision of the Navy Law
impossible, and it is indicative of the extent to which the dis-
illusionment with his aims had spread that, in 1911, he would rule
it out no longer.

Faced with what he thought was a most dangerous threat to his
entire life-work, the State Secretary resolved to employ the biggest
guns he had at his disposal to convince the Kaiser of the need for
an immediate expansion of the fleet. We have seen that in 1899

Tirpitz had begun to build a fleet which was to be inferior to the Royal Navy by no more than 33 per cent. Once completed, it would act as a political and, if necessary, even as a military lever against Britain's position as a world power. It was to this aim that Tirpitz addressed himself when he saw the Kaiser at Rominten on 26 September 1911. 'The historical verdict on our naval policy', he stated in his report, 'will depend on whether it will achieve its purpose' of gaining a 'good defensive chance' against England and thus prevent an attack by her.[4] Otherwise 'our policy must always show consideration for England and our sacrifices for the Navy will have been in vain'. History's verdict on William's reign would then ultimately be a negative one. In view of these high stakes, Tirpitz continued, only two choices were open to the monarch today: that of 'an agreement [with Britain], of a *voluntary limitation of armaments* on the basis of a 2:3 ratio' or else of a continuation of the arms race 'with the aim of *enforcing* this ratio'. Tirpitz said he preferred the former solution and then suggested that his proposal be published and officially made the basis of Anglo-German negotiations. 'If England accepts the proposal, Germany will be free to reach the [2:3] ratio by means of another naval bill.' If, on the other hand, 'England refuses, she will have to bear the stigma [of refusal] and cannot make any complaints'.

Harking back to his original plans, he added that 'in view of the weakness of our Navy' at the turn of the century it had been inappropriate then publicly to proclaim 'a quantitative formula in relation to the strongest sea power'. 'But the Navy needs slogans which can be understood by the masses', and this is why the risk theory had been invented. More recently, Tirpitz continued, this theory had become 'too vague' and Germany should now 'seize the opportunity of creating a firm basis for the Navy'. This, he believed, was best achieved by announcing the 2:3 formula. This announcement would silence domestic opposition while England would probably treat the German offer 'in a dilatory fashion'. At least she would find it impossible to use this as an excuse to wage war on the Reich since the ratio did not represent an immediate threat. The Kaiser should therefore proclaim the formula as soon as possible. 'After the elections, i.e. in February 1912', a precise building programme would be published to be followed by a navy bill in the autumn of 1912. This bill which more or less the parties had been expecting since 1908 anyway, would increase the building tempo for 1912–17 from two to three ships per annum. Otherwise considerable additional funds would be needed in 1918 at a time when 'the Reichstag had got used to the so much cheaper *Zweiertempo*.' A navy bill in 1912 would forestall the temptation to revise the Navy Law at that later date.

William II gave his approval to this plan without further ado. In particular he was attracted by the manipulative possibilities of the new 2:3 formula. 'The risk idea', he informed Bethmann Hollweg on 30 September 1911, 'has fulfilled its purpose and is dead. We now need another, tangible [and] clearly recognisable aim in order to direct our nation and to meet its demand for maritime prestige'.[5] Moreover he felt that as a sovereign responsible for the well-being of the nation he would have 'to insist on the maintenance of a higher building tempo so that none of the shipyards which had, after all, been created by the Navy, went bankrupt and workers became redundant'.[6] The monarch also did not fail to appreciate that Tirpitz's proposals amounted to a continuation of the naval arms race. He knew that England was unlikely to accept the new formula. But this did not seem to have worried him unduly. 'The British financial situation', he said, 'would force the British to be accommodating' and in the end they might even be glad to seize the chance of reducing the arms burden.[7] It was not merely a matter of the further development of the fleet, he wrote to Bethmann Hollweg on 26 September 1911, but involved also 'a question of vital importance to the future foreign policy of the Reich'.[8]

That Tirpitz believed the time had come to implement the anti-British calculations of his original concept emerges from a passage which he deleted from the published version of his Rominten report.[9] Echoing the arguments of the turn of the century, he said 'that once about 60 capital ships of some 25,000 tons are available and ready for war, our present Navy Law will be in accordance with the 2:3 ratio'. This number 'requires 90 capital ships, *based in the home waters*, on the British side ... and both navies will, as far as one can see, financially never be able to afford more than this'. But what was this formidable German instrument to be used for? Again referring to the beginnings of the naval programme, he raised this question once more in a letter to the Reich Chancellor of 7 October 1911.[10] 'When the current naval policy was embarked upon', he wrote, 'all relevant decision-making factors were clear about the fact that we would have to pass through a danger zone.

Then [as now] the ultimate question was: either to abdicate as a world power or to take risks.' The proposed navy bill implied, politically speaking, 'that Germany cannot remain in a permanent position of political dependence on England'; in military terms the 2:3 ratio meant 'that in the case of war we must at least have a promising chance of a defensive victory (*Defensivchance*)'.

Not surprisingly Bethmann Hollweg was profoundly disturbed by Tirpitz's all-or-nothing brinkmanship. In his view, the bill could be justified only with reference to the Moroccan Crisis and the tensions between Britain and Germany.[11] In these circumstances, he replied, the Chancellor and the Foreign Office would not only have to defend the bill in the Reichstag, but would also have to reckon with 'the eventuality of a war with England'. Would Tirpitz please let him know if the Navy were prepared for such a war? The State Secretary and the Chief of the Admiralty Staff, August von Heeringen, could not but reply that 'our chances in a war against England are not good under the present conditions'.[12] Bethmann Hollweg had won a first tactical victory. But the Reich Navy Office programme contained yet another flaw which worked to the Chancellor's advantage. Although Tirpitz and the Kaiser were opposed to this, the 2:3 ratio could also be interpreted to refer merely to a building tempo ratio—two German capital ships per annum against three British ships. Tirpitz argued that, if this principle were adopted, Germany would 'voluntarily abandon the possibility of reducing the military gap' between the Royal Navy and the Imperial Navy.[13] And if the gap could not be closed, he continued, 'the entire naval policy of the past 14 years has been in vain'. It was for this reason that Tirpitz was so keen to get additional ships which avoided a tempo of two ships, due to start from 1912. This had been the rationale of his policy since 1908.

Very probably Bethmann Hollweg had long discovered this curious ambiguity in Tirpitz's 2:3 formula himself, and it is possible that he abandoned his earlier negotiations with England not only because he realised that the State Secretary was obstructing an agreement, but also because he thought that 1912 would be a more propitious time for a diplomatic move. With the tempo dropping to two ships, he would be in a better position to offer the British an understanding on the basis of a 2:3 *building* ratio. There was some reason to believe that England might be prepared to grant political concessions in return for a relaxation of German naval pressure in the North Sea. The demolition of Tirpitz's armaments policy was, after all, a considerable bargaining proposition. By the middle of September, Tirpitz had a strong suspicion that the German Foreign Office intended to reduce the size of the fleet to 40 ships[14] and demanded an immediate announcement of his naval programme for 1912. He thought this all the more important 'because Your Excellency [i.e. Bethmann Hollweg] will no doubt be asked about it before the elections'.[15] For Bethmann Hollweg, on the other hand, any postponement of the announcement would help him not only to circumnavigate the awkward financial question, but also to keep the door open for his negotiations with England. It was for these two reasons that the inter-departmental discussions on the 1912 Budget assumed a crucial importance. If Bethmann Hollweg succeeded in preventing any naval increases from appearing in the budget proposals, to be published before the end of the year, domestic speculation about the future of the Navy could be expected to die down. At the same time, the publication of the proposals without navy increases would signal the British government that the Chancellor was trying to pave the way for diplomatic negotiations.

Finally, with the size of the navy budget again becoming an important issue, Bethmann Hollweg gained an ally who, as William II put it, certainly matched Tirpitz in 'bloodymindedness': Wermuth. The State Secretary of the Reich Treasury had made some headway since 1909 in his attempts to provide Reich finances with a more solid foundation.[16] But this achievement was constantly endangered by the great appetite of the Navy for more money which, he believed, could be satisfied only at the risk of upsetting the entire political system. When Wermuth therefore learned in the early summer of 1911 of the preparations for a navy bill, he immediately raised objections. Financial and domestic considerations, he wrote to Tirpitz on 19 June, would make it impossible to contemplate another increase of the Navy's budget.[17] Tirpitz was hence not completely unprepared when he met his colleague from the Reich Treasury on 9 October.[18] It was nevertheless a lot of water which Wermuth poured into Tirpitz's wine. The Reich Navy Office had been hoping to float most of the money through a loan. Wermuth flatly refused to support this unsound idea. The funds, he said, would have to be raised through additional taxes. Tirpitz was not opposed to this in principle if the 'required sum of new taxes' could be procured, but he realised that this touched upon a most delicate domestic problem. As Wermuth informed him, any announcement of the bill would have to be accompanied by a statement on 'how the costs were to be met', and 'as things stand now' indirect taxes were available only on a minor scale. The remaining sum would have to be levied by means of an extension of the death duty to which the agrarians were violently opposed.

What Tirpitz found even more worrying was that Wermuth insisted on a co-ordination of all fiscal planning in the hands of the Reich Treasury. The proposed navy bill, he was told, necessitated 'a new finance plan running over a longer period'. This, Wermuth continued, made it essential to establish what expenditure the other Reich offices intended to claim over the next few years. Only on the basis of these figures could the total amount of new taxes required to cover these claims be estimated. Against this idea Tirpitz lodged an emphatic protest, arguing that it represented a 'new departure'. If adopted, it would spell the 'death of any new army or navy bill'. In this he was certainly right. As we have seen, it had been one of the most important characteristics of Wilhelmine policy that financial considerations had been subordinated to a long-term armaments programme. But this state of affairs had wrought havoc to the finances of the Reich. It had led to domestic strife and intensified the crisis of the entire political system. Although Tirpitz did not put it in these terms, his concluding remarks to Wermuth show that over the past decade his armaments programme had done nothing to improve the position of the monarchy: even if the Reichstag, he said, were dissolved repeatedly and an election campaign were fought over the question of Germany's defence policy, an improvement in the situation could not be expected. The composition of Parliament would become 'even more democratic' and an era of conflict would 'plunge the German Reich into quite unpredictable difficulties'. Could one in these circumstances pursue any other policy than that proposed by Wermuth? It was the only logical conclusion to be drawn from the failure of Tirpitz's grand design.

This was also Bethmann Hollweg's view when Tirpitz reiterated his criticism of Wermuth's finance plan in a letter to the Reich Chancellor.[19] He said he wanted at least a postponement of the whole issue of the future of Germany's armaments policy until after the elections. This was confirmed by Müller, the Chief of the

Naval Cabinet, who saw the Chancellor on 13 October. Bethmann Hollweg quite understood, Müller reported to the Kaiser on the following day, 'that we must move ahead with the fleet; but he would also have to think of [the problem of] finances and of the political impression [an expansion of the fleet would make] on England'.[20] In view of this and of the strong position which Wermuth had in the Reichstag, Müller added, Tirpitz advised that one should try to win over the Chancellor and his stubborn financial expert. Or, to put it less diplomatically: Tirpitz was evidently hoping that William II would force Bethmann Hollweg to announce the navy bill without delay. Unfortunately for Tirpitz, this was not the outcome of the conference which the Kaiser had with his Chancellor on 15 October.[21] Instead the monarch agreed with Bethmann Hollweg that an official announcement of the bill or of the 2:3 ratio was politically dangerous. And, if the deputies raised the question on their own initiative, the Chancellor was to reply: 'The Reich government will introduce a navy bill if and when it is deemed necessary.'[22] Bethmann Hollweg on his part merely promised the Kaiser to table the bill in the spring of 1912—'provided it is then feasible'.

Tirpitz was hardly pleased, but refused to give up his struggle for an early announcement of the navy bill. He now tried to influence the wording of Bethmann's reply to a Reichstag interpellation, and indeed to engineer that interpellation. On 16 October 1911 the Reich Navy Office got in touch with the Centre Party.[23] Directly or indirectly a number of leading Catholic deputies became involved in these soundings; but neither Matthias Erzberger nor Adolf Groeber and Count Georg von Hertling showed much enthusiasm. However much Erzberger, for example, approved of the *great objective* which the bill was supposed to bring about, namely the mythical *alliance with England*, he did not like Tirpitz's timing. He realised that an early publication of the bill would 'inevitably also raise the financial question'.[24] This would in turn lead to 'the very awkward question of a death duty' which Hertling in particular did not wish to touch so shortly before the elections 'under any circumstances'.[25] According to Bethmann Hollweg, 'the Centre Party would in Hertling's view flatly refuse' the introduction of such a tax; and so would the Conservatives. One of the protectors of the agrarians, the Prussian Minister for Agriculture Klemens von Schorlemer-Lieser, expressed his enthusiasm for the principle of the navy bill. But when Müller quizzed him more closely, Schorlemer added: 'Yes, but of course, I consider it out of the question that the bill will be put before the present Reichstag.'[26]

With party enthusiasm for Tirpitz's proposals so decidedly lacking, it is not surprising that the hoped-for interpellation never came about. Although the Reich Navy Office tried to mobilise the press, not even the heated exchanges during the debate of the Moroccan treaties at the beginning of November 1911 culminated in the question whether the government intended to do something about Germany's naval strength.[27] The Chancellor was most gratified. But in order to make absolutely certain that the announcement of Tirpitz's bill did not slip into the 1912 budget through the backdoor, he proceeded to take up Wermuth's idea of drafting a long-term financial plan. It had the obvious advantage that, if all other Reich authorities were to be asked to submit their estimates for the next few years, more time would elapse before the complete picture could be put together. The Army, in particular, which swallowed the largest portion of the Reich budget, could be expected to take weeks to produce its projections. Moreover this raised further problems for Tirpitz as the Army leaders were now set upon expansion which would eat into the Navy's percentage of the defence budget.

In order to understand why the Army was suddenly prepared to contemplate massive increases and to abandon the principle of numerical stagnation, this reversal of previous policies must be put into the context of the international development since 1905. Witnessing the gradual collapse of Wilhelmine naval and world policy and the isolation of the country with growing discomfort, the military had found it more and more difficult to see themselves merely as defenders of the internal *status quo*. At a time when the military balance of power in Europe appeared to be shifting against Germany, it became less and less possible to uphold the principles of homogeneity and reliability as the sole guidelines of Army policy. Slowly the arguments of the General Staff, which had never ceased to worry, as was its duty, about the military balance, gained the upper hand over the political considerations of the War Ministry and the Military Cabinet. With the ascendency of men like Erich Ludendorff, Moltke's right-hand man from 1908 to 1912, the international posture of the Reich assumed priority. Ludendorff was convinced that military developments pointed irrevocably to modern mass armies and that Germany would, therefore, be forced 'to exploit her manpower resources to the last' and 'to turn the existing reserve formations into really large combat units which are genuinely operational'.[28]

Such proposals required much more money than the Reich, vexed by a chronic financial deficit and a costly naval armaments policy, had available. Could the monarchy really afford to continue a course which, initiated more than a decade ago, had meanwhile had such disastrous effects on its international and domestic position? Was it not better to concentrate on European goals rather than to chase after a colonial chimera? These were questions which Schlieffen had left to his successor to answer. In March 1909, the semi-official *Militärwochenblatt* had carried an article on the 'Army in chains',[29] and in July 1910 Ludendorff postulated unequivocally:[30] 'Any state which is involved in a struggle for its survival with utmost energy, must use all its forces and resources if it wants to live up to its highest duties'. The number 'of our enemies', he continued, 'is so great that it could become our inescapable duty' to use, 'in certain cases', every available soldier from the first moment. 'Everything depends on our winning the first battles.' The immediate implication of these urgent demands was that the priorities of Germany's armaments policy had to be redefined if the government could not find the money to satisfy both Tirpitz and Moltke. The realisation that the fleet would be useless in a war against England and had begun to do more to upset the stability of the political system than to support it, added fuel to these arguments.

In 1910, naval expenditure had reached the figure of 400 million marks, almost half of the Army's. Yet it was no secret that, if war came against England, the Reich would have to wage it against Britain's continental allies. Was it not more reasonable to concentrate on the defeat of France and not to dissipate one's limited financial resources? These tendencies were almost bound to receive a fresh boost after the Second Moroccan Crisis when Moltke was once again outvoted on the issue of an immediate preventive war— his first choice. After this defeat Tirpitz's attempt to introduce another navy bill and thus to gain an even bigger slice of the financial cake was bound to arouse indignation. As early as 1910 Eduard von Capelle had predicted a storm in the event that the Navy were again given preference over the Army.[31] 'The fire', he wrote about Army feeling, 'which has been burning under the ashes until now would then burst into bright flames.' Such, he added, were also the attitudes of many Conservatives. Although Tirpitz had known for some time that the agrarians favoured the fleet only as long as it promised to give them economic rewards, their key position within the Prusso-German political system now turned them into the most dangerous opponents of his entire concept. If they formed an alliance with the military, the federal governments and the Chancellor, the agrarians would undoubtedly be influential enough to enforce a reorientation of Germany's armaments policy.

It is against this background that Heydebrand's speech during the debate of the Moroccan treaties at the beginning of November 1911 deserves careful analysis. 'What safeguards our peace', he thundered, 'is not flexibility, agreements [and] understandings, but only our good German sword and the feeling that we are hoping to look up towards a government which will not allow this sword to rust when the appropriate time has come.'[32] In other words, Heydebrand demanded, more or less openly, that the land forces should be given priority over the Navy. All other differences of opinion apart, this was the point where the leader of the Conservatives and the Chancellor were in complete agreement. 'Germany', Bethmann Hollweg insisted in his own speech in the Reichstag, 'can conduct a strong policy in the sense of *Weltpolitik* only if she maintains her power on the Continent. Only the weight which we can throw into the scales as a continental power' enabled the country to pursue its global commercial interests and colonial policies.[33] All its overseas engagements, he continued, would be destroyed 'if we do not remain strong at home'. Germany would undermine her own position 'if we acquired outposts for whose security we would have to dissipate and weaken our continental forces'.

The Army took the point. Two weeks later the responsible departmental head in the Prussian War Ministry informed the Budget Committee of the Reichstag about recent additions to the French army in the form of North African troops.[34] In his report, the Hanseatic Delegate quoted him as having spoken of the '"heightening of the black peril"' and concluded: 'We shall have to prepare ourselves to meet this considerable increase in French military power.' When, at the end of November, Bethmann Hollweg asked Josias von Heeringen, the War Minister, if the changes in the power constellation required an expansion of the Army, Heeringen replied that he had already been asking himself this same question.[35] The last quinquennial appropriations had been inadequate, he said, and 'the political-strategic situation' had since 'shifted to Germany's disadvantage'. He would have to discuss the size of the prospective army bill with the Chief of the General Staff before entering into negotiations with the Navy to co-ordinate the claims of the two branches of the armed forces. The following days were filled with the production of memoranda by the War Ministry and the General Staff justifying the need for an army bill.[36] Everybody was agreed that Germany's political and military position had worsened and that, if war came, its outcome would be decided on the European continent. It was not difficult to see that these arguments were directed against Tirpitz and the armaments policy which Germany had pursued for more than a decade, although few were as frank about this as Wermuth. At the beginning of December he told the Saxon Ambassador that he considered some improvements of the fleet desirable, but was opposed to any large-scale expansion of the Navy.[37] This would only lead to Britain's moving ahead twice as fast. Germany, he concluded, was after all a land power. For this reason he would favour a strengthening of her Army.

Having suspected for some time that the Army might become a serious rival of the Imperial Navy in the struggle for scarce financial reources, Tirpitz manoeuvred cautiously. When he visited the Kaiser at Hubertusstock in the middle of October, the State Secretary was very reticent about his naval plans while General Hans von Plessen, the Adjutant General of William II, was present.[38] However, by the end of November discretion was no longer enough. Through August von Heeringen, the brother of the War Minister, he learned on 30 November that Bethmann Hollweg had approached the Army.[39] There could now no longer be any doubt that the Army was to be used as a battering ram against the Navy'.[40] On the following day Tirpitz left a message at the Reich Chancellery urging Bethmann Hollweg to announce immediately that deliberations were in progress about an early expansion of both the Army and the Navy.[41] Moreover he tried to persuade the War Minister, as it turned out without success, 'to join forces with me against the Bethmann–Wermuth principle' of playing the Army off against the Navy.[42]

With Josias von Heeringen remaining adamant and the Chancellor refusing to comply with Tirpitz's request, the Kaiser once again became the Navy Secretary's last resort. William II, he threatened, would have to understand that he, Tirpitz, would find himself in an impossible position if the 1912 Budget contained no reference to his naval bill.[43] Failure to announce the bill would 'block it altogether'.[44] Müller and apparently also the Kaiser gained the impression that the State Secretary was deliberately dramatising the situation and preferred to wait for Bethmann Hollweg's account. Reporting in the afternoon of the same day, the Chancellor stressed the political advantages to be gained from a postponement of the announcement Tirpitz wanted so desperately.[45] The 1912 Budget, he argued, was 'healthy' and would 'in its present shape and form make a good impression if published before the elections'. As soon as Army and Navy increases were fitted into it, the introduction of a 'large bundle of new taxes' including a death duty would be unavoidable. 'It will be very difficult to table the bill without these tax proposals prior to the elections'. But all Conservatives and now even the 'Liberals', he added, had raised their voice against new taxation. Finally Heeringen would find it impossible 'to complete his estimates until 15 December'. In view of these difficulties, Bethmann Hollweg recommended, the military bills should be introduced as a supplementary budget in the winter of 1912–13. The most he could do was to 'introduce a modest increase (two ships)' to be published before the elections.

There followed a long discussion of these proposals at the end of which the Chancellor promised to re-open negotiations with the Army and the Navy. It seems that he did so not only because, as a loyal servant of the monarch, he had no other choice, but also because he had discovered a weakness in Tirpitz's insistence on the need for six capital ships to fill the gap of 1912–17. This number was, after all, deemed necessary to reach the anti-British aim of the naval programme. But the Iron Budget, the other goal which Tirpitz had been working towards ever since the turn of the century, required only two new ships. Bethmann Hollweg set about reducing the size of the navy bill and succeeded in whittling it down to four ships.[46] On 23 December, William II approved this concession. Tirpitz obeyed, but insisted that this was as far as he could go.[47] If the State Secretary had expected that the Chancellor would now at last bring himself to publish the navy bill, he was quickly disappointed. Just before Christmas the *Norddeutsche Allgemeine Zeitung* carried an article which emphasised the need for

a strengthening of the Army. Bethmann Hollweg's public commit-
ment to the proposed expansion of the Navy was still not in sight.
What was worse, by reducing the bill from six to four ships
Bethmann Hollweg had made a breach in Tirpitz's programme and
now hoped to exploit it further. On 5 January he proposed to the
Kaiser that a large increase of the Army be submitted to the
Reichstag in the spring of 1912 and that the navy bill be dropped
altogether.[48] Tirpitz had been suspecting for some time that this
was really what the Chancellor had been aiming for all along and
that he did so not merely for domestic reasons, but also because it
offered him a platform for an Anglo-German understanding.

By the end of the year the German Foreign Office had received a
number of hints that Britain was prepared to talk again. Following
the humiliation of Germany during the Moroccan Crisis, London
appeared to be in a conciliatory mood,[49] and the Germans were
given to understand that there might be room for further territorial gains after the successful completion of the Moroccan treaties.[50]
For the Liberal Cabinet there was, however, only one bargaining
object which was of political interest to them: a limitation of naval
expenditure and an end of the Anglo-German arms race. As the
German Naval Attaché reported on 28 October, the Liberals hoped
to invest the savings from an armaments agreement in 'social legislation' and they were naïve enough to believe that 'Germany would
also benefit from this'.[51] But, as we have seen repeatedly, Tirpitz
did not wish to stabilise the existing order through domestic
reform. He aimed at conserving it with the help of an armaments
programme and was actually planning another escalation of the
naval arms race. His hope was that the latest proposed expansion
of the Navy would force Britain to throw in the towel and to conclude an alliance with Germany on terms most favourable to the
latter. Then the 'great overseas policy' would begin.

In the meantime serious doubts had arisen in many circles about
the wisdom and feasibility of this ambitious concept. The growth of
this opposition to Tirpitz did not escape the British government.
Nor had they failed to recognise that, whereas the normal building
tempo of the Imperial Navy was three capital ships per annum, the
peculiarities of the 1908 Navy Law caused this tempo to drop to
two ships between 1912 and 1917.[52] When in 1910, the British
government therefore mentioned a 2:3 ratio as a possible basis for
an understanding, they had a mutual building tempo in mind

which, like Tirpitz's plans, took account of the *Zweiertempo* of 1912–17, though in a very different way. 'The ratio "3 England to 2 Germany" which sounds so simple and looks like a concession to Germany', the German Naval Attaché reported on 28 October 1911, 'is designed to have no other effect but to fix the German building tempo at "2 ships" per annum.'[53] If this manoeuvre were to succeed, he added, the size of the German fleet would 'automatically' be scaled back from 60 to 40 capital ships. Obviously here was a way to end the onerous Anglo-German arms race by offering colonial concessions in return for a German agreement not to increase the building tempo in 1912.

Consequently the British government began to watch domestic developments in the Reich with growing interest. The German Ambassador reported in the middle of November that Grey had expressed to him his '"highest admiration"' for the way in which Bethmann Hollweg had countered right-wing criticism of the Moroccan treaties in the Reichstag.[54] It is also safe to assume that London registered with some satisfaction the fact that the Chancellor had still not announced another navy bill. At the end of November 1911, Grey made his first concrete attempt 'to appease us with pretences of a colonial future', as Metternich termed it.[55] Speaking in Parliament, the Foreign Secretary hinted at 'his support to secure for us the foundations of a future colonial empire in Central Africa'.[56] 'The disintegration of the Portuguese colonies', the German Ambassador explained, 'is progressing and it seems similarly uncertain if the huge Congo Basin can always remain in the hands of a weak state like Belgium.' The British Foreign Minister, he concluded, 'offers us *de faire courroie du cuir d'autrui* when the right moment has come'.

These words were bound to attract the attention of the German Foreign Office. Was this not perhaps an opportunity to avoid the financial burdens of Tirpitz's navy bill and to gain genuine advantages from the reduced building tempo which, were it not for the Reich Navy Office, was due to start in any case? Kiderlen in particular was fascinated. This deal seemed to come quite close to what he had envisaged ever since 1909. Moreover he was among those Germans who had been dreaming of a Central African empire for some time. At the height of the Moroccan Crisis, on 17 July 1911, he had written to Bethmann Hollweg:[57] 'We must move up to the Belgian Congo so that we shall have a say if that area were carved up....' Richard von Kühlmann, *chargé d'affaires* in the German Embassy at London, put all these arguments into a nutshell when he reported on 8 January 1912.[58] 'After the dangerous tensions of the past summer', he wrote, leading circles in Britain were gradually coming round to the view that there might well be an explosion if England did not conduct a more conciliatory policy vis-à-vis Germany to allow her greater breathing space in the colonial field. There were two large areas 'in which Britain might be able to support German colonial expansion on a large scale without damaging her own vital interests: the Portuguese colonies and the Congo Basin'. Under these circumstances, Kühlmann argued, 'the political relations between Germany and England have once again reached a decisive turning point'. He thought it unnecessary to elaborate why 'the Portuguese colonies would represent an extraordinarily welcome acquisition'. A glance at the map would show that after acquiring these territories the Reich would need but one last cornerstone, the Congo Basin, 'in order to make the great German colonial empire in Central Africa a reality'.

There was, however, as Kühlmann saw it, one prerequisite of such an Anglo-German understanding: 'an at least temporary adherence to the building programme of the [current] Navy Law'. If the building tempo were once more increased, 'the old Anglo-German conflict which has been raging for years' would with absolute certainty flare up again. England would make even greater sacrifices 'to weld the Triple Entente more closely together' and might even try to exert an influence on Italy. 'In short, the rift between the two antagonistic groups would become deeper, the possibility of a friendly understanding would be postponed to a distant future and the likelihood of a violent explosion would be markedly increased.' Kühlmann doubted if an increase of six capital ships, to be available by 1919, could compensate for the political disadvantage of such a development. He therefore preferred the alternative, 'to raise Germany, in friendly agreement with England, to the status of a colonial great power'. This, he thought, ought to 'satisfy any of the justified ambitions of the present generation'.

Unfortunately these prospects did not satisfy William II. When, on 10 January 1912, Bethmann Hollweg tried to persuade the Kaiser 'to limit the navy bill to personnel and secondary armaments—[i.e.] no capital ships', the monarch exploded with anger. He did not receive any help from the Chancellor, he complained bitterly, and would have to carry out his policies with the help of Heeringen, Moltke and Tirpitz.[59] Although this statement said much about decision-making in the German Empire, Bethmann Hollweg did not give up at this point. On the following day he met Müller and the Chief of the Civil Cabinet, Rudolf von Valentini, to whom 'he gave a polished lecture concerning our chances of a peaceful understanding with England'.[60] 'If we did not now construct any additional dreadnoughts', the Chancellor explained, 'we would be in a position to create a great colonial empire (Portuguese colonies, Belgian Congo, Dutch colonies) [and] to drive a wedge between the Triple Entente.' He was not opposed, he continued, to spending money on personnel, submarines and other smaller improvements; it was the additional dreadnoughts which he found so objectionable.

It was thanks to Tirpitz and William II that this plan of Bethmann Hollweg's was finally foiled. Germany, they felt, had to build some additional ships or the Iron Budget, which the State Secretary considered to be the minimum objective of his entire naval policy, would not have been established. The successive navy laws so far provided for fifty-eight capital ships to be replaced every twenty years. At least two more ships were needed to secure the minimum of sixty. Bethmann Hollweg's proposal amounted, as Müller pointed out, to 'a complete breach with the principle of the navy laws' and would deliver the fleet into the hands of the popular assembly again.[61] 'For every single ship', he said, a 'new struggle in the Reichstag' would be necessary. He saw only one last possible 'modification of the navy bill' by postponing the construction of one of the capital ships in such a way that the tempo would alternate between two and three ships per annum.[62] Tirpitz was most reluctant to agree even to this. He wanted to keep this ship in reserve as a 'sacrifice' to the Reichstag should the deputies insist on further cuts.[63] But then the results of the election came to Bethmann Hollweg's aid. They had, as Tirpitz noted down for his report to the Kaiser on 25 January 1912, 'made the situation in the Reichstag difficult, especially as far as the bill is concerned. One hundred and sixty Socialists and Progressives plus 40 [deputies of the] Bavarian Centre Party...'[64] 'In view of future parliamentary difficulties'[65] there was no choice but to modify the bill. Of the original six new capital ships, the Navy had now lost no less than three. Tirpitz felt that he could not possibly make any further concessions.

This was the state of the discussions on the future of German armaments policy when, on 29 January, Sir Ernest Cassel handed Bethmann Hollweg an *aide mémoire* on the British attitude towards negotiations with Germany.[66] Its key passage ran as follows:

(1) Fundamental. Naval superiority recognised as essential to Great Britain. Present German naval programme and expenditure not to be increased, but if possible retarded and reduced. (2) England sincerely desires not to interfere with German Colonial expansion. To give effect to this she is prepared forthwith to discuss whatever the German aspirations in that direction may be. England will be glad to know that there is a field or special points where she can help Germany. (3) Proposals for reciprocal assurances debarring either power from joining in aggressive designs or combinations against the other would be welcome.

Cassel, who was given, as he put it, a 'very cordial' reception in Berlin,[67] was asked to transmit to the British Cabinet that 'the German Government is in full accord with the terms proposed in the draft ... with the following exception: that this year's (1912) estimates must be included in the 'present German Naval Programme' in as much as all the arrangements have already been completed.[68] And in order to inform London about the content of these estimates, Cassel also received a summary of the reduced navy bill as approved by the Kaiser on 25 January.

This second document was immediately analysed by Winston Churchill and Lloyd George who had no doubts that it contradicted the first, 'fundamental', stipulation of the British document. Writing to Grey on the same day, Churchill stated that not only the additional ships, but also 'the matter of a third squadron in full commission' was 'a serious and formidable proposition'.[69] Moreover the 'increases in personnel' would have to be met.

I had intended to ask Parlt. for 2000 more this yr and 2000 next. I expect to have to double these quotas. On the whole the addn. to our estimates consequent upon German increases will not be less than 3 million a year. This is certainly not dropping the naval challenge.

On 3 February the Reich Chancellor was informed via Cassel and Ballin that the German navy bill would make negotiations very difficult.[70] But at the same time Cassel announced that the British War Minister, Lord Haldane, would be coming to Berlin shortly. The Reich government had no choice but to accept. To reject negotiations, William II told Müller on 4 February, would mean a three-front war in the spring of 1912 'and this only because of the construction of three capital ships distributed over six years'.[71] Could these ships be struck off, after all? Müller was ordered to investigate this possibility. But Tirpitz refused to consider it. The bill, he told Bethmann Hollweg on 2 February, was now 'an interconnected whole ... from which individual stones cannot be taken away without endangering the whole.'[72] Moreover he had just learned that Wermuth, through his rigorous policy of saving, had accumulated a small surplus so that the financial objections to a large army and navy bill had lost force.[73] Above all, he had objections on military grounds. 'Our bill', he wrote on 9 February, 'aims at nothing but to bring the existing law up to current technical standards.'[74] According to a memorandum by Harald Dähnhardt of the Reich Navy Office, the three additional ships were needed if the readiness for war was to be maintained.[75] 'The construction of dreadnoughts,' he explained, 'with its devaluation of older ships has completely destroyed the homogeneity of the entire fleet.' It would no longer be possible to combine the active battle fleet with the reserve fleet, so that prospects of surviving the first major encounter would be greatly impaired.

In this fashion, the naval experts combined the various parts of the navy bill into an indivisible whole and used the argument of military necessity to override civilian opposition. However, Dähnhardt's memorandum also renders impressive proof of how far the qualitative and quantitative arms race had meanwhile upset Tirpitz's entire programme. Now it was no longer certain that even the minimum aim, the Iron Budget, might be attained. Faced with this elementary threat to his life's work, Tirpitz had only one interest: to wreck an Anglo-German agreement which jettisoned the navy bill. On 7 February he got his way when the Kaiser announced the introduction of a fleet bill in the Reichstag. The Haldane Mission had failed practically before it had begun. On neither side was there any scope for concessions of the kind which would have made a mutual agreement attractive.[76] In May 1912, the Reichstag ratified Tirpitz's reduced proposals together with a strengthening of the Army. Wermuth admitted defeat and resigned. Bethmann Hollweg decided to stay, convinced that his own resignation would merely make things worse.[77] By 1912 the crisis of the Prusso-German political system had assumed proportions which, it seemed, brought the Reich perilously close to complete internal paralysis and diplomatic stagnation.

There had always been people who advocated an early foreign war to overcome both. That these forces had gained considerable ground emerged indirectly from Bethmann Hollweg's letter of resignation of 6 March 1912 which the Kaiser refused to accept:[78]

> If war is forced upon us, we shall wage it and, with the help of God, we shall not perish in the process. But to unleash a war ourselves without our honour or our vital interests being affected, I would consider a sin against the fate of Germany, even if we could reasonably expect to win a total victory.

There can be little doubt, however, that the Chancellor's preconditions were not far from being fulfilled in the view of those who had traditionally identified their own 'vital interests' with those of the nation as a whole. For some time now, the conservative elites of Germany had been suffering nothing but setbacks. After the 1912 Reichstag elections, they felt more threatened than ever before. If the process of disintegration and isolation continued at a rapid rate, the temptation to launch a war might in fact become so great that they would use their superior power inside Germany to bring it about. This possibility had become even more likely when, in November 1911, the Reich government decided to give the Army priority over the Navy again. For it was the Army which was not only better prepared for war, but which was also led by men who were most intimately connected with the hard-pressed agrarian conservatives. He may not have realised this, but the Chancellor had manoeuvred the country on to a course of war when he used the Army to end the ruinous naval arms race.

7 Retreat to the European Continent

If the discussion of the previous chapters revolved very much around the relations between England and Germany, this was because all other international problems were by comparison of secondary importance. Neither the Tripoli War which the Chief of the Austrian General Staff had been hoping to exploit for a settlement of his country's disputes with Italy, nor the position of the Central Powers on the Balkans and vis-à-vis Russia, but the 'antagonism between England and Germany', as the Austrian Foreign Minister Count Alois Aehrenthal observed in December 1911, was 'the dominant element of the international situation'.[1] This antagonism, he added, would 'probably lead to a European war which is now almost unavoidable'. It was 'for this war that we must save our forces'. The tensions between the first sea power and the strongest land power on the European continent originated in Germany's attempt to force Britain, by means of a costly naval arms race, to recognise German 'equality' as a world power. Some fifteen years before, Tirpitz had argued that this could be achieved. Using economic and Social Darwinist catchwords, he had developed an allegedly 'foolproof' armaments programme which, once completed, would enable the Reich to conduct a 'great overseas policy'. As Tirpitz reminded the Kaiser in April 1914, 'the *Dreiertempo* was the aim which I pursued consistently and tenaciously from the very beginning. This was the tempo with which we were "bound to" gain the necessary maritime prestige vis-à-vis England.'[2] The alternative, which Kühlmann had again outlined in his memorandum of January 1912, of confining oneself to the role of a junior partner of the British Empire, was unacceptable to a man like Tirpitz.

The State Secretary's strategy contained many miscalculations, among which his underestimation of Britain's power as well as her will to resist was the most serious. London took up the German challenge and began to counteract Tirpitz's armaments policy. The Reich government soon had to grapple with Britain's policy of containment and a dangerous arms race. A few years after this arms race had begun with full speed, it became increasingly clear that Germany lacked the breath and stamina to attain her ambitious aims. The cost of the arms race became enormous and raised the delicate question of taxation. It was over this question that the tensions inside the Prusso-German monarchy which it had been possible to stave off for a while by means of a policy of manipulation and distraction, rose to the surface. It became obvious that the existing order was no longer capable of coping with the problems of a rapidly changing industrial society.

It is true that Britain was also groaning under the burden of naval armaments. But there was never the slightest doubt that she would make every sacrifice to uphold her maritime position; nor— and this was even more important for the stability of her political system—would the British government exempt the propertied classes of Britain from carrying the awkward financial burden of armaments.[3] On the other hand, as the 1909 tax reforms showed very clearly, the conservative elites of the German Empire were not at all in a sacrificial mood. The result was that the Imperial Navy gradually lost its catalytic function at home. By 1912 more and more people had come to realise that *Weltpolitik à la* Tirpitz was an impossibility. To be sure, thanks to the 1912 Navy Law the fleet comprised a total of sixty-one ships to be replaced automatically every twenty years. To this extent Tirpitz had achieved his *Marineaeternat*. But the price which the monarchy had had to pay for this was very high indeed: the relationship with England was ruined for good; the domestic situation was a complete shambles. Moreover there was no chance of ever transforming the Imperial Navy into a power-political lever against England. To achieve this goal more than three ships were necessary to fill the gap between 1912 and 1917, and these were never approved.

Looking back on this depressing development in April 1914, Tirpitz admitted that two circumstances had 'unfortunately thrown us back in the past few years'.[4] First, there had been the reduced building tempo of two ships per annum from 1912 to 1917 which the 1912 Navy Law had done little to alter; 'secondly, the exploitation of this gap in the building tempo by the extraordinarily active British Navy Minister Churchill'. Tirpitz did, of course, try to fill this gap. In the winter 1912–13 the Reich Navy Office prepared yet another navy bill to restore an 'uninterrupted *Dreiertempo*'.[5] According to the

German Naval Attaché in London, such a bill was vital if Germany
wanted to keep up, 'at least approximately', with the 16:10 ratio
which Churchill thought would give Britain a sufficiently large
margin of safety for the time being.[6] It is indicative of the extent to
which Tirpitz's programme had disintegrated and his own political
position had declined that this time the resistance of Bethmann
Hollweg and others was immediately successful. To some extent
Tirpitz's failure to gain approval for another numerical increase of
the fleet was due to the continuing deficiencies of the existing naval
establishment. Summarising the effects of the latest Navy Law,
Capelle wrote in May 1912 that 'under the pressure of the army bill
and the financial situation we had to limit ourselves to the utmost'.[7]
As a result, the fleet continued to be understaffed and overworked
and the grumbling against Tirpitz never ended. Nor did the feeling
that the German dreadnoughts were inferior to the British ones in
fighting power and speed cease to have its damaging effect on the
morale of the Navy. At the end of 1912, reports reached Berlin from
London that the Admiralty was experimenting with 15-inch and
even 16-inch guns. The Imperial Navy was still lagging behind and
thirsting for money.[8] The prestige of the once powerful State
Secretary had evaporated.

When, in October 1913, the German Naval Attaché reported
from London that there might be a reduction in the size of the
calibre of guns, William II pencilled in the margin: 'That would be
a blessing!'[9] His brother, Prince Henry of Prussia, had been convinced for some time that the cost of capital ships had become
prohibitive and had given up all hope that the aims of Germany's
naval armaments policy could be fulfilled.[10] By 1913, even William
II was inclined tacitly to agree with this pessimistic view, and his
earlier boasts that victory in the arms race was just around the
corner quietly passed into oblivion.[11] It was by then too obvious
that, aided by the naval agreement with France and the adoption of
the wide blockade as its basic strategy for war, the Royal Navy
would succeed in maintaining its superiority. It did not require the
experiences of the First World War to make the leadership of the
Reich aware of the bankruptcy of Tirpitz's grand design. At first
the State Secretary's opponents enforced a postponement of the
projected navy bill for 1913. In August of that year the Reich Navy
Office was asked to reduce its expenditure for 1914 where possible
and to avoid overspending at all cost.[12]

In April 1914, Tirpitz made a last direct appeal to the Kaiser to secure another 150–200 million marks for the Navy, to be spent over the following eight years.[13] He reminded the monarch of the 'great historical merits' which William II had earned in creating the Navy. But even this did not help. After Tirpitz's relationship with Bethmann Hollweg had long turned into 'open enmity', the Kaiser and the Army, above all Moltke, also no longer trusted him.[14] For the Reich government, the fleet had become a millstone around the neck of German domestic and foreign policy. 'Because of the Navy', the Reich Chancellor remarked in December 1912, 'we have neglected the Army and our "naval policy" has created enemies around us. We did not need that and could have built ships anyway.'[15] Thus the victory which Tirpitz won over Bethmann Hollweg in the spring of 1912 was a short-lived one, and he wondered time and again if he should hand in his resignation. His failure was all the more depressing since he was aware of the deteriorating position of the Reich. Germany, he believed, found herself 'on the slide downwards (auf gleitender Bahn)'.[16]

But how could this trend be stopped? The solution which the German Naval Attaché had reported to be popular among the Liberals in England, i.e. to reduce armaments and to invest the financial savings in social reforms,[17] required a preparedness to accept social and political change. Yet this was precisely what the conservative elites at the helm of the Prusso-German political system were lacking. They preferred manipulative strategies of distraction and integration designed to preserve the *status quo* against the pressure of a rapidly changing industrial society. Germany's leading groups did not want the monarchy to develop reformist tendencies. This resistance also made it well-nigh impossible to relax the pace of Wilhelmine armaments policy. It was not only that the armaments industry had become far too dependent on government orders and that it was most difficult to reorientate production towards the civilian sector without causing considerable economic dislocation, but also that armaments had proven to be an effective means of social integration. By mobilising defensive instincts against an allegedly very dangerous external enemy, armaments fulfilled a function which the monarchy needed ever more desperately as time went on. But by 1912 it had become clear that the Navy and the ambitious plan which Tirpitz had built upon it did not fulfil this function any more. In this hour of crisis, the conservative elites began to pin their hopes on the Army again. Its prestige, as established in the nineteenth century, was now invoked to serve as the focal point for a *Sammlung* of all forces supporting the *status quo*. Moreover the Army came to be seen increasingly as the instrument with which the erosion of the Reich's international position could be arrested.

There was hence no question of reducing armaments expenditure. What happened was a re-allocation of resources between the Army and the Navy. The economic and social factors militating against a limitation of armaments became very clear when in 1913 Churchill, eager to reduce the financial burdens of the Anglo-German arms race, proposed a 'Naval Holiday'.[18] Not surprisingly Germany rejected these proposals, fearing the repercussions on the ship-building industry.[19] Any cancellation of orders, the Reich Navy Office argued, 'would make itself felt drastically in redundancies and wage cuts', which—it might have been added—would increase social unrest. In view of these obstacles standing in the way of a limitation of German armaments, it is difficult to envisage a realistic alternative to the new emphasis on Germany's land forces, a change which was personified by August Keim, a retired Major-General.

Keim had been one of the most active agitators for the 1893 army bill, the last major bill for the next two decades. Towards the end of the century, he became an enthusiastic supporter of Tirpitz's naval policy and reappeared in the Navy League propagating the idea of German maritime 'equality'. But when Tirpitz's star began to decline, Keim joined the opposition to the Navy. In December 1911, he published an appeal for the founding of the *Deutscher Wehrverein*.[20] In it, he demanded a strengthening of the Army because 'the fate of the German Empire will, in the next war, be decided in the first place on land'.[21] Now that the balance of power had shifted against Germany, the appeal continued, no effort should be spared 'to secure her military superiority on land'. Apparently with the support of the General Staff and of Krupp, the *Wehrverein* was turned into a powerful propaganda weapon agitating for the 1912 army bill and attracting some 100,000 individual and 260,000 corporate members by 1914. Soon after the ratification of the 1912 Army Law, the increases were declared to have been insufficient and the *Wehrverein* began to demand another expansion.[22]

However, by this time the War Ministry no longer needed any prodding. In his New Year's address to the Commanding Generals,

William II assured the Army that the Navy would have to leave the 'main portion of the available funds' to the land forces forthwith.[23] Referring to this speech, Heeringen reminded the Chancellor five days later that the Army should now be given absolute priority over the Navy.[24] Accordingly the 1912 army bill provided for 29,000 additional troops and 'manifold technical improvements'.[25] But it was clear from the very beginning that the expansion would not stop there. A number of measures had merely been 'postponed until 1913' and in the end the 1913 bill became the largest 'Germany had ever seen'.[26] One of the most important factors contributing to this second massive increase within less than two years was the outcome of the First Balkan War. The quick defeat which the Turks suffered at the hands of the Balkan League in the autumn of 1912 upset the *status quo* in south-east Europe. The Serbs in particular managed to expand their territory considerably.

On 13 October, both Moltke and Heeringen had assured the Kaiser that the Army was prepared for 'all political eventualities'.[27] They thought it unnecessary to accelerate the formation of machine-gun companies. But only one day later, the General Staff suddenly demanded 'very considerable increases in personnel' and a 'decisive rise of our peace-time budget for troops and horses'.[28] This memorandum was followed up by a number of appeals which reached the Chancellor in November and December of that year. Bethmann Hollweg in turn asked the War Minister if there was any need for another army bill.[29] Heeringen duly replied that in view of the events in the Balkans he would advise the introduction of such a bill if there were no financial or political objections. Bethmann Hollweg had none and we shall have occasion to investigate the reasons for this later.[30] At this point it is sufficient to note the result of the reorientation of Germany's armaments policy: on 30 June 1913, the Reichstag approved increases of no less than 117,000 men, 14,900 non-commissioned officers and 4000 officers. Tirpitz's simultaneous attempt to get another navy bill passed was vetoed by Bethmann Hollweg who argued that the financial situation and the 'political relations with England' prohibited any further expansion of the fleet.[31] He was supported in this not only by the State Secretary of the Reich Treasury, but also by Gottlieb von Jagow, Kiderlen's successor in the Foreign Office. Jagow felt quite strongly that the country 'must do even more for the Army'.[32] 'The Russian and the Slav danger', he believed, was more serious 'than is generally assumed'. With regard to naval armaments, on

the other hand, he preferred to adhere to the principle: 'let sleep-
ing dogs lie.'[33] If 'more had to be done for our defences', Jagow was
reported to have said, then it would be more important 'to turn to
the Army now'.[34]

One of the most significant consequences of such reappraisals of
German armaments policy was a revival of the continental strategy
of the Bismarckian period. As will be remembered, the foreign
policy of the first Reich Chancellor had been based on the principle of consolidating Germany's position of semi-hegemony on
the European continent while the other powers haggled over
their colonial possessions. With the further development of
industrialisation, the continental concept was gradually superseded
by the naval and world policy of the late 1890s. The final
disintegration of Tirpitz's grand design at the beginning of the
second decade of the new century now caused the traditional
continental strategy to re-emerge. Once it was obvious that the
first attempt to break through to the first rank of the world powers
had failed, the argument that the Reich was above all a land power
and should concentrate on strengthening its European base
became more and more compelling. To military circles this
appeared particularly vital as they were acutely aware of what they
perceived as the 'encirclement' of the Central Powers. They were
convinced that it was a matter of preserving existing positions
rather than gaining new ones. This is also why the Anglo-German
problem which had occupied the centre of the stage for many years
gave way to a new emphasis on Continental questions.

Andreas Hillgruber has argued that the return to the Bismarckian
tradition came too late to succeed fully in the last two years before
the First World War.[35] It proved impossible, he says, to restrain the
high hopes of a future German world empire which had been
aroused by fifteen years of intensive naval agitation. Instead, the imperialist movement, partly influenced also by the events on the
domestic scene, underwent a shift towards greater radicalism in the
course of which war seemed almost the natural way out. Hillgruber's
interpretation of the years 1912–14 has much to be said for it. There
can be no doubt that the Reich formulated its claim to world power
status more categorically than ever in those last years before the
War. Imperialism formed a unifying bond between the parties of the
Right and the centre and was reinforced by a growing feeling that
the costly and divisive arms race with Britain did not yield the

expected dividends. 'We do not want to make futile sacrifices,' Bassermann exclaimed at a meeting of the National Liberal Reichstag deputies in October 1913, 'but we want our place in the sun [to compensate for them].'[36] However, the less the huge investments since the turn of the century were paying off, the more marked became the tendency to think in terms of the radical alternatives of 'world power or decline'.[37] Although this kind of thinking found its strongest expression in small but vocal groups like the Pan-German League it began to gain wider currency in Conservative and middle class circles. And it was not the only field which saw an 'increasing *rapprochement* between the views of the Conservatives and the National Liberals'.[38]

An analysis of the German press in the last years before the War reveals, behind the blaring tone of imperialist propaganda, a programme of expansion by stages. Instead of trying to strengthen Germany's continental position and simultaneously laying the foundations of a colonial empire as Tirpitz had proposed, the monarchy now interrupted its advance overseas and decided to concentrate on its continental position. This position was to serve as the platform from which the Reich could launch, as a second step, its offensive to establish a genuine *Weltreich*. Although this strategy was not refined until after 1914 and was ultimately executed by Adolf Hitler,[39] its contours nevertheless emerged with remarkable clarity in public discussions from about 1911 onwards. At the time of the Second Moroccan Crisis hopes had still been directed towards sizeable gains in Africa. They had been frustrated, as we have seen, by the intervention of Britain in the Franco-German dispute. Neither in Morocco nor in Central Africa did the Reich government succeed in obtaining areas which were, economically or politically, in any way significant. The widespread dissatisfaction did not, however, lead to an even more vigorous expansionist drive for overseas territories. People began to ask themselves where 'the place in the sun which the German people have been promised more than a decade ago' might lie.[40] At the turn of the century the Reich Chancellor would not have had any hesitation in replying that the country's future was to be found overseas. By 1912, most people were no longer so certain that this was the direction in which the country should try to expand.

The Central African empire which Kiderlen propagated during the winter of 1911–12 hence never met with an enthusiastic response. Germany, the *Deutsche Arbeitgeber-Zeitung* wrote in April 1913, did not wish to acquire '*colonial empires lying on the moon*'.[41] A German Central Africa was nothing but a mirage in order to distract 'us stupid Germans from a resolute policy'. Professor Dietrich Schäfer, once one of the foremost advocates of *Weltpolitik*, also rejected the colonial plans of the German Foreign Office and his colleague Ernst Jäckh believed that it was something to be taken up by the next generation.[42] Even August Bebel, the leader of the S.P.D. , remarked that 'Africa and the South Pacific [islands] are useless' because they could never serve as a base for German settlements.[43]

Some of the reasons accounting for the unpopularity of Kiderlen's strategy appear in a comment which William II attached to Kühlmann's memorandum of 8 January 1912.[44] He feared that the delusion of an African empire would merely involve the Reich in conflicts with other powers and distract the Germans from those parts of the world where more vital decisions would be made. Moreover naval history showed that the status of a great colonial power required a large navy; 'the former without the latter is bare nonsense', the Kaiser wrote. But where could Germany turn if she did not possess sufficient naval strength and had to rely in the first place on her Army? Clearly it had to be areas which were accessible by land. For, as Kurt Riezler, Bethmann Hollweg's private secretary, argued, it would be impossible to stop the economic expansion and the *élan vital* of the German nation.[45] At the same time, he continued, 'it is clear that the world-political freedom of manoeuvre of the German Empire will be the greater the more independent its continental position is from the constellation of the great powers'. That was why the Reich must first be 'liberated from the *cauchemar des coalitions*'. In short, Germany should concentrate on the European continent. The years 1912–14 saw the wide discussion of a term which in the commentaries of the liberal and conservative press embodied these ideas: *Mitteleuropa*.[46] An ubiquitous Social Darwinism apart, the common feature of these discussions was that all commentators expected the emergence of large blocs surrounded by high protective tariffs. What had been a subject of speculation in the 1890s, had, in the eyes of many, now become a reality. Gustav Stresemann, a leading member of the *Bund der Industriellen* and the National Liberal Party, drew the logical conclusion from this by demanding, in February 1913, the creation of 'a closed economic area to secure our need for raw materials and our exports'.[47]

Divergent opinions existed as to the nature and shape of a German-led *Mitteleuropa*. Some like the industrialist and National Liberal deputy Hermann Paasche favoured the idea of a customs union, which he propagated in September 1913 at the founding meeting of the German–Austro-Hungarian Economic Association.[48] But even among the less rabid imperialists of the centre a customs union on a central European scale was seen merely as a beginning. Closer economic co-operation among the states of the Continent, or at least some of them, the Secretary General of the *Hansabund* wrote in August 1912, would alone 'enable us and our neighbouring countries to safeguard our export markets in competition with extra-European states [and] in particular with the United States of America'.[49] Only a continental combination would give the Germans a chance of survival against, as Albert Ritter phrased it in his book on 'new aims of central European policy', 'Greater Russia, World Britannia [and] Pan-America'.[50] There was hence considerable support for 'an extension of the Triple Alliance into a central European confederation' which would offer an opportunity 'of giving German overseas policy a broader basis'.[51] Almost inevitably, the south-east of Europe became a focus of these discussions. Whether one thought of a 'Pan-German customs union' or some other organisational form, the Balkan states were invariably included in the *Mitteleuropa* concept and in the imagination of some publicists and leading politicians the German-dominated power bloc soon stretched as far as Baghdad. Robert Kauffmann, the leader of the Young Liberals, demanded a customs union 'reaching from Borkum to Baghdad' and the *Deutsche Volkswirtschaftliche Correspondenz* urged the establishment of a 'pax Germanica over Asia Minor and the Balkan countries' before they fell under British tutelage.[52]

As far as Western Europe was concerned, the idea of including France, Luxembourg and Belgium received support in *Hansabund* and banking circles after the penetration of the industrial area of northern France by German capital had made some headway.[53] Even the agrarian press joined the chorus of *Mitteleuropa* advocates. There had always been a latent dichotomy between agriculture and the overseas imperialism of the industrial bourgeoisie.[54] But now, after the failure of Tirpitz's plan, the monarchy was slowly moving back onto a course of continental expansionism which corresponded with Conservative traditions. At the same time the agrarians had learned to value the stabilising domestic function of imperialism. From their point of view the propaganda for a strengthening of Germany's continental position had the added advantage of distracting attention from the internal problems of the political system. This is also the context in which the growth of racialist feelings must be seen. The exaltation of the Germanic race and its unification in a huge central European bloc served a similar domestic purpose. By proclaiming a Germanic Empire stretching from the North Sea to the Persian Gulf, sweeping changes in the international balance of power were to be brought about in order to prevent a change of the power structure at home.

In summary it can be said, therefore, that the collapse of Tirpitz's naval armaments programme and the renewed emphasis on Germany's land forces was accompanied by an adjustment of the Reich's foreign strategy. The long-term objective, as the Kaiser and Jagow saw it,[55] was to 'participate, by means of our armaments policy, in the division of the Near and Far East'. But this implied that the Army had to be reinforced and Germany's central European position strengthened to such a degree that she commanded a glacis from which further territorial gains in more distant parts of the world could be made as a second step.

There are innumerable statements by publicists and politicians of all political groups, except for the extreme Left, testifying to the emergence of a new approach to international politics: the idea of attaining the 'place in the sun' in two stages. This idea was an implied criticism of Tirpitz's grand design which, it was felt, had been too ambitious. The Reich had to make a second and more 'modest' start. It is true that this criticism of the *Weltpolitik* of the turn of the century became explicit only during and after the First World War. Then, as Tirpitz observed in 1915, military and conservative circles mentioned quite openly that Germany had 'overstretched' herself by embarking upon the expansion of the fleet.[56] Her world and naval policy, he was told, had been 'premature'; the Reich ought to have pursued a power-political strategy on the Continent instead of antagonising England. The monarchy should have 'invested everything in the Army' in order to 'defeat the enemies on the Continent first'. And General Wilhelm Groener is reported to have said in May 1919: 'We have unconsciously

striven for world domination ... *before* we had secured our continental position'.[57]

Nevertheless it appears that the conservative elites of the Reich
came round to this view as early as the last years before the
outbreak of the First World War, but found that it was too late to
put it into practice by peaceful means. That the change of course
did not come about earlier was due to the formidable political,
psychological and economic obstacles imposed by the dynamic
period of *Weltpolitik*. The momentum of the naval movement,
Tirpitz's belief that victory in the Anglo-German arms race was
just around the corner, the pressures of the military-industrial
complex: all militated against a quick abandonment of naval
armaments. Also, the Reich's position was not yet as desperate as it
was in 1913. It is difficult, therefore, to avoid the conclusion that
the axioms of Wilhelmine policy introduced a strong element of
inevitability into the course of pre-1914 German history. As long as
the ruling elites were not prepared to throw their reactionary
principles overboard and devised their political tactics purely from
the point of view of short-term benefits, the Prusso-German political system was bound to slither ever more deeply into a cul-de-sac.
But rather than changing their rigid *status quo* policy, these elites
adhered to it even if it meant higher and higher risks.

To some extent the pressure to play for high stakes was a consequence of the return to a continental strategy. After Tirpitz's
naval and world policy had posed a threat to the balance of power,
which was dangerous enough to unite Germany's neighbours, the
idea of forming a German-led bloc on the European continent was,
from the point of view of the Triple Entente, an even more alarming proposition. Britain, France and Russia had to try and frustrate
these aspirations, just as they had curbed the overseas ambitions of
the Bülow period. To the policy of *colonial* containment was added a
policy of *continental* containment. Considering that the encirclement psychosis in Germany had reached quite disquieting proportions between 1905 and 1911, it was not impossible that the feeling
of being put into a territorial straitjacket might assume the proportions of a hysteria.

This was all the more likely since the *Mitteleuropa* concept presupposed the support of two allies whose political systems were more
than shaky. In fact, sometimes it was not easy to discern whether
Turkey or the Austro-Hungarian Empire was more deserving of the

epithet of 'Sick Man of Europe'. Both states possessed socio-economic structures which were firmly rooted in the pre-industrial era. Moreover they harboured within their frontiers sizeable Slav and other non-German populations. Consequently the social tensions which accumulated inside the two empires were compounded by the dynamite of nationalism. They were threatened in their existence by both social and national revolutionary movements. In particular the centrifugal force of a nationalist separatism among the Slavs put Austria–Hungary and Turkey into a very precarious position. Some of the pillars of the *Mitteleuropa* concept thus stood on shifting ground. It was not impossible that the two multi-national empires might break up under the strain of Slav independence movements. As far as the Ottoman Empire was concerned, collapse was not seen as an immediate disaster for the Reich, provided Germany secured some of the spoils. A change of heart had taken place, however, with regard to Austria–Hungary.

For many years it had been a widespread view that the Austrians were too weak to accompany the Germans on their march to world power status. As late as 1905, William II was of the opinion that the 'internal conditions' of the Habsburg Monarchy were taking a turn which would put a question mark on the value of the Dual Alliance to Germany.[58] It is symptomatic of the alarm which the isolation of the Prusso-German monarchy caused in Berlin that such derogatory verdicts on the state of its alliance partner were soon forgotten. By 1908 the Reich government was doing its best to avoid all diplomatic moves which might weaken the international status of the Dual Monarchy. At the time of the annexation of Bosnia, Bülow, and even more so the Kaiser, had been very indignant, partly because they had been put into the picture by their ally rather belatedly and by no means fully. There were justified fears that Aehrenthal's devious methods would, as the German Ambassador in Constantinople phrased it, drive Austria–Hungary 'into a serious confrontation with Russia'.[59] But unlike William II, Bülow did not allow himself to be carried away by his indignation. He insisted that 'Aehrenthal (and the dynasty behind him) must gain the impression that we shall remain loyal' no matter how precarious the position into which the Habsburg Monarchy would manoeuvre itself might be. The alliance had become too vital for the Reich for it to be allowed to languish. The Russians were never left in doubt about the determination of the Reich government to support Austria–Hungary through thick and thin, as was made very clear in March 1909 when the recognition of the annexation of Bosnia was practically extorted from St Petersburg.

German support for Austria–Hungary remained unflinching in principle when in 1912 the Balkans became the source of a major international crisis. This time it was not one of the great powers which was responsible for the outbreak of unrest in the Balkans. With the exception of Italy, they all favoured the preservation of the *status quo* in south-eastern Europe, at least for the time being. It was with this aim in mind that Russia had supported the formation of the Balkan League after the end of the Bosnian Crisis. The hope was that this alliance between Serbia and Bulgaria would act as a barrier to the *Mitteleuropa* plans of the Central Powers and would facilitate control of the Slav states by the Tsarist empire. Ultimately Turkey was to be included in this bloc, thus giving Russia access to the Mediterranean. As the Russian Foreign Minister Sazonov viewed the plan:[60] 'Five hundred thousand bayonets to guard the Balkans—this would bar the road forever to German penetration [or] Austrian invasion.' The Serbs and Bulgarians felt that they could put such an impressive military force to better use. Both states were interested in an early liquidation of the Ottoman Empire and in particular in the liberation of the Macedonians. When Greece and finally Montenegro joined the alliance a few months later, war against Turkey had become a serious possibility. In spite of repeated efforts, neither Russia nor Austria–Hungary succeeded in the summer of 1912 in preventing a conflict. In the middle of October fighting began, ending a few weeks later with the collapse of the Turkish Army in the European part of the Ottoman Empire

The quick victory of the Balkan League destroyed the balance of power in south-eastern Europe. And yet only the Austrians had an interest in restoring it, for the multi-national Dual Monarchy had most to fear from the outcome of the Balkan War. Ever since the Bosnian Crisis, Austria–Hungary and Serbia had been deadly enemies and with the latter emerging strengthened from the war of 1912, the Serbs, it was thought, might assume a role vis-à-vis the Habsburg Empire similar to the one played by Bulgaria vis-à-vis Turkey prior to the outbreak of war. Had not the Serbian Foreign Minister stated that 'if the disintegration of Austria–Hungary could take place at the same time as the liquidation of Turkey, the solution would be greatly simplified'?[61] Against the background of such feelings of fear and rivalry, it is not surprising that the Dual Monarchy thought of an intervention against Serbia as long as the Serbs were not yet too strong. Count Leopold Berchtold, the Foreign Minister, coolly informed the French Ambassador on 31 October 1912 that Austria–Hungary would know how to uphold her economic and political interests vis-à-vis a Serbian neighbour who was becoming too powerful.[62] Count Ladislaus Szögyenyi, the Austrian Ambassador to Berlin, elaborated four days later on what this implied.[63] His government wanted specific guarantees that Serbia would not work against the Dual Monarchy and that certain justified claims by Roumania were met. Moreover the existing railway network was to be extended as far as Macedonia; Salonika was to be declared a free port. Finally, an independent state of Albania was to be created. The net effect of all these demands would have been to subject south-eastern Europe to Austrian hegemony.

Kiderlen had a sympathetic ear for these aspirations and recommended that this 'moderate and very sensible programme' be supported by Germany. It was left to the Kaiser to formulate the ulterior motives of German policy when he approved Kiderlen's recommendation *'Our aim'*, he wrote, '[is to establish] the Balkan League as a seventh great power in the concert of Europe, closely connected with Austria and the Triple Alliance.' His ideal was the formation of a 'United States of the Balkans'.[64] Unfortunately for the Central Powers things never got that far; nor, as it turned out, was a threat of war a suitable means towards the desired end. This became very clear when, on 2 December 1912, Bethmann Hollweg publicly assured the Habsburg Monarchy of German loyalty.[65] Should Austria–Hungary be attacked by a third party and thus be threatened in her existence, he exclaimed, the Reich government would come to her aid, and would be prepared 'to fight for the preservation of our own position in Europe [and] for the defence of our own future and security'. The Chancellor's words caused considerable alarm in London. The British government decided to remind the Prusso-German monarchy once again of the limits of its restless policy of strength. Assuming quite rightly that Germany could fulfil her alliance obligations towards Austria–Hungary only by waging war on France, Britain warned Berlin that she could not remain neutral in the event of such a major conflict.

After this warning, the Balkan situation was kept in a suspended state, and by the beginning of 1913 the Central Powers had come nowhere near the proposed continental bloc. This did not prevent the Reich government from developing various schemes for a solution of the Balkan question. Jagow and William II felt that a 'combination [of] Serbia, Roumania [and] Greece' under the leadership of Austria–Hungary was particularly promising.[66] One of the arguments which the Kaiser advanced in support of this idea was that such an alliance would make it more attractive for the Turks to join in. In December 1912 the Kaiser had received a report from Constantinople to the effect that chances of tying Turkey more closely to the Central Powers were favourable: '*Avis au lecteur!!* We must forge the iron as long as it is hot.'[67] 'Austria', he said on another occasion, 'would then possess a preponderant influence over three Slav Balkan countries which, under her aegis, could be put round Bulgaria like an iron ring.'[68] But above all, William II concluded his remarks, 'the dreadful wave of Pan-Slavism will be thoroughly divided by the alliance between Austria, Serbia, Greece and Roumania'.

While agreeing that there existed a dangerous threat of Pan-Slavism, the Austrian government was not convinced that William's proposals were the most practicable ones. Haunted by the nightmare of a Greater Serbia, the Habsburg Monarchy preferred the idea of weakening Serbia through the application of military pressure or, in the last resort, through war—a policy which the Kaiser thought would drive 'all Slavs into the arms of Russia'. For the time being these incipient differences of opinion between Berlin and Vienna did not have any serious consequences. Both partners cherished the hope that the members of the Balkan League would soon be at war among themselves over the distribution of the spoils from the First Balkan War. On 28 June 1913, Jagow admitted quite openly that such a conflict would be 'desirable'.[69] The Balkan League should be left 'to stew in its own juice'. Similarly the Austrian government was planning to observe developments from a distance, although military circles continued to think in terms of intervention against Serbia should an opportunity present itself at a later stage.[70]

The Second Balkan War broke out at the end of July 1913 and resulted in a quick Serbian victory over Bulgaria. The Serbs doubled their territory. The Dual Monarchy had suffered another severe setback. Berchtold was overcome by deep depressions and noted in his diary that his country stood at the cross-roads and would from now on have to struggle for its existence.[71] He was not all that wrong. Rather than facilitating the creation of a central European bloc, the events of the past year had merely undermined the external and internal position of the Habsburg Empire. This realisation strengthened in Vienna, as it did in Berlin, the hand of those who argued that only the destruction of Serbia could stop the distintegration of the multi-national empire. But it was also clear that such a war would inevitably involve Russia and would quickly escalate into a major European war. Yet Germany was at this stage not prepared to become an accomplice to Austrian brinkmanship.

The differences of opinion which had been latent so far now came to the surface with Berlin trying to dissuade Vienna from declaring war on Serbia. On 7 July, Jagow took an unduly optimistic view of 'developments in the Balkans', maintaining that 'the Balkan League is split, Russian influence has received a severe blow and the Balkan States, now tearing one another to pieces, will be so weakened by the war that they will need a long time to recover'.[72] At the same time, the Reich government assured the Dual Monarchy of Germany's undiminished support. But this was small comfort to Berchtold who believed that Austria was 'almost completely isolated' in her hour of need.[73] In previous years, he complained to Szögyenyi at the beginning of August 1913, Germany had always tacitly recognised that Austria was in charge of policy-planning with regard to the Balkans.[74] But 'in recent times this principle has been abandoned and one sees fit to conduct one's own policy against our objections in questions which are of eminent importance to us'. What Berchtold did not quite seem to appreciate was that south-eastern Europe had become a vital area of German policy since the collapse of Tirpitz's grand design and that, Jagow's optimism notwithstanding, the Reich government was quite aware of the unfavourable repercussions of the two Balkan Wars on the international position of the Central Powers. Under these circumstances the Reich could no longer afford to take a passive attitude towards the Balkans and had to solve differences of opinion between Vienna and Berlin by imposing its own policy on the weaker ally.

However, by taking Austria–Hungary on the 'leash' (Fischer), it was unavoidable that the fate of the Reich became inseparably connected with the Balkans and the deteriorating position of the Habsburg Empire in that part of Europe. Just as the South-East was seen to be vital to the survival of Austria, the Balkan question assumed a crucial significance for the stability of the Prusso-German monarchy. If the Reich government succeeded in arresting the centrifugal tendencies and even in expanding its sphere of political and economic influence, the Germans would be able to look into the future with some degree of optimism. The impact of the policy of containment would be mitigated and the powerful central European bloc come within reach. William II and his advisers had great hopes that their policy would work, if only because it was the only alternative to retreat. This all-or-nothing approach to the future was not basically new in Wilhelmine policy. But it was no doubt reinforced by the pessimistic spirit which pervaded the official mind of the Habsburg Monarchy. Consequently any political development which could not be celebrated as an overwhelming success was immediately interpreted as a major setback calling into question the existence not only of Austria–Hungary but also of the German Empire. The survival of the monarchy was thought to be at stake and in this situation even war did not seem too great a risk to take. The Liman von Sanders Affair is a good illustration of this peculiar mentality in the Reich.

The defeat of the Turkish army in the First Balkan War led to intensive efforts to modernise the military establishment of the Ottoman Empire. Feeling that they could not succeed in this without foreign help, the Turks turned to Germany. The German Ambassador in Constantinople encouraged his government because he believed this to be a unique opportunity to 'imbue the Turkish people with a German spirit'.[75] In effect, he hoped to make Turkey the junior partner of Germany. The *Mitteleuropa* idea of a Berlin–Baghdad axis appeared to be taking more concrete shape at last. With this aim in mind, the Reich government dispatched Lieutenant-General Otto Liman von Sanders to Constantinople to prepare an agreement of military assistance which was finally signed at the end of October 1913. Liman was made head of the German military mission and lest they forget what their task would be, William II personally enlightened its members on Germany's aims in the Near East.[76] Liman and his aides, he said when he sent them off, should facilitate the 'Germanisation of the Turkish army' and secure a dominant German influence in 'questions of foreign policy'. Finally, they were to further the development of 'Turkish military might in Asia Minor' so that it would act 'as a counter-weight to the aggressive designs of Russia'.

Although there was indeed some truth in this statement in that the Russians were themselves hoping to gain an influence over the Straits, Sazonov was conversely quite justified in suspecting that Liman had been 'entrusted with the task of firmly establishing German influence in the Turkish Empire'.[77] As he told a German journalist: 'You know what interests we have at the Bosphorus, how sensitive we are on that point. All southern Russia depends upon it and now you stick a Prussian garrison under our noses.'[78] This was also the reaction of the Tsar, who said on 6 December 1913:[79] 'To abandon the Straits to a powerful state would be synonymous with subordinating the whole economic development of southern Russia to that state.' William II must have known, therefore, that he was asking for trouble when he sent Liman to Turkey, and trouble did come. The Russian government mobilised its British and French allies, urging strong action against the Reich. A flexible response, Sazonov argued in a memorandum of 5 January 1914, 'will not protect us from the growing demands of Germany and her allies which begin to introduce an ever more unyielding and irreconcilable tone into all questions that touch their own interests'.[80] He demanded a withdrawal of the German military mission. For various reasons Britain did not wish to go that far. By the middle of January, a compromise had been worked out: 'Liman von Sanders was promoted to the rank of field-marshal in the Turkish army and thus became too dignified to command the troops at Constantinople.'[81]

But this outcome did not prevent the German press from interpreting the affair as a major defeat for Germany,[82] with even the left-liberal *Welt am Montag* thundering: 'Why do we pass our giant army bills if in the last resort we do nothing but execute the Tsar's orders?' It was left to William to give the most typical expression to the all-or-nothing mentality which became more and more widespread in Berlin as the summer of 1914 drew closer:[83] 'Either the German flag will fly over the fortifications of the Bosphorus or I shall suffer the same sad fate as the great exile on the island of St Helena.' The trouble was that there was no chance of a German victory on the Straits. On the contrary, in the spring of 1914 tensions arose between the Reich and the Ottoman Empire and the Berlin–Baghdad axis receded further into the background. Nor were Bethmann Hollweg's efforts to penetrate the Balkan states economically and thus to include them into a central European sphere of influence any more successful. Germany's resources were insufficient to compete against French and British capital and, with the exception perhaps of Roumania, the Balkan states never became directly dependent on German or Austro-Hungarian economic power. In the summer of 1913 Berlin had blocked Austrian military intervention in the Balkans and replaced it by its own policy of 'peaceful' political expansion. A year later, this policy had failed, or so at least it appeared to the leading circles in Berlin and Vienna. Everywhere, Germany seemed to be running up against concrete walls. The continental strategy which had been revived to substitute the world political offensive of the Bülow period was also slowly grinding to a halt. Could it be that, after futile sacrifices for the Navy, the giant investments in the Army had also been in vain? Or might they perhaps be useful to build, by force, the continental platform without which Germany could never be a world power and was by some even believed to be condemned to suffocation? If the concept of pacific penetration failed, could a war perhaps create the *Mitteleuropa* bloc? These questions assumed an immediate urgency when considered in conjunction with developments on the domestic scene to which we must return in the following chapter.

8 The Paralysis of the Monarchy at Home

The domestic predicament of the Prusso-German monarchy in the last two years before the War was largely conditioned by the outcome of the 1912 Reichstag elections. The Social Democrats emerged from them as the strongest party, gaining 110 seats while the Left Liberals and the National Liberals lost only a few. For the parties of the Right which had been responsible for the 1909 tax reforms, on the other hand, the poll turned out to be an unmitigated disaster. The Catholics got away comparatively lightly, losing about 10 per cent of their seats. The agrarian Conservatives were hit worst with a total loss of 17 deputies, giving them only one more than the Left Liberals; the Free Conservatives were likewise badly affected and declined from 26 seats to a meagre 16. The right-wing *Wirtschaftsvereinigung* lost 10 seats.[1]

If one takes into consideration the connections which individual deputies had with economic pressure groups, the defeat of the conservative elites is even more staggering. With the growing interdependence between politics and economics it had become more and more accepted that candidates of particular parties received financial support from economic interest groups in return for a promise that, if elected, they would support the aims of these groups. In the 1907 elections no less than 138 deputies had pledged to further the political and economic aspirations of the Agrarian League. Five years later, public identification with the interests of the big landowners often diminished chances of success. Only 78 out of a total of 213 candidates with agrarian sympathies were actually elected.[2] The candidates who had subscribed to the aims of the Central Federation of Industrialists and had accepted money from heavy industry did not fare much better. From the point of view of the Conservatives, the election result was all the more depressing when compared with their propaganda efforts. They had decided to employ, on a vast scale, the same fiercely nationalist and anti-socialist slogans which had been so successful in 1907. But this time the deliberate attempt to polarise German society completely did not pay off. Neither the Second Moroccan Crisis nor the reckless exploitation of fears and resentments against the S.P.D. was sufficient to distract attention from the inequalities and injustices of the Wilhelmine class state which the conservatives were doing their best to perpetuate. To make the disaster complete, the Reich was seized by a wave of inflationary price increases and by the autumn of 1911 people had become more concerned about the cost of living index than about the alleged threat from the Left.[3] Consequently a large number of voters gave their support to that party which had the most savage things to say about the gulf between the rich and the poor and the anachronistic semi-absolutism of the Prusso-German political system.

Heinrich Claß, the leader of the Pan-German League, probably came very close to the truth when he described the mood of 1912 as follows:[4] 'The propertied and educated [classes] feel that they have been disowned politically and silenced by the vote of the masses. The entrepreneurs who, owing to the development of the last decades, have become the pillars of our national economy see themselves exposed to the arbitrary power of the working-class which are spurred on by socialism.' In the eyes of the *Deutsche Industriezeitung* the outcome of the elections was but another feverish outburst in a 'sick body politic'.[5] The victory of the Left might well have been even greater had it not been for the fact that, although large population movements had taken place since 1871 in the wake of the industrial revolution, the distribution of electoral districts had remained practically unchanged. As a result, a vote in the depopulated territories of East Prussia often had many times the weight of one cast in the S.P.D.-dominated industrial centres of the Rhineland.

Despite these and other technicalities of the electoral system which in most cases worked to the advantage of the right-wing parties, the balance sheet was indeed most discouraging for the Conservatives and the Reich government. The broadly-based *Sammlung* had failed and the parties of the Right had lost their majority in the Reichstag. A parliamentary situation which Bethmann Hollweg had always been dreading had now become a reality. He could not introduce legislation which was acceptable to the centre and the Left for fear of conservative opposition; nor, conversely, could he initiate legislation which pleased the Conservatives because the other parties would either reject it or else add provisions which the Right found objectionable. This applied particularly to the Budget where there was now a real danger of the parties of the centre and the Left turning the table on the agrarians and approving taxes detrimental to the conservative position.

If for no other reason than to prevent this from happening, the Right once again had to try and broaden its basis of support. But obviously there was little prospect of joining together parties which had just been involved in a highly emotional election campaign against one another. Any attempt to create a broadly-based *Sammlung* had to start with a rallying of extra-parliamentary forces. This seemed all the more natural since leading agrarians, such as Diederich Hahn, Gustav Roesicke and Elard von Oldenburg-Januschau, had lost their seats in the Reichstag and were thus almost automatically referred back to the Agrarian League. It was from this power base and in conjunction with the Central Federation of Industrialists that they now began to rally the protagonists of the *status quo* in German society. It cannot be said that their arguments were in any way new. Finding that the traditional noise levels were no longer sufficient to move the burgher, they merely employed the old demagoguery in even bigger doses than before. In short, the Right became more and more extreme and this shift made it increasingly unlikely that the political system would be able to find a new equilibrium on the basis of social and political compromise. By 1912 the agrarians and heavy-industrialists were more convinced than ever that the S.P.D. and the trade unions had to be fought tooth and nail. 'The slightest retreat of industry before the demands of the Social Democrats', Paul Reusch, the Director General of the *Gutehoffnungshütte,* wrote in January 1914, would, 'politically and economically, have unprecedented consequences'.[6] This, he added, 'is why I have always made the greatest efforts to cut the ground from under the feet of the Social Democrats and the Social Democrat trade unions ever since I have been active in industry'. Similarly the leader of the Free Conservatives, Octavio von Zedlitz und Neukirch, could see only one task: 'to fight with all forces and all available means the social as well as the bourgeois democracy as the dangerous enemy of our national unity within the [existing] state'.[7] Roesicke, the leader of the Agrarian League, advocated a rigorous 'containment of the democratisation of the Reich' and called for a 'struggle against the power of the revolutionaries'.[8]

In these circumstances, social policy assumed a crucial importance. The patriarchs of the coal and steel industry had been holding for some time that the attempts at reconciling the worker to the monarchical order by introducing social security benefits had failed.[9] These measures, they said, had only served to increase the power of the trade unions, to whet the working-classes' appetite for more welfare and to burden the employers with rising social security costs. As the *Deutsche Volkswirtschaftliche Correspondenz* put it in an article against the 'social political quackery of the last decades and in particular of the past few years':[10] 'The more has been done in the field of social policy, the more Social Democrats have been elected to the Reichstag.' According to the *Deutsche Arbeitgeber-Zeitung* there was only one remedy to this evil, namely to put the clock back again and to reduce social legislation.[11] This was certainly the view of Gustav Krupp von Bohlen und Halbach when he wrote to the Kaiser on 13 March 1912.[12] Krupp was convinced that social legislation merely helped the S.P.D. because the masses would give it all the credit. A 'change of our over-all political situation', he continued, could only be expected from a defeat of trade unionism; only then would the attempts to solve the manifold problems of 'our contemporary political life ... more or less lose their present air of complete futility'.

Of course, Krupp knew that any move to stop or even scale down welfare policies was bound to increase discontent among the working-classes. Not surprisingly, therefore, the campaign against the 'epidemic of social insurance'[13] was supplemented by the demand for repressive measures against restless workers. If they did not advocate the outright proscription of the Social Democrat movement, many heavy-industrialists wanted at least specific legislation to deal with strikes. There was no lack of detailed proposals. On 1 July 1911, for example, the Central Federation of Industrialists submitted a memorandum to the Reich government proposing a change of paragraph 241 of the Penal Code to prevent picketing.[14] The argument was that those who were willing to work needed the protection of the state. 'What our nation needs today', Carl Ziese, the owner of the Schichau Shipyards at Danzig, wrote in February 1913, 'is a law for the protection of non-strikers.'[15] To be sure, given the peculiarities of the Prusso-German constitutional structure, such legislation was not really vital. There were always the wide-ranging emergency powers which the crown had at its disposal, as was shown in the spring of 1912.

At the beginning of March the Ruhr was hit by a miners' strike. There were tussles along the picket-line and the police force proved insufficient to secure access to the pits for those workers who refused to join the strike. Fortunately, there was the Army. Troops were moved in to 'accompany' non-strikers although the Army was careful to use regiments whose soldiers came from the rural areas of Westphalia. On 19 March 1912 the strike collapsed and over 100 workers and miners' wives were tried for insulting strike-breakers, while dozens of other men were gaoled for resisting arrest or for assault.[16] This was clearly the quickest way of dealing with social unrest; but, as Ziese recognised, it was not necessarily the best. In his view, the 'most effective means of combating Social Democracy is ... to settle the workers, to tie them to the soil and to see to it that grandfather, father and son build, and become attached to, a home.'[17] This, he believed, would 'quite automatically generate patriotism, loyalty to country and the state'. Alfred Hugenberg was moved by similar considerations long before he became chairman of the Krupp Board of Directors. He advocated a systematic policy of rural settlement because 'the Social Democrat urban worker has repaid us for the Bismarckian welfare legislation with [nothing but] unpatriotic behaviour and incorrigible discontentedness.'[18]

In this respect, heavy industry could be sure of the support of the agrarians who for both political and economic reasons were worried about the flight of the rural labour force to the cities. Politically a rural settlement policy was seen as 'the best antidote against Social Democracy';[19] economically, it was hoped, it would make East German agriculture less dependent on Polish migratory workers at a time when relations with Russia were growing steadily worse.[20] Finally, the idea of 'internal colonisation' which gained a good deal of popularity in conservative circles must be related to Germany's return to a continental tradition. Just as world policy, naval armaments and social imperialism had been inter-connected, *Mitteleuropa*, concentration on the land forces, and rural settlement programmes must be seen together. Slowly the eyes of the German elites were turning away from overseas colonies and the Navy towards the more thinly populated open spaces of Eastern and South-East Europe. This, it was argued, was the area where the fate of the monarchy would be decided.

Apart from anti-Socialism, anti-parliamentarism was another favourite theme of right-wing propaganda after 1912. This is not

surprising in view of the fact that the universal suffrage had had
such a disastrous effect on the position of the conservative parties
in the Reichstag. 'The worst of all existing voting systems', the
heavy-industrialist *Post* wrote in January 1912, 'is not the Prussian
[three-class system] but the Reichstag suffrage'.[21] What was more
natural than to demand the abandonment of 'Reichstag parliamentarism'?[22] As in the 1890s, there were some who were not averse to
using the Army to achieve this end. Others preferred the idea of
creating new constitutional organs with which to erode the powers
of the popular assembly. 'An organic representation of the large
professional estates (*Erwerbs- und Berufsstände*)' was to be elected
side-by-side with the Reichstag.[23] The idea of creating a '*Ständehaus*'
provoked considerable discussion.[24] Thus the Secretary General of
the Association of the German Iron and Steel Industry, Henry A.
Bueck, declared that the Reichstag and the parliaments of the
federal states merely provided the S.P.D. with an opportunity of
'spreading with impunity their wild agitation, their poisonous
attacks on our constitutional order among the masses ...'.[25] His
colleague Alexander Tille believed that an association of the
'producing estates' including those workers 'who are attached to
the soil and who are loyal to the present social order ...' might be a
suitable counterweight.[26] Claß favoured the establishment of a
'*Reichsrat*' to be composed of the *aristoi* of the nation.[27]

But Pan-Germans like Claß adhered not only to *Ständestaat* ideas
with which they tried to block a parliamentarisation of the Prusso-
German political system, but also propagated anti-Semitic slogans.
There are a number of general studies on racial anti-Semitism and
its scapegoat function.[28] The important point is that resentments
against Jews were deliberately exploited by the ruling elites of
Germany to distract from the internal problems of the Reich. This
was openly admitted by a friend of Claß, Konstantin von Gebsattel,
who in 1918 bluntly proposed to use the Jews as a 'lightning con-
ductor for all injustices' and to blame the collapse of the monarchy
on them.[29] Before the First World War, the anti-Semites were not
quite so outspoken. However, the effect of their activities was
certainly the same. As the crisis of the political system deepened,
there emerged a growing number of people who were prepared to
believe that the Jews were responsible for Germany's difficulties.
What is more: the alleged Jewish conspiracy could be conveniently
linked to the left-wing threat to the monarchy. The Social

Democrats, Claß maintained, operated under 'Jewish leadership'.[30]
This, the *Korrespondenz des Bundes der Landwirte* argued in August
1913, was also true of the Young Liberals.[31] In this way anti-Semitic
feelings combined with anti-Socialism and an incipient anti-
capitalism. Everything became neatly compressed into the bogey of
the 'golden' and the 'red' international.[32] Not all conservatives, to
be sure, subscribed to these ideas. But the most important thing is
that, long before the War, anti-Socialism, anti-parliamentarism,
fanatical nationalism, anti-Semitic racism and various other elements were combined in a more or less coherent ideology. At the
same time the appeal to fear and resentments among the social
groups which felt most threatened by industrialism reached a new
level of intensity after 1912.

It is easy to overestimate the success of this reckless agitation
among groups outside agrarian and heavy-industrial circles. In fact,
it was much less than impressive. Radical right-wing slogans
exerted an attraction only on certain sections of the bourgeoisie.
Anti-Socialist, anti-Semitic and anti-big-business sentiments were
particularly virulent among artisans and in the retail trade.[33] They
tended to dream of a 'restoration of pre-industrial norms and institutions' and believed that the 'social question' was 'essentially the
Jewish question'.[34] In short, here was a potential group of voters
which responded to the emotional propaganda of the conservative
elites and was waiting to be organised. And organised they became.
With the financial support of the Agrarian League and the Central
Federation of Industrialists, the *Reichsdeutscher Mittelstandsverband*
was founded. The new association was proclaimed to be a bulwark
against socialism and social policy in alliance with the agrarians
and heavy industry. It posed as a 'conservative fighting organisation' and counterpart of the *Hansabund*.[35] The main bone of contention between the two middle-class associations was their estimate
of the S.P.D. At the annual meeting of the *Hansabund* in November
1912, Professor Hans Delbrück spoke of the Social Democrats in
terms which differed markedly from the rabid anti-socialism of the
Mittelstandsverband.[36] The S.P.D., he said, was no longer a 'revolutionary party' and was on its way towards becoming a 'radical
bourgeois labour party'. The task was therefore not to ostracise the
Social Democrats but to lead them out of their 'posture of absolute
negation'. But this required a willingness on the part of the government to initiate cautious reforms instead of conducting a policy of
pure reaction with its polarising effects on society as a whole.

Thus the old differences of the 1909–12 period continued, and as long as the Right and the centre could not agree on the character of the Social Democrat movement (revolutionary or revisionist?), and the measures to solve the domestic crisis (reform or reaction?), a broadly-based *Sammlung* had no chance of success. As before it was again the National Liberal Party in which the divergent views of the internal situation led to a dangerous crisis. On the one hand, the representatives of a 'North-German National Liberalism' favoured an orientation towards the Right;[37] the Young Liberals, on the other, advocated co-operation with the Progressives. Though by no means a left-winger, Ernst Bassermann, the party leader, decided to resist the massive pressure to move towards the Right. As he wrote to Bülow in April 1912:[38] 'If the National Liberal Party sails in the wake of Heydebrand and Erzberger, it will lose all its significance for the future ...'.

It appears that he was being unduly pessimistic when he excluded the Centre Party deputy Matthias Erzberger as a potential ally. After the 1912 elections some Catholic leaders began to have doubts about their collaboration with the Conservatives. This alliance had cost the Centre Party considerable sympathies among the Catholic working classes, and rather than accept the loss of further votes to the Social Democrats, the party leadership decided to adopt a more flexible policy. It was due to this manoeuvring between the fronts that the Centre Party succeeded once more in integrating divergent intra-party forces. Centrifugal tendencies in the National Liberal Party, on the other hand, ultimately became so strong that its right wing split off to form the *Altnationalliberale Reichsverband*. Faced with internal dissent over domestic policies, Bassermann now revived the well-worn ploy of nationalism and imperialism in an attempt to paper over the cracks. 'It is the imperialist idea', Professor Friedrich Meinecke observed in May 1912, 'which ultimately holds the party together.'[39] This was traditionally also the point where a tenuous link existed between the centre and the Right which propagated a forceful foreign policy and the creation of a continental bloc from the North Sea to the Bosphorus. Even the Young Liberals were, as one of their leaders wrote in April 1912, 'more inclined towards the Pan-Germans' in matters of foreign policy.[40] And yet, the magnetic force of nationalism and imperialism was not strong enough to reconcile the parties of the Right and the centre.

There was a simple reason for this: however useful the demand for a firm and active foreign policy was as an integrating mechanism,

Germany always lacked the power to assert herself in international politics. Tirpitz had been painfully aware of this deficiency and had proposed armaments as a prerequisite of Germany's ascendancy. Ever since he had begun to build the Imperial battle-fleet and certainly since the onset of the Anglo-French–Russian policy of containment, William's armaments policy had therefore become the hard core of his foreign policy. But this meant at the same time that the advantages which nationalist and imperialist propaganda offered as a stabilising element were constantly counterbalanced by the disadvantages of domestic conflict resulting from the financial burdens which the armaments imposed on the population. With the help of patriotic and expansionist slogans it had always been relatively easy to rally large majorities for so-called defence measures. But the unity which these policies engendered was superficial and hence deceptive. They invariably raised the problem of how the costs of armaments were to be distributed, and it was at this point that it became clear how little the stability of the political system was, in the final analysis, enhanced by imperialist and nationalist agitation. The navy bill of 1908 and the subsequent tax reform of 1909 were a good illustration of this.

In 1912, the Reich government had introduced yet another armaments bill and had again succeeded in persuading the parties of the Right and the centre to accept it. If the strength of this front was not put to a test in 1912, it was mainly because the divisive question of additional taxes did not emerge immediately. By using the surplus which Wermuth had accumulated in 1910–11, by illegally reducing the liquidation of Reich debts to a minimum and by appropriating only what was absolutely necessary, the thorny tax problem could be circumvented. Or, to be more precise, it had been postponed until 1913. For in connection with the 1912 armaments bill, the Reichstag had ratified the so-called Lex Bassermann–Erzberger which stipulated that the government would have to put before Parliament 'a general property tax which takes account of the various forms of private property' before 30 April 1913.[41] The summer passed without incident. But by the winter of 1912–13, the debate on which items should be incorporated in this tax was in full swing.[42] One proposal, which was favoured by the Left Liberals, was to extend the death duty. But as in 1908–9 it met with violent opposition from the Conservatives. A compromise solution which, it was hoped, would reduce tensions between the parties of the centre and the agrarians was put forward by the Free Conservatives. Their plan was to introduce a tax on the gains on property between the death of the father and that of his son. But the Conservatives refused to see the advantages of this solution. Exploratory talks which Bethmann Hollweg had with Heydebrand and Count Hans Kanitz-Podangen revealed that the agrarians were opposed to any sort of capital gains tax. Nor, as the Chancellor noted to his chagrin, did the two party leaders have any ideas of their own as to the direction which 'the solution of the financial question' ought to take.[43] All they could think of was 'that one should squeeze the stockmarket and large industrial transactions'. In other words, their attitude was the same as in previous years: they preferred offending the commercial middle-classes to making sacrifices of their own.

Desperate to stop the polarisation of opinion and under the pressure of the Lex Bassermann–Erzberger deadline, Bethmann Hollweg decided to go ahead without the Conservatives. He prepared a capital gains tax on property, hoping that the Conservatives would agree to it once it came to a vote in the Reichstag. He thought it more important to end 'the bitter struggle among the bourgeois parties' and thus pave the way for a conservative *Sammlung*.[44] At the same time he was wary of becoming dependent on the left-wing majority in the Reichstag which 'would be irreconcilable with the vital needs of the state and the Reich'. Fearing that 'the external and internal condition of Germany' might require the support of the middle-classes 'at any moment', the Chancellor's main concern was to mobilise as many social groups as possible in support of his moderate conservatism. However, it had always been difficult to pursue such a policy and in 1913 it was more difficult than ever. Not only the agrarians resisted the Chancellor's capital gains tax on property, but also the Bundesrat.

The federal states were afraid of the centralising tendencies of Reich politics. Direct taxation, the Prussian Minister of Agriculture argued in November 1912, would increase the influence of 'the power-hungry Reichstag democracy' over the internal affairs of the member states.[45] He was therefore being perfectly logical when he proposed that, instead of it being extended, the death duty on distant relatives, introduced in 1906, be abolished again. Like the Prussian agrarians, whose mouthpiece he was, he could conceive only of retrograde solutions. The other federal governments did not wish to go quite as far as the Minister. Now that the death duty had been partially taken over by the Reich, they did not mind if the remainder was also surrendered. What they were worried about was the attempt by the Reich, as proposed by Bethmann Hollweg's capital gains tax on property, to assume fresh direct tax rights. The Saxon Minister President thought it better not 'to table a property tax in the Reichstag at this stage'.[46] He considered the Chancellor's scheme a mistake 'which would lead to a weakening of the federal states and their parliaments in favour of the Reichstag'. Nor could the new State Secretary of the Reich Treasury, Hermann Kühn, convince him that the crucial question was not whether the proposed property tax constituted an encroachment on the taxation system of the federal states. The real issue, Kühn argued, was whether it was more dangerous to concede a capital gains tax on property or to give domestic politics 'a turn which would sharpen and eternalise the conflict among the bourgeois parties'. Would the Bundesrat, he asked, really like to foster a situation in which established principles of Reich and federal politics were abandoned and 'the radical elements granted an influence over the government and its policies'?[47] Kühn had no doubt that minor tax concessions were infinitely more preferable. Yet the Bundesrat continued to make difficulties.

The various, but irreconcilable tax proposals threatened to become a hopeless tangle when the government decided, on top of it all, to introduce yet another large army bill. As the Reich Treasury found out in the middle of February, the additional cost would be almost one milliard marks and it was obvious that such a huge programme could not possibly be financed without a major tax reform. That the Army's proposals were nevertheless accepted by the civilian authorities with relatively little fuss demonstrates first of all how far the considerations of the General Staff had meanwhile come to dominate German policy-making. However, Bethmann Hollweg was pleased to oblige the military not merely because the army bill made it easier for him to dismantle the remnants of Tirpitz's naval policy; the army bill, he calculated, would also help him to fulfil the stipulations of the Lex Bassermann–Erzberger and might even serve as a catalyst for a *Sammlung* of the Right and the centre. And with the aim of preventing patriotic enthusiasm for improved defences from cooling down again over the question of how these defences were to be financed, the Chancellor had come up with a very cunning idea: the non-recurrent items of the army bill were to be covered by a 'defence contribution' (*Wehrbeitrag*). This contribution would be levied only once so that it could not be stigmatised as being a direct tax. What is more, it could be dressed up as 'a sacrifice, a patriotic gift', as the Bavarian Finance Minister termed it.[48]

Bethmann Hollweg's calculations turned out to be correct. The idea of a defence contribution was given an enthusiastic reception in the press.[49] The contribution was estimated to fetch some 800 million marks so that about 150–200 million were left for which additional taxes had to be found. Apparently the Chancellor hoped that the general enthusiasm would make it impossible for the agrarians to oppose the 'patriotic sacrifice'; moreover it would force them, as well as the federal states, to approve the introduction of a direct Reich tax. But subsequent negotiations showed that he was still far from having achieved a broadly-based *Sammlung*. 'As far as the question of financial cover is concerned', he admitted to his friend Karl von Eisendecher at the end of March 1913, 'I cannot conduct a big bloc policy.'[50] The Conservatives, he added, were lukewarm about the defence contribution and, at the same time, displayed their traditional 'aversion against a death duty'. In the Bundesrat again the south German states continued to resist Bethmann Hollweg's idea of a capital gains tax on property.[51] As the Saxon Foreign Minister phrased it in a letter to the Chancellor at the beginning of January 1913, this opposition was rooted in the 'extremely important *inner-political* consideration that the federal states be maintained as viable and solvent members of the Reich'.[52]

The final result was a somewhat shady compromise: the remaining sum of 200 million was to be made available through higher matricular contributions of the federal states, which in turn were to be raised through increases in direct taxation. Only if the federal parliaments failed to ratify these latter taxes by the end of 1914 would the Reich obtain the right to levy its own capital gains tax. It was, indeed, 'a compromise which satisfies no one' and, Bethmann Hollweg added, 'the Conservatives above all are hopeless people'.[53] While the Chancellor had no choice but to accept the constraints which the political power structure of the Prusso-German monarchy imposed on him, the Reichstag was no longer inhibited by agrarian intransigence. Since 1912, the parties of the centre and the Left were strong enough to force direct taxes through against the opposition of the agrarians if necessary. The defence contribution posed no problem. It received an overwhelming majority. The incantation of the 'encirclement' theme and of the possibility of a 'European conflagration in which the Slavs will confront the Germans' (Bethmann Hollweg in the Reichstag) sufficed to drive the middle-class parties to the side of the government.[54]

Trouble arose, however, when it came to the peculiar compromise by which the Chancellor proposed to cover the recurrent expenditure of the army bill. Liberals and Catholics demanded the immediate introduction of a direct Reich tax. This the Conservatives strictly opposed, and they remained adamant even when their former ally, the Centre Party, tried to mediate. After the breakdown of these attempts the unprecedented happened: the capital gains tax was approved by the parties of the centre and the Left against the Conservatives. The bill gained 280 votes, including those of the S.P.D. Agrarians, Free Conservatives and *Wirtschaftsvereinigung* were left with a depressingly small minority of 63. Of the 92 Catholics, 70 supported the bill and the rest abstained. What had been a possibility ever since the 1912 elections, had at last taken place: a tax law had been approved against the will of the conservative elites of the German Empire. It is important to emphasise that this did not mean that a permanent left-wing bloc extending from the Social Democrats to the National Liberals had been formed. On the contrary, the Left Liberals as well as Bassermann quickly dissociated themselves from the S.P.D.; but they also refused to ally themselves with the intransigent Right, led by the Central Federation of Industrialists and the Agrarian League. As before, there existed several *Sammlung* movements with the Conservatives as far removed as ever from the ideal of a broadly-based *status quo* policy. At one point, the Chancellor may have thought of using the army bill as a pretext for a dissolution of the Reichstag with the aim of waging a nationalist election campaign and of thus shifting the party balance towards the Right again. But the general patriotic enthusiasm for a massive bill quickly undermined any such calculations. 'The chances of [benefiting from] a dissolution', Bethmann Hollweg recognised, 'would have been miserable now.'[55] And then he added: 'It is a curious thing that this Reichstag which is so democratic should approve such a gigantic army bill.'

None the less, the fact remained that the parliamentary basis of the conservative elites had become alarmingly small. They had suffered a major setback and they were hysterical about it. Where would this end? The full extent of agrarian bitterness and of the feeling of living in a quasi-revolutionary period reminiscent of eighteenth-century France emerges from an article which Heydebrand wrote in the *Conservative Correspondenz*.[56] In it the leader of the Conservatives reproached the Reich government for having tolerated the introduction of a Reich capital gains tax on property and thereby having undermined the position of the federal states 'in favour of the democratic convention rule of the Reichstag'. Especially in Prussia, there existed a growing awareness of how 'the Reichstag with its universal suffrage and its ever more radical composition' influenced the government and influenced it in a direction completely different from that which 'the Prussian Diet with its three-class tier and its distribution of electoral districts favouring the eastern landowners' imposed on the Prussian government.[57] In other words, to the manifold existing conflicts which threatened to tear the Prusso-German monarchy apart there was now added an increasing antagonism between the Reich and Prussia, the largest federal state and the stronghold of agrarianism. And the more vigorously parliamentary tendencies asserted themselves in the popular assembly, the more deeply did the conservative power-elites dig themselves in, desperately trying to uphold their untenable position in a rapidly changing industrial society.

Equally the Left–centre alliance on the tax issue was a bad shock for heavy industry. Thus the syndic of the Saarbrücken Chamber of Commerce, Max Schlenker, said at the annual meeting of the economic associations of the Saar industry in June 1913 that the Reichstag had taken decisions on taxes 'which must fill these estates [!] with very serious concern for the future'.[58] The Association of Chambers of Commerce of the Rhenish–Westphalian Industry protested in April 1913 that the capital gains tax represented a 'first step in the direction of a confiscation of the medium-sized and large assets of the burghers'.[59]

The extremism of the Right was enhanced by the outcome of the elections for the Prussian Diet in which the conservative parties lost 14 seats while, despite the three-class voting system, National Liberals, Left Liberals and Social Democrats gained an equally large number. Although the hegemony of the agrarians remained unbroken, these events stimulated a fresh attempt to build 'a bridge between the commercial *Mittelstand*, industry and agriculture', as the *Bautzener Nachrichten* termed it, to combat the threat of genuine parliamentary rule.[60] These bridge-building efforts finally resulted in the formation of the Cartel of the Productive Estates which combined heavy industry, the Agrarian League, the *Mittelstandsvereinigung* and the *Vereinigung christlicher Bauernvereine*. As was to be expected, anti-Socialism and anti-parliamentarism figured prominently in the propaganda campaigns of the Cartel, but the immediate unifying bond was an economic one.

Heavy industry was particularly worried about the possibility of higher social security contributions at a time when, towards the end of 1913, the German economy appeared to be entering a recession. In the winter of that year, no less than 5 per cent of the industrial labour force were out of work, while food prices rocketed. It was this recession which prevented the trade unions from 'achieving improvements in the living conditions of the working-class which ... could have been obtained under normal circumstances'.[61] The employers saw themselves confronted with the demands of the proletariat to redress the balance. It is easy to exaggerate the actual extent of Germany's economic difficulties. But the point is that the exaggerated perception of the situation among businessmen, i.e. their belief that another period of economic difficulties was about to start, became a political factor in its own right and as such influenced the course of events. The events in the parliamentary sphere conglomerated with this economic pessimism to produce a general mood of gloom. Confronted with the seemingly unstoppable rise of the Left, all one could think of was to call on the government to freeze social policy. Fears of the future also motivated the agrarians. They were haunted by the nightmare of a return to the Caprivi period. Sometime in the not too distant future, they knew the tariff question and the renewal of the commercial treaties with Russia and other countries would come up. Would it be possible to uphold the policy of high protective tariffs; or would there be a 'demolition of our present tariff policy' which was expected to hit not only the big landowners but also 'leave the commercial *Mittelstand* which is dependent on the home market without orders'?[62]

Nevertheless the appeal of the Cartel's purely negative programme was limited. It had particularly little attraction for those groups, united in the *Hansabund* and the two Liberal parties, which had opposed the short-sighted policies of the Right ever since the fiasco of 1909. Their formula for overcoming the country's political

and economic difficulties was not retrenchment and further pro-
tectionism, but 'expansion, progress, free commerce, world trade'.[63]
Rather than involving Germany in trade wars which, as we shall
see, the Conservatives were aiming for, they wanted a liberalisation
of commerce and the abolition of the pro-agrarian system of import
certificates.[64] The ultimate objective was to 'strengthen the influence of liberal ideas' and 'to bring about a greater say, perhaps
even the political rule, of the bourgeoisie in the German Empire
and the federal states'.[65] Jakob Riesser especially, the President of
the *Hansabund* and Chairman of the Central Association of Banks,
considered it desirable to 'break the hegemony' of the 'privileged
classes'.[66] For, he added, 'we are still exceedingly far away from the
practical realisation of the equality of *all* estates, professions and
citizens.'

   This did not, of course, mean that Riesser favoured the full-scale
democratisation of the political system. What he was hoping for was
a gradual evolution which would result in greater middle-class
participation in the decision-making process. Nor did the National
Liberals have any 'desire to become ... conservative', as Bassermann
put it in April 1914.[67]

   In short, the basic pattern of German domestic politics remained
unchanged. There existed three large blocs, with the centre coming
under fire from both the Right and the Left. The S.P.D.'s estimate
of the *Hansabund* and the National Liberals was basically an or-
thodox Marxist one. The agrarians and the Central Federation of
Industrialists, on the other hand, identified them squarely as
partners of the Social Democrats. The 'bright red of democracy',
the *Conservative Correspondenz* argued, could hardly be differentiated
from the 'pink or purple of liberalism'.[68] There were, it is true,
various shades of colours in all three camps. But with the approach
of 1914 the essential fact about the internal political scene of the
Reich was that it was deeply split into irreconcilable blocs and that,
as far as the idea of a broadly-based *Sammlung* was concerned, all
efforts at reconciliation ended in failure. It is therefore difficult to
disagree with Arthur Feiler, the economic editor of the liberal
Frankfurter Zeitung, who in assessing the state of the monarchy,
wrote in 1914:[69]

   Thus social tensions are growing and so is the gaping gulf
   between heavy industry and the finished goods industry, between the beneficiaries of our economic policy and those who are

disadvantaged by it, between the propertied and the property-less classes, between capital and labour. And the trend is that this gulf will become even bigger in the course of the recession.

Gustav Schmidt has analysed the political constellation inside Germany during the last years before the First World War and in particular the position of the groups and parties of the centre.[70] He argues, convincingly, that there was a considerable build-up of reformatory pressures after 1912. These groups hoped to exert an influence on the government and to enforce a better coordination between government policy and popular will 'than the dominant elites had brought about so far'.[71] The idea was 'to effect the necessary adjustment of the constitutional conditions to socio-economic changes and [to changes in] the balance of power', a development deemed desirable also in the interest of Germany's defensive capabilities.[72] The centre believed that only if the participation of the middle-classes in politics increased would it be possible to integrate the working-classes into the nation. They were counting on the revisionist wing of the S.P.D. whose exponents were attracted by the basic outlook of the reform movement. If the *Sammlung* of the centre did not get very far, Schmidt continues, it was due to several major obstacles. One of these was that the 'stamina of public opinion' and the 'loyalty of the voter/party member in crisis situations' was always doubtful and therefore inhibited courageous political initiatives. Moreover the S.P.D. was more concerned about a possible loss of ideological purity than about a potential alliance with the social liberals of the centre. Its verbal radicalism notwithstanding, the main aim of the working-class movement in Germany was to 'prolong the *status quo* ... to consolidate the achievements and to make its own position ... impregnable'.[73] This, Schmidt writes, was also the attitude of the Conservatives so that one cannot actually speak of 'an intensification of class warfare or of a pre-revolutionary situation'; but conversely this was not a propitious time for the initiation of reforms.

The salient feature of German domestic politics before 1914 was therefore an almost total impasse. 'There was no room for compromises with neighbouring social groups or even former competitors.'[74] This paralysis was accompanied by a 'permanent battle of ideologies'. The Social Democrats needed the existing monarchical order as the tree to bark at in order to prevent a split in their own ranks into a revolutionary and a revisionist party. The ruling elites, for their part, could not do without the bogey of the 'revolution'. As a matter of fact it was this bogey which made 'the continued existence of the Reich possible after 1890'.[75] On the eve of the First World War, German society was divided into several hostile camps. What made things so dangerous was that these different social forces 'were blocking each other and owing to their position in the power-structure of the Reich were in a position to do so successfully'.[76] The notion of several groups blocking each other and hence blocking a wayout of the deadlock offers 'the key to an understanding of German politics in the last years before the War'.[77] 'The idea of the bloc suggests a polarisation of the social forces in friend-foe formations ... but also the inability to instil political life with a purposeful dynamic.'

In these circumstances, Bethmann Hollweg found himself in a most unenviable position. At the same time as German foreign policy ran up against the resistance of the Triple Entente to the Reich's *Mitteleuropa* plans, his domestic manoeuvrability became similarly constrained. Co-operation with the reform movement was just as unthinkable as it had been prior to 1912.[78] But the strength of the working-class movement and the federal structure of the Reich made repression, as advocated by the extreme Right, equally impossible. It is symptomatic of the profound internal crisis that the idea of a *Staatsstreich* was once again ventilated. As in 1897 it was a military man, Konstantin von Gebsattel, who produced a memorandum demanding the abolition of the universal suffrage and a 'solution of the Jewish question'.[79] The executive, he wrote, was to be provided with full powers to 'end the attacks by Social Democrats and Progressives on religion, monarchy and state'. While the Crown Prince welcomed Gebsattel's proposals, William II, although officially refuting his son,[80] repeatedly talked about a *Staatsstreich* himself. 'The idea that he will ally himself with the Princes', Bethmann Hollweg wrote in 1913, 'in order to chastise the Reichstag and eventually abolish it, or that he will send one of his adjutant generals into the Reichstag, if I am not tough enough, constantly crops up in conversations with me.'[81]

The Chancellor was appalled. Although he did not wish to rule out a *Staatsstreich* as a last resort, he was convinced that, if success was not absolutely certain, it was 'either a stupidity or a crime' to attempt one.[82] And it was precisely the chances of success about

which he was doubtful. He believed that the Reich's federal structure militated against a victorious outcome. Even if a joint plan for
action could be agreed upon, it was, he felt, by no means certain
that the princes would show perseverance. For he expected a revolutionary upheaval to follow a coup and this, in turn, would impose
such strains on the federal governments that the whole political
structure might easily come crashing down. Bethmann Hollweg was
also concerned about the possibility of a foreign war which France
might unleash if civil war broke out in Germany. In short, in the
eyes of the Chancellor the country was now less prepared than ever
to adopt a violent solution of the constitutional dilemma. The
erosion of conservative support, the growth of the Left and last but
not least the expansion of the Army had made a *Staatsstreich* too
risky to be a realistic proposition. Bethmann Hollweg had no choice
but to manoeuvre between the fronts and avoid the introduction of
all legislation which might lead to another Left–centre alliance
along the lines of the 1913 tax compromise. Although the power of
the conservative elites had been weakened, they were still strong
enough to by-pass the Reichstag with its potentially anti-
conservative majorities. From 1913 onwards, government took place
largely by decree and all policies which might backfire on the
Conservatives as the tax compromise had done were shelved.

The trouble was that no complex industrial society can be ruled
like this for any length of time. Domestic paralysis was not a suitable means of preserving the *status quo*. But if the political system
was no longer capable of overcoming its internal divisions by means
of a 'peaceful' strategy of *Sammlung* or, alternatively, a violent one
of *Staatsstreich*; and if, with the creation of a Ludendorffian *levée en
masse*, the Army was no longer a reliable instrument of law and
order, could a foreign war perhaps act as a catalyst for the renewed
stabilisation of the Prusso-German monarchy's deteriorating position both at home and abroad? We have seen repeatedly that this
idea was not alien to influential political and military circles, and
the events of 1913 had done much to reinforce this kind of thinking. Given their feeling that time was running out, but also their
awareness that they still held an edge over their external and internal opponents, the conservative elites became increasingly tempted
to use their superior powers before it was too late.

9 Towards a Military Solution

For a number of years now the condition of the Prusso-German monarchy had been developing from bad to worse. In the diplomatic field, the abandonment of Tirpitz's grand design did not seem to pay off. Anglo-German relations, it is true, improved slightly after 1912, and Bethmann Hollweg believed that an understanding in the colonial field might be used as a springboard for a more general political rapprochement between the two countries when he set out to clear away the wreckage of the Haldane Mission. But his strategy was largely illusory, partly because everybody became aware of the shift of German policy back to the European continent. Not surprisingly, it was in this area that the Central Powers encountered the opposition of the Triple Entente and its smaller allies whenever they tried to lay the foundations of a bloc stretching from Berlin to the Near East. Worse still was that the national independence movements inside the Austro-Hungarian Empire undermined the cohesion and the existing power base of the Dual Monarchy. Some people felt that it was merely a question of time before this heterogeneous multi-national empire broke up. Inside Germany all attempts to form a broadly-based conservative bloc met with failure. The shift towards the Left continued and the country was split into three political camps paralysing each other and the political system as a whole. And since a *Staatsstreich* was rejected as being too dangerous, the only change that could be expected from a conservative point of view was a change for the worse.

The cumulative effect of this was that those who were still attached to the Prusso-German monarchy in its traditional shape and form saw themselves encircled by enemies from all sides and became increasingly convinced that they had to act before their time ran out. Further stagnation, they believed, would only lead to a further deterioration of the situation. In the field of foreign policy a standstill was bound to accelerate the slow erosion of the existing continental position, especially in the Balkans. At home political paralysis would merely increase social tensions and thus help the enemies of the heavy industrial-agrarian complex. This in turn, had important repercussions on the attitudes of the decision-makers. We have seen earlier how they found it increasingly difficult to arrive at a correct estimate of developments. There was above all their constant overperception of, and the subsequent overreaction to, the threat of the Triple Entente.

But the same overperception can be discovered in the attitude of the conservatives to the 'internal enemy'. In a country in which there was very little social or political interchange between different classes and in which the elites, above all the military, led a completely secluded life, the most exaggerated horror stories of the aims of the working-class movement found ready acceptance. Most conservatives did not know, or did not want to know, that the Social Democrats had in practice abandoned their revolutionary Marxist tradition.[1] What counted was that the S.P.D. demanded a greater share of power and responsibility within the political system. This is not to deny that the demands of the Social Democrats were still sufficiently radical to amount to more than a purely superficial change of the existing order. But the point is that the objective condition of pre-war Germany was less important for her future development than the distortions which this condition underwent in the minds of the ruling elites.[2] For an understanding of the conservative groups which had, and continued to have, a decisive say in all basic policy matters, it is vital to take into account the socio-psychological climate which prevailed in Germany in those last years before the First World War.

There is a specific reason for placing a good deal of emphasis on this aspect. Although there can be little doubt that, objectively, the Reich has to bear the main responsibility for the outbreak of the War,[3] the question of why the Kaiser and his government unleashed it in August 1914 continues to be a hotly debated issue. Fritz Fischer, in *War of Illusions*, views the July Crisis of 1914 as the terminal point of a policy upon which the German government embarked quite rationally and in cold blood from the end of 1912.[4] On the other hand, we have seen that the actions of the monarchy over the past decade were determined increasingly by irrational factors. There can be no doubt that, objectively, it was the country's foreign and armaments policy, as pursued since the turn of the century, which had brought about its isolation. But this did not prevent the Kaiser and his advisers from believing quite earnestly that they were being encircled by the Triple Entente. Objectively the conservative elites were primarily responsible for increased tensions inside German society because they were unwilling to accept the need for political change. But subjectively they were convinced, except perhaps for a few cynics, that the 'red' and 'golden' 'internationals' were to be blamed for the sorry state of domestic politics and for the polarisation in the political spectrum. Can one really expect a political leadership which suffered from a profound loss of reality and among which rationality and reason found it so difficult to assert themselves to plan a major war systematically and many years in advance?

Cold-blooded planning for war appears to square poorly with the atmosphere of anxiety and pessimism prevailing in conservative circles before 1914. Their actions rather bear the mark of panic. Both at home and abroad they found themselves on the defensive—cornered and desperate. War was nothing immoral to them, but a legitimate means of carrying out political conflict. In fact the idea of settling disputes by armed force had a long-standing tradition in the history of the Prusso-German elites and their world view was steeped in irrational notions of honour and chivalry. Yet however much such factors may account for the infusion of a dogmatic and highly inflexible element into the decision-making processes of the monarchy, the Kaiser and his advisers were still cool enough to calculate at which point their own position would be not just difficult or desperate, but hopeless. And they would be prone to act before the situation had deteriorated beyond repair; they would resort to violence as long as there was still a chance of victory.

It is this kind of rationality which made the First World War in a peculiar sense a preventive war. Such a war, the *Berliner Tageblatt* wrote in the spring of 1914 referring to a statement by Bismarck, 'resembles a suicide for fear of death'.[5] At the same time, the paper added, circumstances could be imagined in which a state 'is pushed more and more into a corner' and in which 'light and air are cut off'. In such circumstances 'it can be the duty of self-preservation not to allow the enemy the choice of the time when the *coup de grâce* might best be administered'. Pressed hard by Conrad Haussmann in February 1918 as to whether the First World War was a war which had not been forced upon Germany by her neighbours, as official propaganda would have it, Bethmann Hollweg sighed:[6] 'Lord yes, in a certain sense it was a preventive war'. Yet 'if war was hanging over our heads, if it was bound to come two years later much more dangerously and inevitably and if the military say: today it is still possible [to wage it] without defeat, but not in two years' time', did the country have any other choice, he asked. This was basically the same kind of argument which Waldersee had used in 1897 when he recommended that 'it is in the State's interest not to leave it to the Social Democrat leaders when the great reckoning is to begin; rather it should do everything possible to force an early decision. For the moment the State is, with certainty, still strong enough to suppress any rising.'[7] The difference was that 15 years later a *Staatsstreich* was out of the question. The idea of preventive action had become restricted to the field of foreign policy.

The calculating element in German policy between 1912 and 1914 hence does not appear in the long-term preparation for a war to be started at a pre-set date, but in the assessment of the Reich's advantage over the enemy. If this advantage is seen to be narrowing down to a 'critical mass', the temptation to launch a war is likely to become irresistible. Conversely the proclivity to resort to military action will decrease if the room for political manoeuvre can be extended. The critical point will then recede again and the decision-makers will no longer be under an immediate pressure to resort to violence. As we have seen, the Prusso-German monarchy had lost a lot of diplomatic ground and was faced with paralysis in all spheres of domestic politics which required Reichstag participation. However, there was, protected by the Reich Constitution, a wide executive sphere in which the powers of the crown were largely untouched. This sphere, it is true, was also threatened by parliamentary influences. But although no one knew when this threat might become really dangerous, the fact remains that in 1914 William II and his advisers still possessed the exclusive command of the Army as well as the right to declare war. It was not inconceivable that one day the Reichstag would assume these privileges, too. Until this time the most crucial of all questions with which a nation can be faced, i.e. that of war or peace, was in the hands of a small 'strategic clique'.[8] This left a few people with a tremendous advantage over the mass of Germans, but it also left them with the dilemma of having to calculate the size of the country's advantage over the 'external enemy'.

There were those who believed that the critical point had long been reached and that an immediate war was the only way out. A victorious war, they thought, would not only liberate the Reich from the pressure of the 'encirclement', but would also remove the internal deadlock. The historical experience of 1866 tacitly provided a sort of precedent for this concept. These 'militaristic' tendencies had received a fresh stimulus from the outcome of the First Balkan War. It had weakened the position of the Central Powers in south-east Europe and so alarmed the Austrian and the German General Staffs that they pressed for a war against Serbia. When it became clear that the destruction of Serbia would lead to a major conflict, involving the Triple Entente, the Kaiser concluded that the hour of decision was imminent. 'It is a matter of life and death for Germany', he remarked nervously.[9] 'The eventual struggle for existence which the Germans (Austria, Germany) will have to fight in Europe against the Slavs (Russia) supported by the Romans (Gauls) will find the Anglo-Saxons on the side of the Slavs.'

These remarks set the stage for a conference of William II with top naval and Army officers on 8 December 1912 which the Kaiser opened by demanding that Austria–Hungary should make a determined stand against Serbia lest 'she lost control over the Serbs inside the Austro-Hungarian monarchy'.[10] Moltke believed that a war was inevitable—'the sooner the better'.[11] Only Tirpitz opposed the idea and pleaded for a 'postponement of the great struggle by $1\frac{1}{2}$ years'. Moltke's angry reaction was that 'the Navy would not be ready then either and the Army's position would become less and less favourable; the enemies were arming more rapidly than we do, as we were very short of money'. According to Müller the result of the conference was 'pretty much nil';[12] or to put it differently, those who wanted an immediate war were defeated. To some extent, this was due to the vacillation of the Chief of the General Staff himself who said: 'War—the sooner the better', but refused to draw any conclusions from his attitude which, according to Müller, should have been: 'to confront France or Russia or both with an ultimatum which would unleash war with right on our side'.[13] Moreover the meeting recognised that 'the nation' was not yet sufficiently enlightened about the 'great national interests' which were involved for Germany in the event of a war between Austria and Serbia.[14]

Bethmann Hollweg, who had not been invited to the meeting, did not share Moltke's pessimism. For once he was in agreement with Tirpitz. It is safe to assume that Tirpitz, by advocating a post-ponement of action until 1914, pursued a delaying tactic in the hope of avoiding war altogether. Ever since coming to office in 1897, he had been pointing out to the Kaiser and everybody who wanted to hear it that the Reich would have to pass through a 'danger zone' and that diplomatic crises would be inevitable. What was required was a steady foreign policy rather than nervous diplomatic activism and that Britain would then be less difficult. At the same time, Tirpitz had estimated the length of the 'danger zone' and in 1912 he believed he saw some light at the end of the long tunnel. Although this turned out to be an illusion, it is important for an understanding of the conference of 8 December to note that Tirpitz was hoping for an improvement of Germany's strategic and political position in the foreseeable future. The Reich Navy Office reckoned that the naval balance would shift in the Reich's favour and that Britain would then be more amenable to German territorial claims. An alliance with Britain and hence the breaking of the iron ring around Germany would at long last vindicate his armaments policy. Moltke's war could only jeopardise this prospect.

Tirpitz and Bethmann Hollweg were thus agreed in their opposition to an early war and in their hope for an improvement of the monarchy's position. The Chancellor believed it to be his task to try and steer the Reich away from the critical point which Moltke felt had now been reached and to enlarge his government's room for political manoeuvre both at home and abroad. His diplomacy in the Balkans and on the Bosphorus, but also his attempts to initiate a rapprochement with Britain in 1913 must be seen in this context. At the same time he was working to overcome the internal crisis and to form a broadly-based conservative *Sammlung* of the Right and the centre. The 1913 army bill, as we have seen, was partly designed to act as a catalyst at home and to dismantle the naval programme as a disturbing element in his negotiations with London. Finally, the strengthening of the land forces was a vital concomitant of the Reich's *Mitteleuropa* strategy. But as in the case of Tirpitz's naval policy it proved difficult to gain political advantages from a stepping-up of armaments. The size of the 1913 army bill had barely become public when France reacted in kind. Although the government and the German press subsequently tried to blame the arms race on Paris, there can be little doubt that the introduction of the three-year service in France was a consequence of Germany's army bill. In the case of Russia the causalities are even clearer. It was in reaction to Germany's measures of the spring of 1913 that the Tsarist government made preparations for the reorganisation of the Russian army and for increases by nearly 500,000 men. The second half of 1913 also saw the initiation of plans to extend the railway network in western Russia.[15] The reorganisation was to be completed by 1917.

This meant that, although Germany had gained a momentary strategic advantage, it was possible by the end of 1913 to predict when this advantage would be lost. From 1916 at the latest, the balance of power would once again shift in favour of the Triple Entente, so that it was also relatively easy to predict the moment when German strength would reach its critical point. Some time around 1915, the temptation 'to commit suicide for fear of death' would be very great. In the meantime the General Staffs in Berlin and Vienna were busily comparing the relative military strengths of the Triple Entente and the Triple Alliance. On 24 February 1914 Moltke forwarded to the German Foreign Office a memorandum in which he discussed the threat posed to the Reich by Russia's recent armaments.[16] Conrad, his Austrian colleague, was driven by similar fears. On 3 March 1914 he told Colonel Josef Metzger, the head of the Operations Department in the Austrian General Staff, that he was wondering increasingly 'if one should wait until France and Russia were prepared to invade us jointly or if it were more desirable to settle the inevitable conflict at an earlier date. Moreover the Slav question was becoming more and more difficult and dangerous for us.'[17] At a meeting in Karlsbad in the middle of May the two generals had an opportunity of reinforcing one another in their conviction that time was running out.[18] Moltke was convinced that 'to wait any longer meant a diminishing of our chances; as far as manpower is concerned, one cannot enter into a competition with Russia'. Full of gloom, he saw Jagow soon after his return to Berlin, who gained the following impression of the thoughts of the German Chief of the General Staff:[19]

> The prospects of the future seriously worried him. Russia will have completed her armaments in 2 to 3 years. The military superiority of our enemies would be so great then that he did not know how we might cope with them. Now we would still be more or less a match for them. In his view there was no alternative to

waging a preventive war in order to defeat the enemy as long as we could still more or less pass the test. The chief of the General Staff left it at my discretion to gear our policy to an early unleashing of a war.

This solution to Germany's dilemma seemed all the more attractive because, as Moltke had emphasised in March 1914, Russia was not pursuing any aggressive designs at the moment.[20] He did not believe that Russia would try to engage Austria or Germany in a war 'in the near future'. France, he added, would be even less inclined to adopt 'an aggressive posture'. Similarly Conrad advised the German Military Attaché, Count Karl von Kageneck, to act before it was too late. The sooner a war with Russia broke out the better; 'our position will not improve. But one must be clear that it will be a life and death struggle. If we win, Germany and Austria–Hungary will be in control of things; if we lose, the Germans will be taken by the throat. [Then] the Slav peril will come.'[21]

Such appraisals of the German and Austrian position had been appearing in the German press for some time and now did so with increasing frequency. During the campaign for the 1913 army bill commentators had still given prominence to the argument that Germany needed 'stronger armaments in view of the political situation in the world in order to safeguard her existence and to secure peace and the benefits of peace for her economic growth'.[22] The predicament of the Reich, *Der Tag* wrote in April 1913, was best described by the formula: 'Enemies all around—permanent danger of war from all sides.'[23] Other papers tried to predict what this uncomfortable position might lead to and openly wrote about the 'struggle between the Slavs and the Germans which is bound to come sooner or later'.[24] 'On this occasion,' the heavy-industrialist *Post* added in December 1912,[25]

when the German people will risk everything some of those German questions which the founding of the Empire of 1870 has left unsolved will also have to be decided .... This is what the Pan-Slav agitators in Russia, the revenge-thirsting brawlers on the Seine and also the secret wire-pullers in England should make a note of: in and through a world war which is to be unleashed and which, we assume, will be victorious for us, the German people will gain a position in central Europe which will make a repetition of such a general war simply impossible.

This agitation which also exemplifies well the ambiguity of Germany's *Mitteleuropa* offensive reached a first climax in the spring of 1913, at the time of the debate on the army bill. Under the impact of this agitation a fortress mentality spread among the population together with a feeling that in the long run peace offered no solution to the internal and external problems of the Reich. It is rather unwise to take the press comments at their face value. Their hysterical tone seems to indicate that the papers were whistling in the dark. The glorifications of war and the constant sabre-rattling were symptoms of the pathological state of Wilhelmine politics. For, as Bethmann Hollweg once put it, those who felt strong and confident did not have to 'carry the sword in their mouths'. Clearly, the key decision-makers no longer possessed this confidence.

Although in the spring of 1913 much of the agitation for war was motivated by the desire to rally support for the army bill, it also had a lasting effect, which worried Bethmann Hollweg. 'I am', he told Eisendecher at the end of June 1913, 'fed up with war and the clamour for war and with the perennial armaments. It is high time that the great nations calmed down again and occupied themselves with peaceful pursuits, or there will be an explosion which no one desires and which will be to the detriment of all.'[26] This was no doubt correct. On the other hand it was not for the first time that the propaganda for more armaments began to develop a dangerous momentum of its own. The same problems which had beset Bülow during the Anglo-German naval arms race now limited his successor's freedom of action. It was not only that the French and Russian counter-measures could be predicted to offset the effect of the German army increases at some later date, but also that the thrust of public opinion increasingly imposed restrictions on the flexibility of German policy. In fact, this latter problem became so serious that the Chancellor decided to utter a warning in the Reichstag that wars had not always been planned and executed by governments but that 'nations have often been driven into war by noisy and fanatical minorities'.[27] Today this danger, he added, was greater than ever, 'after public opinion, popular mood and agitation have been gaining in weight and influence. Woe be to him whose retreat is not well-prepared.' Unfortunately Bethmann Hollweg's was not. His intention to gain for his government greater room for manoeuvre at home and abroad suffered one setback after the other. By the end of 1913 the war party and the military were fully entrenched.

This became particularly evident in October 1913 when the Prusso-German political system was shaken by the Zabern Affair. The incidents in Alsace–Lorraine offered ample proof that local hostility to the annexation of the province in 1871 was as strong as ever and that, as Countess Marie Radziwill phrased it, there existed an old *'antagonisme latent de deux Allemagnes très différentes'*.[28] In other words, the Prussian military state still formed the hard core of the German Empire, separated from the rest of society. The Affair started when, on 28 October 1913, a lieutenant of the 99th regiment, stationed at Zabern, abusively referred to the Alsatians as *'wackes'*.[29] This remark was reported in the *Zaberner Anzeiger* a week later and caused a wave of indignation. The paper demanded an apology, but the local commanding officer refused to give one, and henceforth trouble never ended. On 9 November the same lieutenant was jeered by a crowd when he was on patrol duty in town. It is typical of the mood in military circles and their loss of reality that the local commander immediately thought that a revolt was in the offing. Sentries were reinforced and all soldiers had their leave cancelled. The civilian *Kreisdirektor* was informed that, if law and order could not be guaranteed by the police, the Army would move in and declare a state of siege. And as if to rehearse for the imposition of military rule, the Army proceeded to arrest a number of soldiers who were suspected of having informed the press. The commanding officer completely overstepped the bounds of legality when he ordered the search of the offices of the *Zaberner Anzeiger* in the hope of finding incriminating evidence and when, on 28 November, he had some thirty civilians arrested, almost all of them on charges of ridiculing the military in public or of insolent behaviour, as it was called.

> As a climax to the day, Reuter [the commanding officer] appeared with some officers and about 60 men on the Schlossplatz and although there was no demonstration whatsoever ordered the people to disperse. Not all obeyed the order, but with a drum

roll and a charge with fixed bayonets, even the most hardy took to their heels.[30]

By this time the incidents had long ceased to be a purely local affair and had led to a confrontation between the head of the civilian administration of Alsace–Lorraine, Count Karl von Wedel, and the provincial corps commander, General Berthold von Deimling. The latter gave his full support to the actions taken by the local regiment and blamed everything on the provocations of the population. Against this interpretation, Wedel had already protested in an earlier report on the first incidents. Now he sent a telegram to the Kaiser, claiming quite unceremoniously that there had been further 'serious excesses and illegalities'. Unless these were redressed, he feared, 'faith in the German sense of justice and in German impartiality will be shaken down to its foundations'.[31] He therefore asked the Kaiser for permission to report to him in person on the situation.

William II was no doubt the central authority who could have made a decision based on justice and political wisdom. It was, after all, blatantly obvious that the military had transgressed their powers. But the Kaiser was guided by other considerations when he turned down Wedel's request and gave his spontaneous approval to Reuter's action of 28 November. The decisive point was that court and military circles in Berlin thought it more important to uphold 'the prestige of the Army which had allegedly been challenged', as Wedel put it in a letter to the Chief of the Civil Cabinet, Rudolf von Valentini.[32] In place of Wedel, who was asked to submit a written report, General von Huene gave the monarch a first account on 29 November, followed by a report from Deimling of 30 November. Both generals complained bitterly about Wedel and the civilian administration in general. The events of 28 November, Deimling maintained, were the 'natural consequence of the weak-kneed and passive attitude' of *Reichsstatthalter* Wedel.[33] The reaction of the Army had been perfectly adequate, even if the legal basis of its intervention was contestable. William II approved this interpretation without reservation. In this view he was duly confirmed by another report which was produced by a commission of inquiry under the chairmanship of Major-General Alfred von Kühne. The monarch had no doubt that it was not the Army which was to be

blamed for the troubles, but that 'three-quarters' of the responsibility lay with the '*Schweinepresse*'.[34] Kühne's reports, it is true, also
had a few critical things to say about Reuter. But it was never made
public that Reuter retired soon afterwards. Nor was it made known
that the lieutenant who had started the whole affair was trans-
ferred to another unit.

On 2 December this splendid officer had caused yet another
incident when, aided by five soldiers, he had tried to arrest a civilian and, in the course of this, had injured the latter with his sabre.
Once more the Army was prepared to accept the excuse that the
arrested had assumed a threatening posture rather than to repri-
mand the officer in question for his excesses. On the contrary, the
incident led to the Army's gaining what, apparently, it had always
been aiming for. On 3 December the Kaiser issued an order to
Deimling that the Army was to be responsible for law and order in
Zabern forthwith, and lest there be a misunderstanding about the
Army's powers he declined to insert in his order a clause that
Deimling should keep 'within the limits of the law'.[35]

With William II having taken a highly partial stand, not only
Wedel's but also Bethmann Hollweg's hands were tied. Wedel's
report of 30 November had convinced the Chancellor that the Army
had committed breaches of the law, and that 'the most pacific
population in the old provinces' had nothing but bitter feelings for
the excesses of the military.[36] The Chancellor therefore thought it
best to suspend Reuter and to dispatch an officer to Zabern to investigate the matter. On 3 and 4 December he told the Kaiser quite
openly that in his view the Army had violated the law 'in a very
serious manner'.[37] The military had, he said, excluded the civilian
authorities and arrogated to themselves powers which were not
really theirs. In the meantime public indignation had spread to
Berlin and Bethmann Hollweg faced a storm in the Reichstag. Yet
the Chancellor knew that he could not possibly join the chorus of
critics. The prestige of the Army had suffered a blow and 'I shall
rather accept a dent in my own reputation than permit the denigra-
tion of the Army'.[38] Under Secretary of State Arnold Wahnschaffe
had moreover learned 'that there was widespread suspicion that the
Kaiser had personally prevented the expiation of the injustice which
had been done'.[39] In these circumstances Bethmann Hollweg considered it his duty to come to the support of the monarch and the
pillar of the shaky Prusso-German political system, the Army.

Nothing was to become public of the profound differences of opinion which existed between Wedel and the military. If the *Reichsstatthalter* resigned at this moment, 'the Chancellor's position', Wahnschaffe noted, 'will be untenable and all the criticism concerning the breach of law will be directed against' the monarch.[40] Valentini held similar views, giving the military the major share of responsibility but adding: 'These are flaws in the constitutional structure and in the world of ideas of our military which we must, under no circumstances, admit to a public hostile towards us.'[41]

Thus Bethmann Hollweg stood before the Reichstag on 2 December knowing that it was 'my duty to defend the authority of the Army with all energy and in all directions'.[42] Arguing that 'the king's coat must be respected under any circumstances', he brushed all military outrages aside and did not mention that Reuter had been sent on leave. So overwhelming was the impression that the Chancellor subscribed to the actions of the Army that in the end even the parties of the centre joined the opposition. S.P.D., Left Liberals and Catholics tabled a motion of no-confidence which found the approval of the National Liberals and was carried by a majority. Philipp Scheidemann, a leading socialist, pointed to British constitutional practice and demanded the resignation of Bethmann Hollweg. But once more it became clear that the Prusso-German Constitutionalism was not to be compared with the parliamentary systems of government in western Europe. He would 'resist with all his powers', the Chancellor retorted sharply, 'that our constitutional conditions be changed in this respect'.[43] He spoke against a 'revolutionary democratisation' of the Army over which the monarch alone possessed the power of command. The Zabern Affair would never be allowed to become a 'battering ram ... against imperial powers'. Indeed, if, as Valentini had written, the Affair had demonstrated 'flaws in the constitutional structure' of the Reich, these flaws formed an integral part of the political system whose most basic weakness was that it was supposed to preserve the rule of a small minority in a rapidly developing industrial society. For, as the War Minister phrased it in a letter to Bethmann Hollweg, 'if we are no longer in the position to move our regiments to wherever we deem it necessary because the population of the border area has objections to this, a situation would be created whose continued existence would most seriously endanger the security of the Reich'.[44] Heeringen had pinpointed the problem and as long as the monarch and his advisers were in a position to do with the Army what they pleased, William II could also afford to regard the discussions in the Reichstag as 'fits' of 'political children' living in a 'mad house'.[45]

Although the vote of no-confidence remained a scrap of paper, the Zabern Affair had the lasting effect of further disillusioning the population with the existing order. 'Politically', the *Kreisdirektor* of Strasbourg wrote at the end of January 1914, 'Alsace-Lorraine is at present a shambles';[46] but the ruins were not confined to that part of the Reich alone. The majorities in the Reichstag and the reactions of the press showed that large sections of the population had become alienated from the monarchy and that the conservative elites no longer controlled the popular assembly. Countess Radziwill noted a widespread disappointment with this *'patrie peu enviable'*, and a profoundly unhappy aristocrat even told her:[47] *'Si j'étais libre et plus jeune, je quitterais ce pays.'* Only the Conservatives fully approved of what had happened in Alsace and for some of them even Bethmann Hollweg's reply in the Reichstag was not firm enough. Heydebrand and Count Kuno Westarp would not have been unhappy to see the Chancellor replaced by a stronger man, although they did not wish to expose themselves in the question of succession.[48] To a man like Westarp, the Affair moreover offered fresh evidence that the Alsatians were still far from considering 'the Army a valuable part of the nation which is to be given particular support'.[49] They did not yet see themselves at one with the Army, he wrote, whereas such an identification 'is a deeply-rooted tradition for us Prussians'. Since other sections of the population were showing a similar lack of identification, the Zabern Incidents merely contributed to a deepening of the domestic split which paralysed the country and polarised the political system as a whole.

Whereas the crown and the conservative groups supporting it had further isolated themselves from the rest of the country, the Army's position *within* the decision-making machinery had been strengthened. The military and their supporters were in a 'victorious mood', as the State Secretary for Alsace–Lorraine informed Bethmann Hollweg.[50] To Eisendecher the Chancellor complained in February 1914 about the 'boundless arrogance' prevailing in military circles, while Wedel endured his defeat silently. Being himself a former general, Wedel found it impossible 'to take sides against the military'.[51] The Army, he felt, was the 'firm bulwark of the monarchy and the Fatherland' and nothing was to be done that would weaken its power. When, in January 1914, Reuter was cleared of the charges against him, the *Reichsstatthalter* submitted his resignation. The question was, so the right-wing Social Democrat deputy Ludwig Frank exclaimed on 23 January in the Reichstag, whether Germany 'should advance towards a *Rechts-* and *Verfassungsstaat* (state of law) or move backwards to a police and military state'.[52] But the answer had already been given by the conservative elites on whose power the future direction of German policy was largely dependent and who, so far, had shown themselves incapable of learning from past mistakes. 'In Prussia', *The Times* summarised the situation on 14 January 1914, 'the Army is supreme and, through Prussia, the Army rules Germany. This is the first lesson of the [Zabern Affair] for those who lightly imagine the German Empire to be even as other states.'[53]

This applied increasingly also to the pressures brought to bear on the foreign policy of the Reich. On 2 March 1914, the *Kölnische Zeitung* published an article by its correspondent in St Petersburg discussing the state of Russian domestic politics.[54] By the autumn of 1917, Richard Ullrich reported, Russia's financial and economic difficulties would, with the aid of French credits, have been overcome. This as well as Tsarist agricultural policy which was designed to preserve the position of the big landowners would generate 'expansionist aspirations' towards Persia, Turkey and Russia's western frontier. As early as the spring of 1913, General Pavel von Rennenkampf, the commander-in-chief at Vilna, would have loved to invade East Prussia and 'to leave the prosperous German country on the other side of the border to his pillaging horsemen'. Today the Russians admitted quite openly that they were 'arming for war against Germany' and that they were thinking of turning the Army 'which they would possess in a few years time' against their western neighbours. Ullrich concluded that official Russo-German relations would 'assume a quite different face' if those 'gentlemen would realise that in future they would have to reckon with a firm will, rather than a conciliatory attitude on the German side'.

What is remarkable is that this article coincided with another one published on the previous day in the *Schlesische Zeitung*, containing a report on the allegedly very powerful war party at the Tsarist court.[55] 'A war', the paper argued, 'does not normally break out when one expects it, but it comes like a thief in the night. This is why we must never allow ourselves to be lulled into a false sense of security and must always be prepared.' Although there was a semi-official denial in the *Norddeutsche Allgemeine Zeitung* that government circles had anything to do with Ullrich's article, the suspicion remained that the campaign was officially inspired. The Russian Ambassador, at any rate, learned from various confidential sources that 'the growing power of Russia is arousing the gravest fears in Berlin'.[56] Although Jagow told him that the outcome of the Liman von Sanders Affair was the 'main cause for the outburst of indignation', Sergei Sverbeyev knew that the real problem lay elsewhere:

> In the view of government circles here, our siege artillery will be ready in 1916 and from this moment onwards Russia will become a terrible rival which Germany will, allegedly, find it very difficult to cope with. [In view of this it would not be surprising] if one tried to intimidate us. [Moreover, Germany would make every effort] in order to be prepared for the case of a military conflict with us.

Apart from the fact that in the spring of 1914 the military were gaining ground in the decision-making machinery more rapidly than ever, there is circumstantial evidence that the Army was behind the anti-Russian press campaign and that it was trying to add the weight of 'public opinion' to its old argument about the need for quick military action. Ullrich, to begin with, was a former officer who had been retired in 1905 after being seriously injured during a commission as an observer in the Russo-Japanese war.[57] The correspondent of the *Schlesische Zeitung*, on the other hand, was a retired captain who had once worked in the General Staff.[58] In May, a few weeks after Tirpitz's request for more money had been turned down, Moltke submitted a memorandum to the Kaiser in which he argued that as from 1917 Russia would be ready for a quick war in the west.[59] He had no doubts that in view of this and of the expected deterioration of Germany's position the existence of the country was at stake. He demanded 'that we train *every* German who is fit for military service'.

These remarks, together with the above-mentioned exchanges between Moltke and Conrad, seem to indicate that the Army was not only taking an extremely gloomy view of the future, but was also thinking of another all-out strengthening of its forces. This was bound to meet with the approval of the heavy-industrialists who were worried about the economy—so much so, in fact, that the Austrian historian Josef Redlich suspected them of complicity.[60] This was also what struck the Social Democratic *Vorwärts* about the campaign:[61] 'For many years, one declared a war between Germany and England to be inevitable and demanded, year after year, a strengthening of the fleet. Now Russia is turned into the aggressive enemy. The armaments industry (*Rüstungstreiber*) always needs a bugbear to generate the necessary [atmosphere of] anxiety in which even their maddest claims are granted.' That this strategy was effective and further incited public feelings of hysteria, was confirmed by the *Frankfurter Zeitung* on 4 March 1914.[62] 'Broad circles of the population', the paper wrote, 'have allowed themselves to be seized by a nervousness which offers the armaments enthusiasts and war fanatics the fertile soil into which to put the seeds of new army increases.' What the *Frankfurter Zeitung* found remarkable was how quickly the agitators had changed their tune. A few years ago, it observed, Britain was the arch enemy; now Russia and France were identified as the most dangerous opponents whose attack was to be pre-empted.

This observation points to an important mechanism propelling the military-industrial complex in Germany. New enemies had to be found all the time, not necessarily in order to wage war against them, but because without them a vital sector of the economy and indirectly of the monarchy as a whole would suffer a setback. There was, however, yet another factor which helps to explain the anti-Russian campaign of the spring of 1914 and to which Ullrich had alluded in his article. 'In three years' time,' he wrote, 'when we must conclude a new commercial treaty' with the Russians, the Tsarist Empire would create difficulties in this sphere also.[63] Ullrich's remark touched upon a subject which did not immediately concern the Army nor heavy industry, but the agrarians. It has already been mentioned that the Junkers had been agitating for some time for the maintenance of the high protective tariffs of 1902 and had warned against a return to the policies of the Caprivi era. As has been mentioned above, Caprivi had lowered Germany's tariff barriers in 1892. It was due to the fierce opposition of the agrarians to this that he subsequently lost his post and that the government promised to revise agricultural tariffs.

In 1902 grain tariffs were increased once again from 3.50 marks to 5.00 marks per two cwt. Although this revision destroyed all hope of the Reich ever adopting a socially pacifying 'cheap food' policy, like Britain, the advantage of high tariffs was obvious: it secured the economic survival of a small pre-industrial minority at the expense of the consuming masses. The drawback was that this did not endear the workers to the Wilhelmine class state so that the Kaiser and his advisers had to try to win them over by means that had long been blunted.[64] Nor was another policy, devised to keep up food prices for the benefit of the big landowners, likely to find favour with the masses: the actual export of grain. To understand this it must be remembered that in 1905 Germany and Russia had signed a commercial treaty which was particularly favourable to the Germans. Weakened by the defeat in the Far East, St Petersburg had to concede, *inter alia*, low tariffs on German agricultural produce. This concession was an incentive to the Junkers to export grain, regardless of the fact that the Reich was by no means self-sufficient and was therefore forced to import foodstuffs at a price which, thanks to the 1902 tariffs, was kept artificially high. But what made German grain exports even more lucrative was the system of *Einfuhrscheine* (import certificates).

Originally this system had been introduced to cover exports which were to re-enter the German market, e.g. grain which was shipped from East Prussia via the Baltic Sea to the industrial Rhineland. Subsequently, however, the government lifted the proof of identity for such exports. All grain exports were issued with a certificate, regardless of whether or not they were destined for the internal market. This certificate could now be used by the exporter to avoid payment of duties on grain entering Germany from, say, America, and later the certificates could even be submitted to cover such goods as coffee or petroleum. Since in most cases exporters and importers were not identical and importers were interested in obtaining these certificates, a market developed on which the certificates could be sold. In other words, by being issued with an *Einfuhrschein* whenever they exported grain, the big landowners were, in fact, paid a veiled export premium.

That these advantages acted as a powerful stimulus to the East Elbian grain export can be seen from the following figures: in 1902 as little as 6500 tons of rye reached Russia from Germany. By 1908, two years after the ratification of the commercial treaty, the figure was at 142,200 tons and in 1913 even at 231,000 tons.[65] In that same year certificates with a market value of some 150 million marks were distributed—a handsome subsidy for the agrarians.[66]

Last but not least as a result of this export premium, German grain exports to Russia became a deadly competitor for Russian agriculture, whereas the latter was deterred from the German market by high protective walls. In 1902, before the abolition of the Caprivi tariffs, Russian grain exports to Germany had amounted to 842,000 tons. Ten years later, this figure had sunken to a meagre 269,000 tons.

A further point of friction in Russo-German relations was the employment of Polish seasonal workers on the East Elbian estates. Obviously these workers were particularly cheap from the Junkers' point of view. They had to feed them only during harvest time and they did not impose any additional financial burdens on them in the way of social security and welfare benefits. It was not that the Poles could expect better treatment from the Russian land-lords. But what angered the latter was that Polish migration depleted the labour market when workers were needed and after their return from Germany, they burdened Russia's pocket for the remainder of the year.

It is not surprising that this state of affairs, combined with German agricultural policy, generated a good deal of resentment among the Tsarist landowning aristocracy. As they were just as closely interconnected with the bureaucracy and the Army and just as threatened by decline as the Prusso-German elites, one important reason for the growing antagonism between Berlin and St Petersburg can be found in the peculiarities of the two countries' commercial relations. Ultimately the ideological affinities of the two monarchies, their revulsion against change and their desperate attempts to preserve an old-fashioned order, counted for less than these political and economic differences. 'It hardly requires any mention', *Deutscher Aussenhandel* wrote in April 1914, 'that in view of the high-grade political tension between the two countries any conflict in the field of commercial policy implies a serious test of peace.'[67] Yet, precisely this conflict was almost bound to break out when, in 1916–17, the commercial treaty came up for renewal. The Prussian agrarians had few illusions that the Russians would once more submit to a German *Diktat,* and Russian policy in the spring of 1914 gave the Reich an inkling of what the future held in store.

At the beginning of March, a meeting of exporters from south Russia, held at Kiev, resolved that the Tsarist Empire should 'liberate itself from its economic dependence on Germany which is

humiliating for a great power'.[68] Moreover they pleaded for closer
relations with countries which did not impose protective agricultural tariffs and demanded compensatory measures 'against the
open or hidden export premiums for German industrial syndic-
ates'. Finally, they added, the Russian seasonal workers should be
given the full protection of German welfare legislation if it were
found to be impossible to find 'attractive employment' for them in
Russia itself. And as if to demonstrate that these demands were to
be taken seriously, the Russian parliament, the *Duma,* approved
immediate tariff increases on grain of 30 copecs per *pud.*[69] The
agrarians in Germany could thus hardly fail to gain the impression
that any future commercial agreement with Russia would end the
existing advantages. There existed in the Reichstag a left-wing
majority which threatened to support a lowering of the high tariff
walls. Caprivi-ism was rearing its head again! At the same time it
was to be expected that the Russians would insist on the abolition
of the export premium, while safeguards for the Polish seasonal
workers promised to raise production costs. In short, profits were
almost certain to decline. More estates would go bankrupt and the
Baltic Sea ports faced, as *Deutscher Aussenhandel* put it, an 'economic
catastrophe'.[70] In addition to the growth of left-wing movements,
the Junkers were now exposed to the possibility of a trade war with
Russia. The closure of the frontier to Polish seasonal workers was
likely to be bad enough. But what would happen if St Petersburg
used the weight of its Army to bully the Reich into making concessions? Inevitably such fears fanned agrarian hatred of Russia,
and Heydebrand demanded that a determined stand be made
against her.[71] In St Petersburg, he said, people would understand
'very well the language of force'.

In this way, the military fears of the General Staff coincided with
the apprehensions of the big landowners, both of them vital pillars
of the Prusso-German political system. To the experience of being
cornered at home and of operating an immobilised governmental
machinery was added the feeling of isolation and of living on 'the
eve of a trade war'.[72] At home the advantages of their superior
power position seemed to be dwindling fast. The conservative elites
were still in control of the physical forces of the state and, as the
Zabern Affair had shown, they were very much aware of this.
Abroad their only reliable and significant ally was a multi-national
empire, Austria–Hungary, which was torn by separatist and social

revolutionary forces. Any edge which the Central Powers still had over their continental neighbours was quickly disappearing. The existence of the monarchical order was at stake which meant that high risks had to be taken. In short, the depressing predicament of the monarchy served to reinforce the arguments of those who preferred war to the agony of a slow political death. If waged in time, war offered a chance of victory, providing the Reich with the continental platform which it had failed to gain since 1912. At the same time, a war promised to solve the internal problems in the Bismarckian fashion of 1866. 'A fresh and uninhibited war', the arch-conservative *Ostpreussische Zeitung* wrote as early as December 1912, would immediately decimate the 110 Social Democrats in the Reichstag.[73] Sometimes, the editor of the *Deutsche Arbeitgeber-Zeitung* elaborated in February 1913, war was 'the only remedy to cure existing illnesses'.[74] Above all, the agrarians, as Bethmann Hollweg observed on June 1914, 'expected a war to turn domestic politics in a conservative direction'.[75]

The Chancellor, on the other hand, was convinced that this was a mistaken assumption. He believed 'that a world war with its unforeseeable consequences will greatly strengthen the power of social democracy, since it preaches peace and will topple many a throne'.[76] This was all the more likely because it was quite possible that the Reich would lose such a war and defeat would seal the fate of the Prusso-German monarchy.

10 The July Crisis of 1914

If one reviews the state of German policy in the early summer of 1914, it is not difficult to understand why the Chancellor should have been overcome by pessimistic thoughts. 'The more distant future is quite dark', he wrote to his friend Wolfgang von Oettingen in 1913 and, according to his son, he doubted, on another occasion when overlooking the park of his estate at Hohenfinow, north-east of Berlin, 'if there were any purpose in planting new trees; in a few years the Russians would be here anyway'.[1] The past four years, he sighed, 'have dealt harshly with me and the last winter and spring with their great tasks have made me weary'.[2] 'Especially the men who should lighten my burden professionally, H[is] M[ajesty] and the Conservatives, make things as difficult as they can', he added. But it was not only that there was paralysis at home for which the conservative elites of Germany were primarily responsible. Thanks to the Entente policy of containment, Bethmann Hollweg's room for diplomatic manoeuvre had also diminished while the Reich remained chained to a disintegrating multi-national Austro-Hungarian Empire and allied to a mediterranean state which was far from reliable. As Georg von Waldersee, the Chief Quarter-master in the General Staff, put it in the middle of May 1914:[3] 'At the moment Italy is *still* on the side of the Triple Alliance and Emperor Francis Joseph's personality *still* holds the hotch-potch Danubian Monarchy together .... But for how long? Will these things perhaps not change in favour [of the Entente Powers] quite soon?'

As a private individual sitting in front of his Hohenfinow fire-place, Bethmann Hollweg might have been free to indulge in a gloomy fatalism. But as Chancellor of the Prusso-German monarchy he could not afford to remain passive, if only because the worried military were constantly breathing down his neck and, with their incessant talk of a preventive war, were also infecting the Kaiser. In these circumstances Bethmann Hollweg could no longer

196

sit back cultivating a feeling of 'uneasiness' when reading Moltke's memoranda about the Russian peril.[4] He had to *do* something unless he was prepared to relinquish the reins of government to the military. This pressure for action to arrest a deteriorating domestic and foreign situation received a tremendous boost when, on 28 June, Archduke Francis and his wife were assassinated by Serbian nationalists at Sarayevo and when William II, after receiving a first report on the events from the German Ambassador in Vienna proclaimed his famous 'now or never'. 'The Serbs', he wrote 'will have to be straightened out, *and soon*.'[5]

The international crisis which now followed and which led to the outbreak of the First World War can usefully be divided into three phases. The first phase marked the evolution of a fairly precise plan for action and the decision to implement this plan. During the second phase the Central Powers set out to execute their concept until it became clear towards the end of July that it had been mismanaged. A major war now seemed the only escape out of the cul-de-sac in which the Reich found itself. There is yet another basic point which must be made at the beginning of this chapter: it will be noticed that only a very small circle of men was involved in the crucial decisions which ended in war. Neither party leaders nor the representatives of economic pressure groups were drawn into the secrets of the Court, the German Foreign Office and the General Staff. But this does not contradict our previous analysis. On the contrary, a good deal has been said so far about the constitutional and structural peculiarities of the Prusso-German monarchy, its concentration of great power in the hands of the Kaiser and a small arch-conservative elite and the manipulative strategies they had traditionally resorted to. In particular the decision to wage war had remained the exclusive prerogative of the monarch. It is not surprising, therefore, that when it came to making this decision no more than a dozen people were consulted while, again characteristically enough, the rest of the population was manipulated into supporting it.

One of the most crucial aspects of the first phase of the July Crisis was that the 'hard-liners' had now definitely gained the upper hand. Talking to Stumm a few days before the Sarayevo incident, Victor Naumann, a Berlin journalist, noted 'that one no longer took quite so negative an attitude towards the idea of a preventive war not only in Army and Navy circles but also in the Foreign Office as

one had done a year ago'.[6] Stumm had spoken of the Russian threat
in 'very serious terms' and had added that 'war, "which Germany
could have whenever she wanted to"', was no longer 'unthinkable'.
After the assassination of the Archduke, the moment seemed to
have come for the great reckoning. As the Saxon Ambassador to
Berlin learned on 2 July, the military began to press once more 'that
now, with Russia not yet ready' and France 'very preoccupied with
her domestic problems and her financial calamity', Germany should
not shrink from waging war.[7] The prevalence of this view was
confirmed (though it was put somewhat more diplomatically) by the
German Ambassador to Vienna when he saw Emperor Francis
Joseph and the Austro-Hungarian Foreign Minister Berchtold.[8]
Both men were told emphatically that the Reich would support
Austria unwaveringly 'whenever it were a matter of defending her
vital interests' (*Lebensinteressen*) whose definition the Reich would
leave to her leaders. Berchtold, moreover, was directly encouraged
to make 'an active move against Serbia'.

The prodding was needed. The Austro-Hungarian government
was far less determined to use the Sarayevo murders for a move
against Serbia than were the Kaiser and his entourage. In Vienna,
only Conrad advocated immediate action. Francis Joseph, on the
other hand, preferred to wait for the results of the official investi-
gation into the assassination, while Count Karl Stürgkh, the
Austrian Minister President, and Count Stefan Tisza, his Hungarian counterpart, pleaded for 'keeping a cool nerve'.[9] Berchtold,
finally, feared that 'Germany and Roumania would leave us in the
lurch'.[10] In order to verify the German attitude at the highest level,
Francis Joseph decided to write a letter to William II which the
latter received on 5 July. The Kaiser's reply was his famous 'blank
cheque' in which he assured the Austrians of his unconditional
support. The Dual Monarchy should not hesitate to take action
against the Serbs.

Much has been written about this assurance and there can be
little doubt that it was intended to give *carte blanche* for a 'punishment' of Serbia which was believed to be deeply implicated in the
plot to assassinate the Archduke. The country was to be attacked
without long-winded diplomatic preliminaries.[11] The Kaiser and
his advisers were also aware that such a violent solution implied
the danger of an intervention by Russia which, in turn, would
unleash the whole mechanism of alliance commitments and lead

to a major war. Everything, so Count Georg von Waldersee, the Chief Quartermaster, informed the Saxon Military Attaché on 3 July, now 'depends on how Russia reacts to the Austro-Serbian business'.[12] Should the Russians react by military means, he added, 'we could, from today to tomorrow, [ourselves] be involved in a war.' It would be wrong to assume that this prospect particularly alarmed the German military. The General Staff, so the Saxon Military Attaché concluded, thought this to be a propitious time for a war with Russia. Without war, an improvement of the German position could not be expected in the future. In view of this, the Army had only one concern, namely to be prepared for all eventualities as the Kaiser had ordered them to be when he saw the representatives of the armed forces on 5 and 6 July.[13] They left it to Bethmann Hollweg and the German Foreign Office to deal with the political aspects of the problem, if they could.

The Chancellor had meanwhile evolved a plan for action which, compared with the sledge-hammer politics of the military, was somewhat more sophisticated. In fact, it was so persuasive that the Kaiser and the Army agreed to leave its execution in his hands while they went on holiday, to see what would become of it. As William II explained the plan to Capelle, Tirpitz's representative, 'the Austrian Government will demand the most far-reaching satisfaction from Serbia and will, as soon as this is not given, move its troops into Serbia'.[14] He thought that an intervention by Russia was unlikely 'because the Tsar will not lend his support to royal assassins and because Russia is, at the present moment, militarily and financially totally unprepared for war', and France would be in similar difficulties. For this reason, he had told Francis Joseph that he could rely on Germany. He believed 'that the situation would be cleared up within a week, because of Serbia's backing-down....' This was also what the Kaiser had told the War Minister Erich von Falkenhayn when they met on the previous afternoon (5 July). Here William mentioned that the period of tension would probably last a little longer, namely 'three weeks'.[15]

In other words, the other great powers were to be presented with the destruction of Serbia before anything could be done to prevent it. Bethmann Hollweg, as Kurt Riezler, his private secretary, put it in his diary, first wanted to achieve a *'fait accompli'* and then to be 'friendly towards the Entente'.[16] In this case, he added, 'the shock can be endured,' for 'in case of warlike complications between

Austria and Serbia, he and Jagow believed that it would be possible to localise the conflagration.'[17] The advantages of this plan—the strengthening of the Central Powers, the weakening of Russia and of Pan-Slavism, the soothing of the Right at home—were so obvious that the Chancellor was, on 5 July, mandated to try it out. Even Moltke, who was on holiday and was merely kept informed by Waldersee, was prepared to acquiesce. 'Austria', he commented on what he heard from Berlin, 'must beat the Serbs and then make peace quickly, demanding an Austro-Serbian alliance as the sole condition. Just as Prussia did with Austria in 1866.'[18]

There were, however, several preconditions for the *fait accompli* to be successful. First of all it was important that the Triple Entente did not become suspicious of the Central Powers and take immediate counter-measures. For this reason, the military authorities were ordered 'to avoid, for the time being, all steps which are liable to arouse political attention or to cause extra costs'.[19] Accordingly Moltke was ordered to stay where he was, and so were Tirpitz and the Chief of the Admiralty Staff, Hugo von Pohl, both of them likewise already on holiday. 'At the explicit request' of the Foreign Office, Waldersee immediately took his vacation whereas the Kaiser who had made 'an absolutely quiet [and] resolute impression' on Capelle, went on his scheduled trip to Kiel to start his annual Norwegian cruise.[20] Two days later, on 8 July, Falkenhayn also left, first for an inspection tour and 'then for a holiday'.[21] On the day of his departure he signed a letter to Bethmann Hollweg which shows that the Army, like the Navy, was trying not to be concerned about the immediate crisis, but was rather making plans for another expansion of its size to become effective in 1915–16, i.e. for the time when the Russian increases were expected to pose a genuine threat.[22] In addition to these plans Falkenhayn submitted proposals for an improved training of reservists and against socialist anti-Army propaganda.

Apart from the appearance of absolute calm, speed was another prerequisite of the success of Bethmann Hollweg's concept. The assassination had aroused widespread indignation in Europe and a 'punishment' of Serbia would have met with a good deal of understanding. But Austria had to react soon. If the reaction were delayed for too long, suspicions were bound to arise that the Dual Monarchy, with Germany behind her, was pursuing more far-reaching aims. Herbert Butterfield has shown that this was most probably the attitude of the British Foreign Office and that it was largely the slow speed with which the Austrians and Hungarians prepared their move that destroyed Grey's calculations.[23] The slowness of their preparations certainly helped to destroy Bethmann Hollweg's plan.

However, it would be a serious mistake to assume that the Reich Chancellor was unaware of the great risks his action involved. He realised that even if there were no delays or leaks, the Austro-Hungarian attack on Serbia might well escalate into a major war. He appreciated in particular that the expected international shock might prove too much for Russia whose position in the Balkans would be directly affected by the Austrian move. 'An action against Serbia', Riezler reported Bethmann Hollweg as saying on 7 July, 'can lead to world war'.[24] The Chancellor also had no doubt that, 'whatever the outcome' of such a war, it would turn 'everything that exists upside-down'. It was, he added on 14 July, 'a leap into the dark', and yet he felt he had no choice but to take the risk in full awareness of its consequences.[25] The 'leap into the dark', Riezler recorded, was most difficult for Bethmann Hollweg to take, and yet he considered it his 'gravest duty' (*schwerste Pflicht*).

The Riezler Diaries contain a number of statements which elucidate why Bethmann Hollweg saw no alternative to accepting the risk of a world war. 'The secret intelligence,' the Chancellor's private secretary wrote on the day after the 'blank cheque' had been issued, '…gives a shattering picture.'[26] The Entente powers knew 'that Germany was "completely paralysed". Austria is becoming increasingly weaker and more and more immobile. The subversion [of the Dual Monarchy] from the north and the southeast [has] progressed very far…. The military might of Russia is growing fast.' There was, he added, 'secret intelligence about the Anglo-Russian naval negotiations'* which indicated that Germany would have 'to reckon seriously with British attempts to land in Pomerania in case of war…' This, he thought, was 'the last link in the chain' (*letztes Glied in der Kette*). Russia, above all, would henceforth step up her demands and would try to employ 'her tremendous explosive force'.[27] 'The future belongs to Russia which is

---

*Since May 1914 Britain and Russia had been exploring the possibility of a naval agreement about which the Germans were well-informed. They had a spy working for them in the Russian Embassy at London who transmitted the Russian Ambassador's correspondence to Berlin.

growing and growing and is becoming an ever-increasing nightmare to us.' 'In a few years time', Tsarist demands could no longer be 'warded off, even less so if the present European [power] constellation remains'. Unless the Reich stiffened Austria's back now, she would seek 'a *rapprochement* with the Western powers whose arms are wide open, and we shall lose our last military ally'.[28]

This assessment of Germany's position was depressing enough. But what appeared to make action, even at the risk of a world war, so imperative was that the crisis involved a Balkan problem. If war came, it would come 'from the east' so that Germany would have 'to fight for Austria, rather than Austria for us'.[29] In this case the Reich would have 'a chance of winning'. We shall see below that this hope was based not only on military calculations, but also on the realisation that a war against Russia would be popular among all classes and would hence present an opportunity of overcoming the internal problems of the monarchy. If, on the other hand, so Riezler added on 8 July, the Balkan crisis did not escalate into a major war because 'the Tsar does not want it or [because] a dismayed France counsels peace, we still have the prospect of splitting the Entente.'[30]

There are a number of less well-documented and more indirect considerations which led the Chancellor to adopt his risky strategy. Apart from the military who were pushing him forward, it was now also the attitude of the Kaiser which, to some extent, forced his hand. We have seen repeatedly that, in earlier years, William II had been a counterweight against the 'militarism' of the General Staff. Obviously, the Kaiser had most to fear from a people's war which, even if successful, was likely to increase popular pressure on the crown. It appears that on this point the monarch was in agreement with Bethmann Hollweg. However, as time passed, the constant deterioration of the Reich's position both at home and abroad did not fail to make an impression on William. Moltke's inveterate production of alarmist memoranda exerted a positively demoralising influence on the once optimistic and self-confident monarch. When Max Warburg, a Hamburg banker and friend, met him a week before the Sarayevo murders, he found him 'profoundly disturbed' about the political situation and 'more nervous than usual'.[31] Now, after the assassination of the Archduke, he decided to demonstrate that he had strong nerves. 'This time,' he assured Krupp repeatedly when they met at Kiel in the evening of 6 July, 'I shall not chicken out.'[32] It was almost pathetic, Krupp thought, to see how William tried to prove that he was not a coward. But there can be little doubt that this mental state of the Kaiser also pushed his Chancellor into accepting the highest risks.

It has been argued that, because objectively the chances of success were so slim, Bethmann Hollweg did not seriously believe his *fait accompli* strategy would work.[33] All that his moves in the first half of July were designed to achieve was to create the most favourable conditions for a major war. It appears that this is an *ex post facto* argument which does not take sufficient account of the evolution of the crisis as experienced by the actors involved in its (mis)management. The available evidence rather seems to suggest that the Chancellor genuinely hoped for a German victory short of a great war. It was not, it is true, a well-calculated hope, but it was precisely the uncertainty of success which caused him to pray for it all the more fervently. There is another psychological factor which is likely to have stirred Bethmann Hollweg into action: it is not only that he hoped a major conflict could just about be avoided, but also that the possible eruption of such a conflict seemed some distance away. This distance encouraged a kind of dare-devil attitude on the part of the German leadership which turned into growing nervousness as the date of the Austro-Serbian clash drew closer.

In the meantime, Bethmann Hollweg and the German Foreign Office tried very hard to prod Vienna into speedy action. On 7 July the Austro-Hungarian Ministerial Council met under the chairmanship of Berchtold to discuss the next moves.[34] Berchtold opened the meeting with the news that 'both Emperor William and Herr von Bethmann Hollweg assured us most emphatically of Germany's unconditional support in the eventuality of a war-like complication with Serbia'. He realised, he continued, 'that a passage at arms with Serbia could result in a war with Russia'. On the other hand, it should be borne in mind that, in view of Russia's attempts to unite the Balkan states in order then 'to be able to play them out against the [Dual] Monarchy at the suitable moment', Vienna's position would 'deteriorate increasingly'. This, Berchtold added, was all the more likely 'since passive toleration' of such a development would inevitably 'be interpreted by our [own] South Slavs and by the Roumanians as a sign of weakness'. Austro-Hungarian weakness would, moreover, increase the magnetic force of the two neighbouring states on the minorities within the multi-national Empire.

According to Berchtold there was only one logical conclusion to be drawn from this state of affairs: 'to steal the march on our opponents and, by a timely settling of accounts with Serbia, check the development which is already in full swing'. It was Tisza who now raised his voice against Berchtold's proposal to launch a 'surprise attack on Serbia without any preliminary diplomatic preparation'. He did not wish to object to a penal expedition in principle. But, as he wrote to Francis Joseph on the day after the meeting, an invasion of Serbia 'would, as far as can humanly be foreseen, lead to an intervention by Russia and hence to a world war'.[35] He could therefore never agree to an unceremonious marching into Serbia, as proposed by Berchtold and 'to his regret also discussed in Berlin' between the representatives of the two allied governments. If this radical solution were adopted, 'we would in his opinion thoroughly discredit ourselves in the eyes of Europe', and, with the exception of Bulgaria, encounter the hostility of all Balkan states. In these circumstances Austria–Hungary should first present Serbia with a list of demands and

> issue an ultimatum only if Serbia did not fulfil them. The demands must be stiff but not impossible to meet. If Serbia accepted them we would have scored a brilliant diplomatic success and our prestige in the Balkans would soar. If [on the other hand] our demands were not fulfilled, he, too, would vote for military operations. But he would have to state straight away that any such operations, though they might result in a diminution of Serbia, must never aim at her destruction, because, without a life-and-death struggle, this could never be tolerated by Russia and because he himself as Hungarian Prime Minister could never agree to the annexation, by the Monarchy, of any part of Serbia.

Above all, Tisza concluded, the Dual Monarchy should not allow itself to be pushed into war.

His arguments found little sympathy with his colleagues. They felt that 'a purely diplomatic success' would be 'worthless', even 'if it were to end in a glaring humiliation of Serbia'. Instead they resolved that Serbia should 'be presented with such far-reaching demands' as to make their rejection certain. This would then 'clear the road for a radical solution by way of military operations'. However, the ministers were prepared to accept Tisza's procedural point 'that mobilisation should take place only after concrete demands have been placed before, and rejected by, Serbia and an ultimatum has been presented'. Tisza was satisfied with this compromise provided that the terms for Serbia, though stiff, would not immediately and 'clearly betray our intention to make impossible demands'. Otherwise, he added, 'we should have an untenable juridical basis for a declaration of war'. For this reason 'the text of the note must be very carefully thought out and he would attach importance to having it submitted to him before it were sent off'. Similarly Francis Joseph, who received Tisza's own summary of his objections together with an oral report by Berchtold on 9 July, was inclined to hold 'that *concrete demands would have to be put to Serbia*'.[36]

This outcome of the discussions on the Austro-Hungarian side had fatal repercussions on the German idea of a *fait accompli* in two respects. For one, the decision to give the whole manoeuvre an elaborate diplomatic cover and to word the first note to Serbia very carefully meant a considerable delay. Whereas Berlin expected the Austro-Serbian war and the subsequent international storm to be over in, at most, three weeks, it was now fairly certain that the drafting of the note would itself take a good deal of time. Consequently the link between the assassination of the Archduke and the 'punishment' of Serbia would become more and more tenuous and European public opinion less and less likely to see it. Moreover there was an increased danger that something would leak through to London, Paris or St Petersburg. Secondly, Tisza's suggestion to divide the diplomatic preliminaries into two parts—first a note and then an ultimatum—stretched Bethmann Hollweg's programme even further, giving the other powers additional time for intervention. Objectively, therefore, the Reich Chancellor's surprise action—the defeat of Serbia to be followed by a peace offensive towards the Entente with a view to localising the conflict to the Balkans—was doomed to failure when, on 7 July, the Austro-Hungarian Ministerial Council adopted Tisza's cumbersome two-stage proposal. It may be that it was this virtual coincidence of the decision to wage war against Serbia at the conscious risk of a world war on 5 July and the practical inevitability of such a major war as a result of the procedure adopted only two days later, which induced Fritz Fischer to assume that the Central Powers wanted a *world* war all along.

However, it appears that this is too linear an interpretation of German and Austrian intentions. In the two weeks that followed the Austrian Ministerial Council, Berlin continued to hope that localisation would work. In fact, it was during this period that Bethmann Hollweg and the German Foreign Office became fully conscious of the need for speed. Thus Jagow informed the Austrian Ambassador to Berlin of his fear 'that the sympathetic support for, and the interest in', the Austrian note might subside if it took too long to send it.[37] To prevent this delay, members of the German Embassy in Vienna paid frequent visits to the Austro-Hungarian Foreign Ministry where the 'formulation of suitable demands' had become 'the main concern'.[38] By the middle of July, Berchtold was himself acutely aware of the problem of timing, but at the same time he pointed to a dilemma. 'On the one hand,' he wrote, 'we must now prevent a flagging of public interest in the Monarchy which is favourably inclined towards our policy; on the other hand, [we must] not, by systematically escalating the language of our press organs, give rise, among other powers, to the idea of mediation.'[39] It was apparently for this latter reason (and thus quite in line with Bethmann Hollweg's plan) that on 13 July Conrad, the Chief of the Austro-Hungarian General Staff, went on holiday, followed two days later by Alexander von Krobatin, the War Minister.[40] Meanwhile the German Foreign Office was likewise doing its best 'to portray the situation as harmless from a European point of view'.[41]

Berlin tried to do even more than this. Bethmann Hollweg and his advisers not only realised that the delay of the note threatened to bring about the premature intervention of other powers, but also that the two-stage diplomatic procedure, as suggested by Tisza and adopted by the Ministerial Council on 7 July, generated exactly the same danger. It was with the aim of reducing the chances of great power mediation *after* the demands had been handed over to Serbia that the two diplomatic despatches were now compressed into one. As Berchtold told the German Ambassador on 10 July, 'the deadline for the [Serbian] reply must be kept as short as possible'.[42] He mentioned '48 hours' although he saw that 'even this small time-limit' would give Serbia enough time 'to obtain instructions in St Petersburg'. This manipulation obviously overrode Tisza who had always insisted on a careful, step-by-step preparation of the attack on Serbia. The Hungarian Minister President was understandably not enthusiastic. But in the end even he became convinced that his own argument was inconsistent and by the middle of July he had given his approval to a 48-hour ultimatum.[43] This was not the end of his objections, however. On 17 July, Bethmann Hollweg was informed that 'negotiations with Count Tisza are still going on',[44] and it was only on 19 July that the Ministerial Council met again to approve the draft of the communication to Serbia.[45] The ministers agreed that it should be transmitted to Belgrade in the afternoon of 23 July, i.e. almost three weeks after the 'blank cheque' had been issued and four weeks after the assassinations at Sarayevo.

The reasons for Tisza's stubbornness emerged most clearly on the nineteenth. They are of interest here only because they illuminate once more the great risks which Berlin and Vienna were consciously taking. As far as the diplomatic preparation of the *fait accompli* was concerned, the Hungarian Minister President merely fought a rearguard action. He now spoke of merely one 'ultimatum' himself. But he insisted that 'the action against Serbia' must not be started with the aim of conquering territory and that, apart from minor frontier adjustments which were militarily justified, 'not a [single] piece of Serbia' would be annexed by the Dual Monarchy. 'He would make this demand,' he concluded, 'not only for reasons of domestic policy, but in particular also because he was personally convinced that Russia would [otherwise] have to fight back *à outrance*.' Moreover an early assurance to the other powers that Austria–Hungary did not intend to annex territories would be 'one of our best trumps to improve our international position'. Riezler, when hearing about this proposal, agreed; he hoped that it might persuade the Russians to come to the conference table rather than to mobilise.[46] Although Tisza finally got his way on this point, the net effect of all these negotiations was that valuable time, a vital factor in Bethmann Hollweg's strategy, had been lost.

Nevertheless this does not explain why the Ministerial Council of 19 July decided to delay the transmission of the ultimatum until the twenty-third. To account for this, another factor must be mentioned which had apparently been overlooked, or cast aside as irrelevant, at the beginning of July: the state visit of Raymond Poincaré, the French President, to Russia from 20 to 23 July. On 13 July, Berchtold had told the German Ambassador that he hoped 'to reach agreement with Tisza on the wording of the note to be addressed to Serbia' and that he would submit the draft to Francis

Joseph for final approval on 15 July.[47] The note could 'then be handed over in Belgrade without delay [and] hence prior to Poincaré's departure'. Riezler gave the reason for this:[48] 'Then [we shall gain] a better chance that France, recoiling from the real possibility of war, will counsel peace in [St] Petersburg.' But on 14 July it became clear that it was impossible to complete the operation 'on the sixteenth or on the eighteenth', partly because of the technical problems,[49] yet apparently also because of the trouble with Tisza. This meant that the ultimatum would become public while the French President was in St Petersburg. There was hence a real danger that Poincaré and Nicolas II would co-ordinate their reactions to the Austro-Hungarian move, and to avoid this danger, it was decided not to transmit the ultimatum until the French party had left Russia again.

The upshot of the difficulties which the original plan had been encountering since 5 July was that the *fait accompli* was by this time highly unlikely to be achieved. It seems that slowly but surely this also began to dawn on Bethmann Hollweg and his advisers. With the date of the ultimatum approaching, apprehension spread in the German Foreign Office and the Reich Chancellery. This was particularly true of Jagow. Meeting him on 20 July, the day after the final decision had been taken in the Vienna Ministerial Council, the Deputy Chief of the Admiralty Staff, Rear-Admiral Paul Behncke, found him to be 'unsure of himself, fidgety and timid'.[50] The interview consisted of 'endless discussions or, to be more precise, twaddle without anything concrete emerging'. Jagow gave a description of 'the general political situation in nervously applied, rather gloomy colours' and declared that 'a general European conflict was by no means out of the question'. It was obvious that the German house of cards was beginning to collapse.

The Chancellor, Riezler noted on 20 July, was becoming 'taciturn' while, at the same time, trying to keep a stiff upper-lip.[51] Pondering over the causes of the present predicament of the Prusso-German monarchy, he discovered one of the main reasons to be the 'aimlessness [of German policy], the need for small prestige gains and the pressure to take all currents of public opinion into consideration'.[52] The right-wing parties 'which, by making a lot of noise (*Radau*) over foreign policy, are aiming to maintain and foster their position in the party spectrum' had, he felt, to bear some of the blame. Finally, there were 'the earlier mistakes [of conducting an] Ottoman policy against Russia, a Moroccan one against France [and of building a] fleet against England, [i.e. of pursuing a policy of] irritating everybody, of blocking everybody's way and yet not really weakening anyone'. This was indeed what the Kaiser's grandiose *Weltpolitik* had come to only some fifteen years after it had begun. Yet, it was too late now to draw the logical conclusion from such insights into the roots of the German dilemma. The Kaiser and the military were unlikely to accept another diplomatic defeat. Soon they would be coming back from their holidays to look at what Bethmann Hollweg had made of his blitz plan, and if it did not work, they would take over to escalate the crisis into the sort of major war which they had been advocating for some time.

What choice was there for Bethmann Hollweg but to hope and pray that his *fait accompli* could still be achieved? On 16 July he wrote to Count Siegfried von Roedern that 'in case of an Austro-Serbian conflict the main question is to isolate this dispute'.[53] Five days later he informed the German Ambassadors in Paris, London and St Petersburg:[54] 'We urgently desire a localisation of the conflict; any intervention by another power will, in view of the divergent alliance commitments, lead to incalculable consequences.' The Saxon *chargé d'affaires* to Berlin was told on 17 July that 'one expects a localisation of the conflict since England is absolutely peaceable and France as well as Russia likewise do not feel inclined towards war'.[55] Writing a day later, Jagow confirmed that 'we wish to localise [a] potential conflict between Austria and Serbia'.[56] And Riezler noted in his diary:[57] 'If the Serbian business comes off well without Russia's mobilisation and hence without war', Germany might perhaps come to an arrangement with her over the question of stabilising the Dual Monarchy.

Once the date for the ultimatum had been set, the German Foreign Office took steps to ensure such an outcome. On 19 July the semi-official *Norddeutsche Allgemeine Zeitung* published an item which had been personally drafted by Jagow.[58] It appealed to the 'united interest of Europe' in preserving, as on previous occasions, the peace in the Balkans. This European solidarity, the commentary continued, would 'seem to make it desirable and imperative that disputes which might arise between Austria–Hungary and Serbia remain localised'. Behncke was told on 20 July that, on the day of the ultimatum, Germany's diplomatic representatives would inform the Triple Entente 'that we consider Austria's steps against

Serbia justified and would, above all, advocate a localisation of the conflict'.[59] The German Ambassador in St Petersburg would be directed to stress 'that Serbia is a source of wild anarchist activities and that it is in the interest of monarchism in general to curb this'.

There is an interesting account of a discussion with Jagow which illustrates how the German Foreign Office was, by 20 July, becoming increasingly aware of the danger that the *fait accompli* might not work and how it reacted to this by thinking up quite fantastic schemes to prevent the war from escalating into a world war.[60] Jagow, in particular, began to look for additional diplomatic devices with which to force the other powers into passivity. The first point to be noted about his 'peace' moves is that by this time they no longer included Russia. In view of the many twists and delays which the original plan had suffered, he had, apparently, abandoned almost all hope that the Tsarist Empire could be kept out of the developing conflict. But what about England? The Army had long accepted that the British Empire would side with its European allies against the Central Powers. It is typical of the complete lack of understanding and the resultant underestimation of capitalist-parliamentary political systems on the part of the Prussian military caste, that this did not seriously worry them. Unaccustomed to thinking in the categories of 'total war' of the twentieth century,[61] Moltke told Jagow on one occasion that he considered the British Expeditionary Force a negligible quantity:[62] 'We shall be able to handle the 150,000 English [in addition to the French Army]'.

Bethmann Hollweg and his advisers were more sceptical and wondered if Moltke really appreciated the wider implications of a world war. On 9 July the Under Secretary of State in the German Foreign Office, Arthur Zimmermann, took the view that, if localisation did not work and if a continental war proved unavoidable, Britain would 'stand on the other side'.[63] This continued to be a widely held opinion during the next two weeks.[64] But with the day of the delayed ultimatum approaching, Jagow, Stumm and Bethmann Hollweg suddenly refused to accept the obvious. Thus Jagow and Stumm told Behncke on 20 July that Britain would at first take a wait-and-see attitude before emerging as Germany's enemy at a later stage. And perhaps she might even stay out altogether.[65] But it then turned out that the two diplomats were themselves no longer quite convinced of this. For, much to Behncke's astonishment, they suddenly put forward the idea that 'we should tell England we would immediately occupy the Netherlands if she entered the war'. Behncke replied that, in his view, this was the surest way of getting Britain into, rather than keeping her out of, the war. The subsequent discussion showed, however, that Jagow's threat was not intended to be carried out. Instead he proposed to use it 'as a bluff', although he must have realised that it was a peculiarly ineffective one.

Nevertheless Jagow's idea was more than an indication of the fumbling and far from cold-blooded way in which the whole crisis was now being managed in Berlin. It was part of a larger, though equally ineffective, strategy of bluff which was integral to Bethmann Hollweg's risk concept and which had been formulated by Riezler in the autumn of 1913.[66] By encouraging an Austro-Serbian conflict and going to the brink of a major war, Bethmann Hollweg hoped to make a gain which would reinforce the deteriorating position of the Central Powers. But towards the end of July it was all too depressingly clear that, what Riezler had identified as being the great danger of German policy, had come true: the Chancellor had 'bluffed himself into an impasse' (*festgeblufft*).[67] Neither Russia nor Britain were prepared to tolerate the defeat of Serbia, Bethmann Hollweg's *fait accompli*. If it took some time for their reaction to emerge, it was largely because the Entente Powers thought that peace could be preserved if Serbia satisfied practically all the demands contained in the Austro-Hungarian ultimatum. Yet by 27 July it was obvious to them that this was not the kind of localisation which Berlin and Vienna were interested in. The Serbian reply to the Austrian ultimatum had hardly been handed over when the Dual Monarchy made preparations for the mobilisation of the Army. On the twenty-seventh, it was resolved to declare war on Serbia not later than 29 July, 'mainly to block any attempt [by the other powers] to intervene'.[68] At the urgent request of the German government the date was then even moved forward by 24 hours to 28 July.

When the Russian Foreign Minister saw the Tsar on 25 July, he was already full of suspicion that the Austrians, pushed on by the Germans, were committed to invading Serbia.[69] The demands of the ultimatum, he said,

> bear no relation either in form or in content to those omissions
> for which a measure of blame might possibly be imputed to the

Serbian Government. Though it was admissible to request the latter for an enquiry to be instituted in Serbia on the basis of the facts brought to light in Austria–Hungary by the enquiry into the murder in Sarayevo, there can nevertheless be no justification for the posing of political demands which would be unacceptable to any state. The clear aim of this procedure—which is apparently supported by Germany—is the total annihilation of Serbia and the disturbances of the political equilibrium in the Balkans.

This and 'the establishment of Austrian hegemony in the Balkans' would have to be prevented. It was with this objective in mind that, on the same day, the Russian Crown Council resolved to *prepare*, as a precautionary measure, the partial mobilisation of the military districts of Odessa, Kiev, Kazan and Moscow. On the day of the Austrian declaration of war against Serbia, 28 July, St Petersburg ordered the actual mobilisation of those four districts. What Bethmann Hollweg had recognised as a potential danger and consciously accepted as a risk all along, had at last come about: it was impossible to localise the conflict. Unless the Central Powers were prepared to reduce the original goals of their action, a major war was unavoidable. Yet Bethmann Hollweg's position was too weak to beat a retreat.

On 26 July, Moltke and the other military leaders were all back in Berlin to note that the Chancellor's plan for a *fait accompli* had misfired. There are two reports by the Saxon and the Bavarian Military Attachés which offer a good insight into what went on in Berlin between 26 and 28 July.[70] According to the Bavarian report the top leadership was divided into two camps: 'The War Ministry and the General Staff, on the one hand, the Reich Chancellor and the Foreign Office on the other.' Both wings were united only in their 'disgust that Austria had tackled her preparatory measures with so little energy that it would take yet another two weeks before the operations would start'. But this was about the extent of their agreement. Falkenhayn, supported by Moltke, the report continued, 'urgently desires military measures which are in keeping with "the tense political situation" and the "threatening danger of war".' Moltke

wants to go even further. He uses all his influence that the singularly favourable situation be exploited for military action. He points to the fact that France finds herself in nothing less than military difficulties [and] that Russia feels everything but secure; moreover, [it is] the propitious time of the year with the harvest largely gathered in [and] the annual training [of reservists] completed.

The Saxon account mentioned the Chief of the General Staff as having said 'that we shall never hit it again so well as we do now with France's and Russia's expansion of their armies incomplete'. 'Against these driving elements' in the officer corps, the Bavarian Military Attaché elaborated, stood Bethmann Hollweg, trying 'to apply the brakes with all his energy'. He wanted to avoid everything that might lead to similar military preparations in France and Britain and hence 'set the ball rolling'.

The Chancellor was fighting an up-hill struggle, and he knew it. After the failure to achieve his *fait accompli*, Moltke's plan gained an irresistible momentum. The primacy of politics, which had always enjoyed but a precarious existence in the Prusso-German monarchy, was definitely discarded and the old *Militärstaat* asserted itself. Politics were relegated to the position of a hand-maid charged with helping to secure an early military victory which, it was hoped, would solve all of Germany's internal and external problems. Bethmann Hollweg's emotional response to the final ascendancy of the Army was one of despondency. As Riezler recorded on 27 July, he now saw the 'force of fate, stronger than the power of humans, hanging over Europe and our people'.[71] The practical effect of this decisive shift in favour of waging a *major* war was that the Chancellor and his political advisers became less and less concerned with finding a peaceful solution to the crisis. Instead they made increasing efforts to create conditions for such a war which were as favourable as possible to the Central Powers. They appreciated, and perhaps more so than the generals, that for a complex industrial society to become involved in a great conflict certain preconditions had to be fulfilled, especially when this society was as unstable politically and as dependent on supplies from overseas as Germany. It was clear that the war could not be won if the country remained as divided by class warfare as it had been over the past years. Moreover its economic life was at stake if Britain intervened to impose a blockade.

Following the failure of his strategy, Bethmann Hollweg therefore tried, with increasing vigour, to fulfil two tasks: to unite the nation and to keep Britain out of the war. There were two aspects to the first task. On the one hand, it was essential that the leaders of the S.P.D. and the trade unions should not influence the mass of the population against war and consequently be arrested by the Army under the provisions of the state of siege; obviously this would merely turn them into martyrs. They had to be persuaded instead to proclaim their support for Kaiser and Reich and thus to set an example to the population. Any other policy towards the working-class movement would, indeed, have led to a fatal split of German society coincidental with an extreme external crisis. That the danger of such a split was very real was due not only to the blatant class bias of official Wilhelmine policy before 1914, but also to the peculiarities of the regulations governing the state of siege which, as we have seen, put all power into the hands of the military and more particularly the local army commanders. We have also had occasion to observe that the Army, the last bastion of monarchism, was all too prepared to use its powers for the arrest of Social Democrat leaders and the suppression of the left-wing press.

In fact, the 'radicals' in the officer corps had been hoping ever since 1905 that an early war would, so to speak, kill two birds with one stone. Unlike the Kaiser who thought of solving the domestic threat to the monarchical order first and then of tackling the danger of external containment, leading officers proposed to remove both menaces with one stroke. As late as 1910, one of the local commanders whose military district included the highly industrialised Ruhr area had made specific preparations for the arrest of all socialist leaders and journalists in the event of war.[72] That William II, too, was very conscious of the far-reaching possibilities which the state of siege regulations offered became clear when, towards the end of July 1914, the Sarayevo Crisis was about to reach its climax. If the socialists continued their anti-war propaganda, he said, 'I shall proclaim the state of siege and have the entire leadership *tutti quanti* locked up.'[73] And Riezler noted that 'there are generals who want to meddle immediately and shoot "in order to teach the Reds a lesson".'[74]

The Chancellor and his advisers knew that this would be a disaster. On 23 July he told Riezler that the S.P.D. leadership could be won over only through personal negotiations and assurances.[75] But what was even more important was that the government 'demands guarantees from the military against the follies of the

"Red-baiters" in uniform'. Such guarantees were, indeed, very desirable. But in order to be absolutely certain that individual commanders did not flout the government's recommendations, Bethmann Hollweg and the Reich Office of the Interior tried to obtain an agreement that the application of the state of siege would be limited to certain territories. With this aim in mind, Clemens von Delbrück, the State Secretary concerned, scheduled a meeting of the various Prussian and Reich authorities for 24 July.[76] Yet the Army was reluctant to allow its powers to be curtailed in this manner.[77] All the War Minister was prepared to do was to inform the local commanders that the political parties must not be driven into opposition by means of arrests and bans on newspapers. On 25 July, he sent off a circular, entitled 'Criteria for the Preparation of the State of War and for the Exercise of Executive Powers', which ordered the generals to take up a passive attitude and to observe the left-wing press closely.[78]

On the following day talks began with Social Democrat deputies who were presumably told of the content of Falkenhayn's directive. With war apparently inevitable, Bethmann Hollweg personally took charge of the negotiations. On 28 July, he met Albert Südekum, a leader of the S.P.D.'s right wing, and told him that it was vital at this moment for the Social Democrats to abandon their opposition to official policy.[79] Strife and criticism at home, the Chancellor argued, would merely strengthen the influence of the war party in St Petersburg and would also undermine his own position vis-à-vis the hard-liners in Berlin. Südekum was impressed. On the following day he wrote a letter to Bethmann Hollweg informing him that he had meanwhile talked to members of the S.P.D. Executive. The government, he said, could rest assured that there existed no plan for, or threat of, a general strike, sabotage or any other action.[80] Simultaneously the Party Executive sent a strictly confidential letter to the editors of all socialist newspapers exhorting them to take up a position of moderation and reserve in their writings.[81] Südekum's assurance enabled Bethmann Hollweg to declare at the meeting of the Prussian State Ministry on 30 July that, as far as the leadership of the working-class movement was concerned, 'nothing is to be feared'.[82] Falkenhayn immediately informed the local commanders.[83] Apparently worried that his earlier orders might be disregarded and the truce be jeopardised, he felt it his 'duty to bring this to [their] attention so that the military commanders can take this into consideration for their policies'.

After Bethmann Hollweg had successfully discharged the first part of his attempt to unite the nation for a major war, there were still the Social Democrat masses to be manipulated into accepting the inevitability of a conflict. Prior to the Bethmann–Südekum accord, the left-wing press had been very critical of the policies of the Central Powers and so, presumably, were its readers. On 25 July, *Vorwärts* had published an appeal by the S.P.D. Executive which condemned in sharp words 'the frivolous war provocation of the Austro-Hungarian government'.[84] The Reich government was urged to avoid 'any war-like interference'. Two days later, the paper warned that a major war would result in a social revolution.[85] The influence which such campaigns exerted on the masses was, from the point of view of the monarchy, frightening enough. But to make things worse, the Party Executive called on its members to demonstrate against Austria–Hungary and for peace. One such demonstration took place in Berlin on 28 July. There were heavy clashes with the police which gave rise to grave apprehensions about what was in store in the event of war. To this extent, the truce with the S.P.D. *leadership* offered little comfort. The government had to prepare the way for slogans which diverted the population from its anti-war and anti-Austrian posture. The Austro-Serbian conflict which had now begun to escalate into a major conflagration had to be turned into a defensive war, with Russia appearing as the vile aggressor.

On 27 July, Müller recorded in his diary that 'the tenor of our policy [is] to remain calm to allow Russia to put herself in the wrong, but then not to shrink from war if it were inevitable'.[86] And the Chancellor advised the Kaiser:[87] 'In all events Russia must ruthlessly be put into the wrong.' Yet this was possible only if the Tsarist Empire mobilised before Germany. Although he was gradually developing a fixation about his own military time-table for a major war, even Moltke was prepared to accept the importance of this condition. 'War [must] not be declared on Russia', Conrad was informed on 30 July, 'but [we must] wait for Russia to attack.'[88] Once the Russian mobilisation had been declared, the Reich could safely follow suit and the war would begin, as Waldersee later described the view prevailing in the General Staff, 'by itself'.[89]

As is well-known, on 30 July St Petersburg did the Reich government this favour by turning the partial mobilisation of the twenty-ninth into a general one. This decision has frequently been assumed to have been the crucial step which unleashed the First World War and some historians have therefore apportioned the major share of responsibility to Russia.[90] But more convincing in this case are the arguments of Fritz Fischer. He has not only carefully analysed the decision-making inside the Russian government, but has also pointed to the fact that, to Germany, the Tsar's mobilisation order was the last straw only because the Central Powers were by then bent on waging a European war and were, for domestic reasons, merely waiting to be given a pretext for starting it.[91] Bethmann Hollweg told the Prussian State Ministry on 30 July that 'although the Russian mobilisation has been declared, her mobilisation measures cannot be compared with those of the West European states .... Moreover Russia does not intend to wage war, but has only been forced to take these measures because of Austria.'[92] Yet this insight did not induce the German government to seek a peaceful way out of the crisis. Instead the Russian mobilisation was used to gear the masses at home towards the idea of a defensive war against the deadly enemy in the east.

The announcement of Russia's decision certainly had the desired effect on the German public. When on 2 August the allegation was added that Russian patrols had trespassed on German territory, the attitude of the entire press, including the Social Democrat papers, changed completely.[93] The seemingly inevitable war now appeared to be a defensive crusade against the dark forces of Slavdom and oppressive Tsarist autocracy. It was a tide which the Social Democrat leaders found impossible to resist. However, some of them were overcome by dark premonitions, like Ludwig Frank, a 'revisionist' deputy, who wrote as early as 29 July:[94] 'Even workers can be heard to say that Russia is a barbaric country, the international trouble-maker deserving defeat! But this seductive view is erroneous.'

Bethmann Hollweg, on the other hand, was not vexed by such qualms. He had discharged the first part of his political task. The nation was united. 'The morning papers', Müller wrote on 1 August, 'reprint the speeches made by the Kaiser and the Reich Chancellor to an enthusiastic crowd in front of the *Schloss* and the Chancellor's Palace. Brilliant mood. The government has succeeded very well in making us appear as the attacked.'[95] What the peace-time domestic and diplomatic manoeuvres of the monarchy had never succeeded in bringing about, had now become a reality: the bitter political feuds and the dangerous cleavages of the Wilhelmine class-state had been forgotten. The workers, the outcasts of Prusso-German society, naïvely boarded the freight-trains which carted them off to the front to defend the existing order—ready victims of a cunning manoeuvre of political deception by which a small group of men succeeded in veiling their decisive part in the outbreak of the First World War, and continued the cover-up for more than another generation.

On the other hand, the Chancellor's second political mission of securing British neutrality ended in failure. The advantages to Germany of Britain's abstention from the prospective continental war were obvious. But it was not only London's memories of the reckless course of German world and armaments policy since the turn of the century and the suspect manoeuvres of German diplomacy after the delivery of the Austro-Hungarian ultimatum which destroyed all hopes of British neutrality; it was the way in which the General Staff had prepared its war against Russia that made Britain's intervention a certainty. Moltke's strategy was based on the famous Schlieffen Plan which envisaged that, in the event of a conflict with the Tsarist Empire, Russia's ally, France, was to be attacked.[96] While the bulk of the German Army was engaged in a swift campaign in the west, no major operations were to take place on the eastern frontier. The General Staff expected that it would take weeks for the cumbersome Russian war machine to be ready. By that time, however, France would be defeated and, if this did not in itself bring an end of the war, the troops would now be available for a second strike in the east.

Yet in order to assure a quick victory the Schlieffen Plan provided for an extensive outflanking movement by the Army's right wing through southern Belgium and Luxembourg. The violation of Belgian neutrality, guaranteed by Britain in a treaty of 1839, was an integral part of the Reich's strategy. This meant that, if the invasion of France through Alsace–Lorraine made a British response very likely, the German march through Belgium and Luxembourg made it absolutely certain. The ascendancy of the 'radicals' in Berlin who wanted war not only against Serbia, but also against Russia therefore touched off an irreversible chain reaction which ended with Britain's entry into the war on 4 August. Bethmann Hollweg had been initiated into the plans of the General Staff for some time and was thus aware of the mechanism. It is not surprising that, after he had reconciled himself to the inevitability of a continental war, he tried to interrupt the chain reaction short of a

British involvement. Apparently he hoped, as Jagow had done on 20 July, that somehow it might at least be possible to keep England out during the first phase of the war. Whatever his hopes, on 29 July the Chancellor made the British Ambassador a last, desperate offer to the effect that Germany would not annex any French territory if Britain remained neutral.[97] Sir Edward Goschen promised to forward the proposal to London.

There was, of course, no hope of it being accepted. But the subsequent Crown Council at Potsdam showed how far a cool appreciation of the harsh realities had once again become displaced by wishful thinking. William II had learned from his brother, who had just returned from London, that the King had given his word 'that England will remain neutral in the event of war'.[98] On the other hand, Prince Henry had quoted Grey as having stated that 'the matter would be different if we were to crush France'.[99] It is indicative of the Kaiser's inability to grasp the most basic principles of the British parliamentary system that this contradiction at first rather puzzled him, until he pretended that the King occupied the same quasi-absolutist constitutional position as he did. The King's word, he said, was enough as far as he was concerned. It would have been wiser to accept the word of Grey who had just warned the German Ambassador in London that, if war broke out between France and Germany, 'the British Government would, *under the circumstances, find itself forced to make up its mind quickly. In that event it would not be practicable to stand aside and wait for any length of time.*'[100] Bethmann Hollweg had no doubt about the implications of this statement: 'The hope for England [was now] zero.'[101]

The Chancellor's house of cards had collapsed before it had been completed. The Schlieffen Plan saw to it that the Central Powers would not only have to fight against Russia, but also against France and the British Empire. There was no alternative strategy since the *Aufmarsch* in the east had been shelved in the spring of 1913. By 4 August 1914 Europe found itself engulfed in a war which was unprecedented and lengthy. It strained the social fabric of its participants to the utmost, ultimately leading to the defeat and bankruptcy of the Central European monarchies with their peculiar political systems. In the long run, not even the emergency situation of a war was able to arrest the disintegration of the Prusso-German Constitutionalism. In 1919 a parliamentary republic was established in its place. Its first president was a Social Democrat.

Chronological Table

1871	18 January	William I proclaimed German Emperor
	16 April	Reich Constitution received
	10 May	Peace Treaty signed at Frankfurt with France
1875	22–27 May	German Social Democratic Party founded
1878	June–July	Congress of Berlin
	18 October	Anti-socialist laws passed
1879	12 July	Agricultural and industrial tariffs introduced
	7 October	Austro-German Alliance signed
1881	18 June	Three Emperors' League between Russia, Germany and Austria–Hungary
1882	20 May	Triple Alliance formed (Italy joins Germany and Austria–Hungary)
1887	18 June	Reinsurance Treaty between Russia and Germany to replace expired Three Emperors' League
1888	9 March	Frederick III succeeds William I
	15 June	William II succeeds Frederick III
1890	15 March	Dismissal of Bismarck
	18 June	Reinsurance Treaty lapses
	1 October	Anti-socialist laws not renewed
1891	27 August	Franco-Russian Entente
1892	1 February	Germany signs commercial treaties with Italy, Belgium, Switzerland and Austria–Hungary
	17 August	Franco-Russian Military Convention
1893	17 January	Franco-Russian Alliance signed
	18 February	Founding of Agrarian League (B.d.L.)
	13 July	German Army bill accepted
1894	10 February	Russo-German commercial treaty signed

220

	26 October	Hohenlohe succeeds Caprivi as Reich Chancellor
1895	29 December	Jameson Raid
1896	3 January	William II sends telegram to Kruger
1897	15 June	Tirpitz nominated State Secretary for the Navy
	20 October	Bülow nominated State Secretary in the German Foreign Office
1898	10 April	Reichstag ratifies First Navy Law
	30 April	German Navy League founded
	September–November	Fashoda Crisis
1899	May–July	First Hague Peace Conference
	12 October	Boer War opens
1900	January	'Bundesrath' Affair
	14 June	Reichstag accepts Second Navy Law
	June–August	Boxer Rising
	17 October	Bülow nominated Reich Chancellor
1901	22 January	Edward VII becomes king
	October–December	Collapse of Anglo-German alliance negotiations
1902	30 January	Anglo-Japanese Alliance formed
	25 December	Reichstag accepts higher agricultural tariffs
1903	16 June	Reichstag elections with gains for S.P.D.
1904	4 February	Russo-Japanese War opens
	8 April	Entente Cordiale between France and Britain
	28 July	Russo-German commercial treaty signed
	3 October (–1908)	Herero and Hottentot insurrection in German South-West Africa
	21 October	Dogger Bank Incident
	23 November	Russo-German alliance negotiations break down
1905	1 February	German commercial treaties with Russia and Austria–Hungary ratified
	31 March	William II visits Tangiers
	30 April	Anglo-French military conversations
	27 May	Battle of Tsushima (Russian Navy routed)
	6 June	Delcassé falls from power

	23 July	Treaty of Björkö
	28 September	Morocco Conference agreed
	5 October	*Dreadnought* laid down
	5 December	Campbell-Bannerman forms Liberal ministry
1906	1 January	Moltke succeeds Schlieffen as Chief of German General Staff
	12 January	Landslide victory of Liberals in British elections
	16 January	Algeciras Conference opens
	8 April	Algeciras Act signed
	May	Tax reform passes Reichstag
	5 June	Third Navy Law (Novelle 1906) ratified
	13 December	Bülow dissolves Reichstag
1907	1 January	Crowe's memorandum on German foreign policy
	25 January	Reichstag elections
	February	Bülow Bloc formed
	15 June	Second Hague Peace Conference opens
	31 August	Anglo-Russian Entente
1908	16 February	William II writes to Lord Tweedmouth
	8 April	Asquith becomes Prime Minister
	14 June	Fourth Navy Law (Novelle 1908) ratified
	12–13 August	Hardinge visits William II at Kronberg
	6 October	Annexation of Bosnia and Herzegovina by Austria–Hungary
	28 October	*Daily Telegraph* publishes interview with Kaiser
	10–11 November	Reichstag debates on *Daily Telegraph* Affair
1909	9 February	Franco-German agreement over Morocco
	12 March	British Navy bill accepted after Navy Scare
	24 March	Collapse of Bülow Bloc
	12 June	Hansabund founded
	24 June	Bülow tax reform bill defeated
	14 July	Bethmann Hollweg succeeds Bülow
1910	15 January	British general elections
	6 May	Edward VII dies

	27 May	Reform of Prussian three-class voting system fails
1911	21 May	French occupy Fez (Morocco)
	1 July	*Panther* sent to Agadir
	21 July	Lloyd George warns Germany in Mansion House speech
	29 September	Tripoli War between Italy and Turkey
	4 November	Morocco Agreement signed
	9–10 November	Reichstag debates Morocco Agreement
1912	January	Reichstag elections with S.P.D. emerging as the strongest party
	7 February	Kaiser announces Army and Navy bills
	8 February	Haldane arrives in Berlin for talks
	13 March	Balkan League between Serbia and Bulgaria formed
	21 May	Military bills and Lex Bassermann–Erzberger passed by Reichstag
	29 May	Greece joins Balkan League
	17 October	First Balkan War
	8 December	William II calls military conference at Potsdam
1913	5 January	Jagow succeeds Kidelen-Wächter in the German Foreign Office
	26 March	Churchill proposes 'Naval Holiday'
	4 June	Prussian Diet elections
	30 June	Second Balkan War opens
		German Army bill and Tax Compromise accepted
	7 August	French Army bill ratified
	10 August	Peace of Bucharest ends Second Balkan War
	28 August	*Kartell der schaffenden Stände* proclaimed
	18 October	Churchill again proposes 'Naval Holiday'
	October–November	Zabern Affair
	9 December	Liman von Sanders Commission seen off by Kaiser
	14 December	Liman von Sanders arrives in Constantinople

1914	May	Anglo-Russian naval talks begin
	28 June	Assassination of Francis Ferdinand and his wife at Sarayevo
	5 July	Hoyos Mission; Kaiser issues 'blank cheque'
	6 July	William II leaves for Norwegian cruise
	7 July	Austro-Hungarian Ministerial Council meets
	8 July	Ultimatum to Serbia prepared
	15 July	Conrad goes on holiday
		Poincaré and Viviani leave for St Petersburg
	19 July	Austro-Hungarian Ministerial Council approves ultimatum to be handed over on 23 July
		Jagow plants article in *Norddeutsche Allgemeine Zeitung* advocating localisation of Austro-Serbian conflict
	20 July	Poincaré and Viviani arrive in St Petersburg
	21 July	Francis Joseph approves ultimatum
		Text of ultimatum sent to Berlin
	23 July	Austria–Hungary hands over ultimatum
		Poincaré and Viviani leave St Petersburg for state visit to Oslo and Copenhagen
	24 July	Austria–Hungary informs France, Russia and Britain of ultimatum
		German ambassadors transmit note in Paris, London and St Petersburg that conflict be localised
		Paul Cambon proposes conference
		Grey's first proposal to mediate
		Delbrück meets Reich and Prussian authorities
		Russian Council of Ministers considers partial mobilisation
	25 July	Serbia replies to ultimatum
		Vienna breaks off diplomatic relations with Belgrade
		Moltke and Falkenhayn return to Berlin

William II orders return of Fleet

French Ministerial Council urges immediate return of Poincaré and Viviani

Grey again proposes mediation

Jagow forwards Grey's proposal to Vienna

Russian Crown Council approves resolutions of Ministerial Council; Tsar orders preparations for mobilisation to be made

26 July Russia asks Germany to exert moderating influence on Austria–Hungary

Grey proposes Four-Power conference of ambassadors in London

Austria mobilises on Russian frontier

France takes precautionary military measures

27 July Austria–Hungary decides to declare war on Serbia

William II returns to Potsdam

France accepts Grey's proposals

Bethmann Hollweg rejects idea of Four-Power conference

British attitude hardening; Royal Navy to be kept together

Poincaré cancels visits to Copenhagen and Oslo

28 July Austria–Hungary declares war on Serbia and shells Belgrade

Prince Henry of Prussia reports to William II on his conversations with George V

William II issues 'Halt-in-Belgrad' appeal

William II appeals to Tsar's monarchical solidarity

Russia orders mobilisation of four western military districts

Grey hoping that Austria–Hungary and Russia can be brought to negotiate

Bethmann Hollweg meets Südekum (S.P.D.)

29 July   Vienna refuses to enter into negotiations with Serbia

Tschirschky transmits Kaiser's '*Halt-in-Belgrad*' proposal

Poincaré and Viviani return to Paris

Germany informed of Russian partial mobilisation

Germany warns Russia

Moltke demands general mobilisation

Bethmann Hollweg makes move to keep Britain neutral

Grey informs Lichnowsky that Britain could not remain neutral in the event of a con-tinental war; again he proposes mediation

Russian general mobilisation ordered, but revoked by Tsar late that same evening

30 July   Austria–Hungary agrees to negotiations with Russia, but refuses to delay opera-tions against Serbia

Moltke presses for general mobilisation

Berliner Lokalanzeiger announces German mobilisation, but issue is withdrawn; offi-cial denial

Prussian State Ministry meets

Austria–Hungary orders general mobilisa-tion for 31 July

Russian general mobilisation ordered for 31 July

31 July   Vienna rejects international conference and orders general mobilisation

Russian general mobilisation becomes known in Berlin at noon

Kaiser proclaims 'state of imminent war' one hour later

Germany refuses to mediate and issues ulti-matum to Russia

French Ministerial Council decides to order mobilisation for 1 August

1 August	German ultimatum to Russia expires; Germany declares war on Russia and mobilises
	Continued hopes in Berlin that Britain might stay neutral
2 August	German troops occupy Luxembourg; Berlin transmits ultimatum to Belgium
3 August	Italy remains neutral
	Germany declares war on France
	Belgium rejects German demands
	German-Turkish treaty concluded
	Britain mobilises army; Cabinet decides to issue ultimatum to Germany
4 August	German troops invade Belgium
	British ultimatum transmitted to Berlin
	Ultimatum expires at midnight; British Ambassador asks for passport

Bibliography

The best general study is J. JOLL, *The Origins of the First World War* (1984). More detailed information on the diplomatic moves and alliances may be found in L. ALBERTINI, *The Origins of the War of 1914* (1965); I. GEISS (ed.), *July 1914* (1972); IDEM, *German Foreign Policy, 1871–1914* (1976); J. REMAK, *The Origins of World War I* (1967); B.E. SCHMITT, *The Coming of the War* (1930).

The country volumes in the Macmillan Series 'The Making of the Twentieth Century' relating to the origins of the First World War are now complete, covering Britain (Z. STEINER), Germany (V.R. BERGHAHN), Austria-Hungary (S.R. WILLIAMSON, Jr.), France (J. KEIGER), Russia (D. LIEVEN), and Italy (R. BOSWORTH).

The debate on Fritz Fischer's publications (see below) is traced in: J.A. MOSES, *The Politics of Illusion* (1975); H.-W. KOCH (ed.), *The Origins of the First World War* (1984); J.W. LANGDON, *July 1914. The Long Debate, 1918–1990* (1991).

General studies of the German Empire: H.-U. WEHLER, *The German Empire, 1871–1918* (1985); V.R. BERGHAHN, *Germany, 1871–1914. Economy, Society, Culture, and Politics* (1993).

Other books of particular importance among those listed below are marked with an asterisk.

1. PUBLICATIONS OF OFFICIAL DOCUMENTS

British Documents on the Origins of the War, 1898–1914, ed. G. P. Gooch and H. Temperley, II vols (London, 1927 ff.).

Die Grosse Politik der Europäischen Kabinette, 1871–1914, ed. by J. Lepsius, A. Mendelssohn Bartholdy and F. Thimme, 40 vols (Berlin, 1922 ff.).

Documents Diplomatiques Français, ed. Ministère des Affaires Etrangères, 32 vols (Paris, 1929 ff.).

Julikrise und Kriegsausbruch 1914, ed. I. Geiss, 2 vols (Hanover, 1963/4); with an abridged version in English under the title *July 1914* (London, 1967).

Kriegsrüstung und Kriegswirtschaft, ed. Reichsarchiv, 2 vols (Berlin, 1930).

Österreich-Ungarns Aussenpolitik von der Bosnischen Krise 1908 bis zum Kriegsausbruch 1914, ed. L. Bittner *et al.*, 8 vols (Vienna, 1930).

2. BIOGRAPHIES, DIARIES, SPEECHES, MEMOIRS AND WORKS
   CONTAINING SOURCE MATERIALS

V.R. BERGHAHN and W. DEIST, 'Kaiserliche Marine und Kriegsausbruch 1914', *Militärgeschichtliche Mitteilungen*, 1(1970) 37 ff.

*IDEM (eds), *Rüstung im Zeichen der Wilhelminischen Weltpolitik* (Düsseldorf, 1989).

TH. VON BETHMANN HOLLWEG, *Betrachtungen zum Weltkriege*, 2 vols (Berlin, 1919).

K.E. BORN and P. RASSOW (eds), *Akten zur staatlichen Sozialpolitik in Deutschland, 1890–1914* (Wiesbaden, 1959).

B. VON BÜLOW, *Reden*, 4 vols (Berlin, 1930).

W.S. CHURCHILL, *The World Crisis, 1911–1914* (London, 1964).

F. CONRAD VON HÖTZENDORFF, *Aus meiner Dienstzeit*, 5 vols (Vienna, 1921).

E. DEUERLEIN (ed.), *Der Bundesratsausschuss für die auswärtigen Angelegenheiten* (Regensburg, 1955).

IDEM (ed.), *Briefwechsel Hertling-Lerchenfeld, 1912–1917* (Boppard, 1973).

K. VON EINEM, *Erinnerungen eines Soldaten, 1853–1933* (Leipzig, 1933).

*M. EPKENHANS, 'Großindustrie und Schlachtflottenbau, 1897–1914', *Militärgeschichtliche Mitteilungen*, 43 (1988) 65–140.

*K.D. ERDMANN (ed.), *Kurt Riezler* (Göttingen, 1972).

F. FELLNER (ed.), *Schicksalsjahre Österreichs. Das politische Tagebuch Josef Redlichs*, 2 vols (Graz-Köln, 1953).

H. GOLDSCHMIDT, *Das Reich und Preußen im Kampf um die Führung* (Berlin, 1931).

W. GÖRLITZ (ed.), *Der Kaiser...* (Göttingen, 1965).

IDEM (ed.), *The Kaiser and his Court* (London, 1961).

C. FÜRST ZU HOHENLOHE-SCHILLINGSFÜRST, *Denkwürdigkeiten der Reichskanzlerzeit* (Stuttgart–Berlin, 1931).

A. HOPMAN, *Das Logbuch eines deutschen Seeoffiziers* (Berlin, 1924).

E. JÄCKH, *Kiderlen-Wächter. Der Staatsmann und Mensch*, 2 vols (Berlin–Leipzig, 1924).

A.E.O. KLAUSSMANN (ed.), *Kaiserreden* (Leipzig, 1902).

H. VON MOLTKE, *Erinnerungen, Briefe, Dokumente, 1877–1916* (Stuttgart, 1922).

W. MUEHLON, *Ein Fremder im eigenen Land* (Bremen, 1989).

H. POGGE VON STRANDMANN (ed.), *Walther Rathenau. Tagebuch 1907–1922* (Düsseldorf, 1967).

N. RICH and M.H. FISHER (eds), *Die Geheimen Papiere Friedrich von Holsteins*, 4 vols (Göttingen, 1963; trs. Cambridge, 1955–63).

* J.C.G. RÖHL (ed.), *Philipp Eulenburgs politische Korrespondenz*, 3 vols (Boppard, 1976–83).

B. SÖSEMANN (ed.), *Theodor Wolff: Tagebücher, 1914–1919* (Boppard, 1984).

A. VON TIRPITZ, *Erinnerungen* (Leipzig, 1919).

* IDEM, *Der Aufbau der deutschen Weltmacht* (Stuttgart–Berlin, 1924).

IDEM, *Deutsche Ohnmachtspolitik im Weltkriege* (Hamburg–Berlin, 1926).

R. VIERHAUS (ed.), *Das Tagebuch der Baronin Spitzemberg* (Göttingen, 1961).

A. VON WALDERSEE, *Denkwürdigkeiten*, 3 vols (Stuttgart, 1922–3).

R. GRAF ZEDLITZ-TRÜTSCHLER, *Zwölf Jahre am deutschen Kaiserhof* (Stuttgart–Berlin–Leipzig, 1924).

3. SECONDARY WORKS

L. ALBERTINI, *The Origins of the War of 1914* (London, 1965).

E.N. ANDERSON, *The First Moroccan Crisis, 1904–1906* (New York, 1928).

C. ANDREW, *Théophile Delcassé and the Making of the Entente Cordiale, 1898–1905* (London, 1968).

K. BACHEM, *Vorgeschichte, Geschichte und Politik der deutschen Zentrumspartei*, 8 vols (Köln, 1927 ff).

M. BALFOUR, *The Kaiser and his Times* (New York, 1972).

K. BARKIN, *The Controversy over Industrialisation* (Chicago, 1970).

V.R. BERGHAHN, *Der Tirpitz-Plan* (Düsseldorf, 1971).

IDEM, *Rüstung und Machtpolitik* (Düsseldorf, 1973).

J. BERTRAM, *Die Wahlen zum Deutschen Reichstag vom Jahre 1912* (Düsseldorf, 1964).

H. BLEY, *Bebel und die Strategie der Kriegsverhütung* (Göttingen, 1973).

E. BÖHM, *Überseehandel und Flottenbau* (Düsseldorf, 1972).

H. BOLDT, *Rechtsstaat und Ausnahmezustand* (Berlin, 1967).

IDEM, *Deutsche Verfassungsgeschichte* (München, 1984).

K.E. BORN, *Staat und Sozialpolitik seit dem Sturz Bismarcks* (Wiesbaden, 1957).

R. BOSWORTH, *Italy and the Approach of the First World War* (London, 1983).

E. BRANDENBURG, *Von Bismarck zum Weltkriege* (Berlin, 1925).

L. BURCHARDT, *Friedenswirtschaft und Kriegsvorsorge* (Boppard, 1968).

M. CATTARUZZA, *Arbeiter und Unternehmer auf den Werften des Kaiserreichs* (Stuttgart, 1988).

L.J.R. Cecil, 'Coal for the Fleet That had to Die', *American Historical Review* (July 1964) 990 ff.

Idem, *Albert Ballin* (Princeton, 1967).

R. Chickering, *Imperial Germany and a World without War* (Princeton, 1976).

*Idem, *We Men Who Feel Most German* (Boston, 1984).

J.H. Clapham, *The Economic Development of France and Germany* (Cambridge, 1936).

M.S. Coetzee, *The German Army League* (Oxford, 1990).

G. Craig, *The Politics of the Prussian Army* (New York, 1964).

Idem, *Germany, 1866–1945* (Oxford, 1978).

G.D. Crothers, *The German Elections of 1907* (New York, 1941).

V. Dedijer, *The Road to Sarajevo* (London, 1967).

L. Dehio, *Deutschland in der Weltpolitik im 20. Jahrhundert* (München, 1955; trs. London, 1959).

W. Deist, *Flottenrüstung und Flottenpropaganda* (Stuttgart, 1976).

K. Demeter, *Das deutsche Offizierkorps in Gesellschaft und Staat* (Frankfurt, 1964; trs. London, 1967).

J.R. Dukes and J. Remak (eds), *Another Germany* (Boulder, 1988).

*G. Eley, *Reshaping the German Right* (New Haven, 1980).

Idem, *From Unification to Nazism* (London, 1986).

*Idem and D. Blackbourn, *The Peculiarities of German History* (Oxford, 1984).

*M. Epkenhans, *Die wilhelminische Flottenrüstung, 1908–1914* (München, 1991).

R.J. Evans (ed.), *Society and Politics in Wilhelmine Germany* (London, 1978).

Idem, *Rethinking German History* (London, 1987).

R.J.W. Evans and H. Pogge von Strandmann (eds), *The Coming of the First World War* (Oxford, 1988).

E. Eyck, *Das Persönliche Regiment Wilhelms II* (Zürich, 1948).

S.B. Fay, *The Origins of the World War*, 2 vols (New York, 1928).

A. Feiler, *Die Konjunkturperiode 1907–1913 in Deutschland* (Jena, 1914).

F. Fischer, *Germany's War Aims in the First World War* (London, 1967).

*Idem, *War of Illusions* (London, 1973).

Idem, *Wir sind nicht hineingeschlittert* (Reinbek, 1983).

R. Fletcher, *Revisionism and Empire* (London, 1984).

S. Förster, *Der doppelte Militarismus* (Wiesbaden, 1985).

D. Fricke *et al.* (eds), *Die bürgerlichen Parteien in Deutschland*, 2 vols (Leipzig, 1968–70).

*I. Geiss, *German Foreign Policy, 1871–1914* (London, 1984).

R. Gellately, *The Politics of Economic Despair* (London, 1974).

M.R. GORDON, 'Domestic Conflict and the Origins of the First World War', *Journal of Modern History*, 46 (1974) 191–226.

G. GRANIER, 'Deutsche Rüstungspolitik vor dem Ersten Weltkrieg', *Militärgeschichtliche Mitteilungen*, 38 (1985) 123–62.

J.A.S. GRENVILLE, *Lord Salisbury and Foreign Policy* (London, 1964).

D. GROH, *Negative Integration und revolutionärer Attentismus* (Frankfurt, 1973).

W.L. GUTTSMAN, *The German Social Democratic Party* (London, 1981).

O.J. HALE, *Publicity and Diplomacy* (London, 1940).

G.W.F. HALLGARTEN, *Imperialismus vor 1914*, 2 vols (München, 1963).

F. HASELMAYR, *Diplomatische Geschichte des Zweiten Reiches*, 6 vols (München, 1961).

B. HECKART, *From Bassermann to Bebel* (New Haven, 1974).

* K. HILDEBRAND, *The Foreign Policy of the Third Reich* (London, 1973).

IDEM, *Bethmann Hollweg* (Düsseldorf, 1970).

A. HILLGRUBER, *Die gescheiterte Großmacht* (Düsseldorf, 1980).

W. HUBATSCH, *Der Admiralstab und die obersten Marinebehörden in Deutschland* (Frankfurt, 1958).

I.V. HULL, *The Entourage of Kaiser Wilhelm II* (Cambridge, 1982).

* K. JARAUSCH, *The Enigmatic Chancellor* (Princeton, 1972).

* J. JOLL, *The Origins of the First World War* (London, 1984).

H. KAELBLE, *Industrielle Interessenpolitik in der Wilhelminischen Gesellschaft* (Berlin, 1967).

D. KAISER, 'Germany and the Origins of the First World War', *Journal of Modern History*, 4 (1983) 442–74.

* E. KEHR, *Battleship Building and Party Politics in Germany* (Chicago, 1975).

IDEM, *Economic Interest, Militarism and Foreign Policy* (Berkeley, 1977).

J. KEIGER, *France and the Origins of the First World War* (London, 1983).

* P.M. KENNEDY, *The Rise of the Anglo-German Antagonism* (London, 1980).

M. KITCHEN, *The German Officer Corps* (Oxford, 1968).

H.W. KOCH (ed.), *The Origins of the First World War* (London, 1984).

G. KRUMEICH, *Armaments and Politics in France on the Eve of the First World War* (Leamington Spa, 1984).

L. LAFORE, *The Long Fuse* (Philadelphia, 1965).

I.N. LAMBI, *Free Trade and Protection in Germany* (Wiesbaden, 1963).

IDEM, *The Navy and German Power Politics* (London, 1984).

* J.W. LANGDON, *July 1914* (Oxford, 1991).

D. LIEVEN, *Russia and the Origins of the First World War* (London, 1983).

W.E. LIVEZEY, *Mahan on Sea Power* (Oklahoma City, 1954).

W. LOTH, *Katholiken im Kaiserreich* (Düsseldorf, 1984).

A.T. Mahan, *The Influence of Sea Power Upon History* (London, 1889).
A.J. Marder, *Anatomy of British Sea Power* (London, 1940).
Idem, *From Dreadnought to Scapa Flow*, 5 vols (London, 1961 ff.).
G. Martel (ed.), *Modern Germany Reconsidered* (London, 1992).
A.J. Mayer, *The Persistence of the Old Regime* (London, 1981).
H.C. Meyer, *'Mitteleuropa' in German Thought and Action* (Den Haag, 1955).
S. Mielke, *Der Hansabund* (Göttingen, 1976).
W.J. Mommsen, 'Domestic Factors in German Foreign Policy', *Central European History*, 6 (1973) 3–43.
G.W. Monger, *The End of Isolation* (London, 1963).
J.A. Moses, *The Politics of Illusion* (London, 1975).
J.A. Nichols, *Germany after Bismarck* (Cambridge, Mass., 1958).
I. Nish, *The Anglo-Japanese Alliance* (London, 1966).
E. Oncken, *Panthersprung nach Agadir* (Düsseldorf, 1981).
A. Peck, *Radicals and Reactionaries* (Washington, 1978).
H. Pogge von Strandmann and I. Geiss, *Die Erforderlichkeit des Unmöglichen* (Frankfurt, 1975).
R. Pommerin, *Der Kaiser und Amerika* (Düsseldorf, 1986).
R. Poidevin, *Les relations économiques et financières entre la France et l'Allemagne de 1898 à 1914* (Paris, 1969).
W. Pöls, *Sozialistenfrage und Revolutionsfurcht im Zusammenhang mit den Staatsstreichplänen Bismarcks* (Lübeck–Hamburg, 1960).
H.J. Puhle, *Agrarische Interessenpolitik und preußischer Konservatismus im wilhelminischen Reich* (Hannover, 1967).
H. Raulff, *Zwischen Machtpolitik und Imperialismus* (Düsseldorf, 1976).
J. Remak, *The Origins of World War I* (New York, 1967).
Idem (ed.), *The First World War* (New York, 1971).
J. Retallack, *Notables of the Right* (Boston, 1988).
G. Ritter, *The Sword and the Scepter*, 2 vols (Miami, 1969–71).
J. Röhl, 'Staatsstreichplan oder Staatsstreichbereitschaft', *Historische Zeitschrift*, 203 (1966) 610 ff.
Idem, *Germany without Bismarck* (London, 1967).
Idem, 'Admiral von Müller and the Approach of War', *Historische Zeitschrift*, 4 (1969) 651 ff.
* Idem, Kaiser, *Hof und Staat* (München, 1987).
Idem and W. Sombart (eds), *Kaiser Wilhelm II* (Cambridge, 1982).
A. Rosenberg, *Imperial Germany* (London, 1966).
R. Ross, *The Beleaguered Tower* (Notre Dame, 1976).
J.J. Ruedoerffer [i.e. K. Riezler], *Grundzüge der Weltpolitik in der Gegenwart* (Berlin–Stuttgart, 1916, first publ. 1914).
* K. Saul, *Staat, Industrie und Arbeiterbewegung* (Düsseldorf, 1974).
W. Schieder (ed.), *Erster Weltkrieg* (Köln, 1969).

K. Schilling, 'Beiträge zu einer Geschichte des radikalen Nationalismus in der Wilhelminischen Ära, 1890–1909', Ph.D. thesis (Köln, 1968).

G. Schmidt, 'Innenpolitische Blockbildungen in Deutschland am Vorabend des Ersten Weltkrieges', *Das Parlament* (Beilage) (13 May 1972) pp. 3 ff.

* Idem, *Der europäische Imperialismus* (München, 1985).

B.E. Schmitt, *The Coming of the War, 1914* (New York, 1930).

G. Schöllgen, *Imperialismus und Gleichgewicht* (München, 1984).

Idem, *Das Zeitalter des Imperialismus* (München, 1986).

Idem, *Escape into War?* (Oxford, 1990).

D. Schoenbaum, *Zabern 1913* (London, 1982).

C.E. Schorske, *The German Social Democratic Party* (Cambridge, Mass., 1955).

H. Schottelius and W. Deist (eds), *Marine und Marinepolitik* (Düsseldorf, 1972).

W. Schüssler, *Die Daily-Telegraph-Affäre* (Göttingen, 1952).

B.F. Schulte, *Die deutsche Armee, 1900–1914* (Düsseldorf, 1977).

Idem, *Europäische Krise und Erster Weltkrieg* (Frankfurt, 1983).

D.P. Silverman, *Reluctant Union* (Philadelphia, 1972).

E.G. Spencer, *Management and Labor in Imperial Germany* (Berkeley, 1988).

* D. Stegmann, *Die Erben Bismarcks* (Köln, 1970).

J. Steinberg, *Yesterday's Deterrent* (London, 1965).

Z.S. Steiner, *The Foreign Office and Foreign Policy* (Cambridge, 1969).

Idem, *Britain and the Origins of the First World War* (London, 1977).

F. Stern, *Bethmann Hollweg und der Krieg* (Stuttgart, 1968).

Idem, *Gold and Iron* (New York, 1978).

O. Graf zu Stolberg-Wernigerode, *Die unentschiedene Generation* (München, 1968).

W. Struve, *Elites against Democracy* (Princeton, 1973).

M. Stürmer, 'Staatsstreichgedanken im Bismarckreich', *Historische Zeitschrift*, 209 (1969) 566 ff.

Idem, *Das ruhelose Reich* (Berlin, 1918).

* Idem (ed.), *Das Kaiserliche Deutschland* (Düsseldorf, 1970).

S. Suval, *Electoral Politics in Wilhelmine Germany* (Chapel Hill, 1985).

S. Tirrell, *Agrarian Politics after Bismarck's Fall* (New York, 1961).

L.C.F. Turner, *Origins of the First World War* (London, 1970).

H.P. Ullmann, *Der Bund der Industriellen* (Göttingen, 1976).

E. von Vietsch, *Bethmann Hollweg* (Boppard, 1969).

B. Vogel, *Deutsche Rußlandpolitik* (Düsseldorf, 1973).

H. -U. Wehler, *Bismarck und der Imperialismus* (Köln, 1969).

* Idem, *The German Empire, 1871–1918* (Oxford, 1985).

K. Wernecke, *Der Wille zur Weltgeltung* (Düsseldorf, 1970).

S.R. Williamson, Jr., *The Politics of Grand Strategy* (Cambridge, Mass., 1969).

* Idem, *Austria-Hungary and the Origins of the First World War* (London, 1991).

K. Wilson, *The Policy of the Entente* (Cambridge, 1985).

P. Winzen, *Bülows Weltmachtkonzept* (Boppard, 1977).

* P.-C. Witt, *Die Finanzpolitik des Deutschen Reiches von 1903 bis 1913* (Lübeck–Hamburg, 1970).

E.L. Woodward, *Great Britain and the German Navy* (Oxford, 1935).

K. Wormer, *Großbritannien, Rußland und Deutschland* (München, 1980).

E. Zechlin, *Die Staatsstreichpläne Bismarcks und Wilhelms II* (Stuttgart, 1929).

H.-G. Zmarzlik, *Bethmann Hollweg als Reichskanzler* (Düsseldorf, 1957).

References

INTRODUCTION

1. See F. Fischer, *Germany's War Aims in the First World War* (1967); idem, *War of Illusions* (1973); summaries of the Fischer Debate may be found in: J.A. Moses, *Politics of Illusion* (1975) and J.W. Langdon, *July 1914* (1991).
2. S.R. Williamson, Jr., *Austria-Hungary and the Origins of the First World War* (1991).
3. All of Kehr's key publications are now available in English translation. See E. Kehr, *Battleship Building and Party Politics in Germany, 1894–1902* (1975); *Economic Interest, Militarism, and Foreign Policy* (1977). For a summary of the 'Kehrite' position see W. J. Mommsen, 'Domestic Factors in German Foreign Policy', *Central European History* (March 1973) 3–43, who also first coined this term. A debate on the applicability of this label can be found in: G. Eley, 'Die "Kehrites" und das Kaiserreich', *Geschichte und Gesellschaft*, 1 (1978) 91–107; H.-J. Puhle, 'Zur Legende der "Kehrschen Schule"', ibid. 108–19. Roger Fletcher later introduced the concept of the 'Bielefelders' since some protagonists taught at the University of Bielefeld. See R. Fletcher, 'Recent Developments in West German Historiography: The Bielefeld School and its Critics', *German Studies Review*, 3 (1984) 451–80. See also J.N. Retallack, 'Social History with a Vengeance?', ibid. 423–50; R.G. Moeller, 'The Kaiserreich Recast?', *Journal of Social History*, 4 (1984) 655–83. See also the contributions by M.R. Gordon, 'Domestic Conflict and the Origins of the First World War', *Journal of Modern History*, 2 (1974) 191–226; A.J. Mayer, 'Domestic Causes of the First World War', in L. Krieger and F. Stern (eds), *The Responsibility of Power* (1967) pp. 286–300; D. Kaiser, 'Germany and the Origins of the First World War', *Journal of Modern History*, 4 (1983) 442–74.
4. See A. Hillgruber, *Die Zerstörung Europas* (1988); K. Hildebrand, 'Staatskunst oder Systemzwang?', *H.Z.*, 228 (1979) 624–44; idem, 'Julikrise 1914. Das europäische Sicherheitsdilemma', *Geschichte in Wissenschaft und Unterricht*, 36 (1985) 469–502; M. Stürmer, 'Deutscher Flottenbau und europäische Weltpolitik vor dem Ersten Weltkrieg', in *Deutsches Marineinstitut und Militärgeschichtliches Forschungsamt* (eds), *Die deutsche Flotte im Spannungsfeld der Politik, 1848–1985* (1985) pp. 57ff.; G. Schöllgen, *Escape into War?* (1990).
5. See, e.g., L. Dehio, *Gleichgewicht oder Hegemonie?* (1948); idem, *Deutschland in der Weltpolitik des 19. und 20. Jahrhunderts* (1955).
6. See H.-U. Wehler, *Bismarck und der Imperialismus* (1969); idem, *The German Empire, 1871–1918* (1985).
7. See the works cited in note 4 above.
8. See note 4 above.
9. See R.J. Evans, *In Hitler's Shadow* (1989); C.S. Maier, *The Unmasterable Past* (1989); P. Baldwin (ed.), *Reworking the Past* (1990).
10. See the accounts by Moeller, Retallack, and Fletcher cited in note 3 above.
11. Thus James Sheehan in his review article in *Journal of Modern History*, 3 (1976) 567.

12. R.J. Evans (ed.), *Society and Politics in Wilhelmine Germany* (1978), p. 23.
13. See, e.g., G. Eley, *Reshaping the German Right* (1980); R. Chickering, *We Men Who Feel Most German* (1984); M.S. Coetzee, *The German Army League* (1990); W.L. Guttsman, *The German Social Democratic Party* (1981); E. Evans, *The German Center Party* (1981); J.C. Hunt, *The People's Party in Württemberg and Southern Germany* (1975); A.J. Peck, *Radicals and Reactionaries* (1978); J.N. Retallack, *Notables of the Right* (1988); D. White, *The Splintered Party* (1976); S. Mielke, *Der Hansabund* (1976); H.-P. Ullmann, *Der Bund der Industriellen* (1976); D. Blackbourn, *Class, Religion and Local Politics in Wilhelmine Germany* (1980); D. Silverman, *Reluctant Union* (1972); R.J. Evans, *The Feminist Movement in Germany* (1976); A. Hackett, *The Politics of Feminism in Wilhelmine Germany* (1979); J. Quataert, *Reluctant Feminists in German Social Democracy* (1979); R. Levy, *The Downfall of the Anti-Semitic Political Parties in Wilhelmine Germany* (1975); J. Reinharz, *Fatherland or Promised Land* (1975). See also the anthologies by G. Martel (ed.), *Modern Germany Reconsidered* (1992); J. Dukes and J. Remak (eds), *Another Germany* (1988).
14. See, e.g., K.-J. Bade, *Vom Auswanderungsland zum Einwanderungsland* (1983); D. Blasius, *Ehescheidung in Deutschland* (1987); R.J. Evans, *Death in Hamburg* (1987); R. Spree, *Health and Social Class in Imperial Germany* (1988); L. Niethammer, *Wohnen im Wandel* (1979); R.J. Evans (ed.), *The German Family* (1980); J.C. Albisetti, *Schooling German Girls and Women* (1988); J.C. Fout (ed.), *German Women in the Nineteenth Century* (1984); M. Mitterauer, *Ledige Mütter* (1980); B. Franzoi, *At the Very Least She Pays Her Rent* (1985); M. Mitterauer, *Sozialgeschichte der Jugend* (1986); J. Ehmer, *Sozialgeschichte des Alters* (1990).
15. See, e.g., V. Lidtke, *The Alternative Culture* (1985); C. Klessmann, *Polnische Bergarbeiter im Ruhrgebiet* (1978); H.-H. Liang, *The Social Background of the Berlin Working-Class Movement* (1980); J. Mooser, *Arbeiterleben in Deutschland* (1984); R.C. Murphy, *Guestworkers in the German Reich* (1983); D. Crew, *Town in the Ruhr* (1979); W. Ruppert, *Der Arbeiter* (1986); R.J. Evans (ed.), *The German Working Class* (1983); J.S. Roberts, *Drink, Temperance and the Working Class in Nineteenth-Century Germany* (1984).
16. See, e.g., C. Huerkamp, *Der Aufstieg der Ärzte im 19. Jahrhundert* (1985); J. Kocka, *Bürgertum im 19. Jahrhundert* (1988); K. Gispen, *New Profession, Old Order* (1989); H. Kaelble, *Soziale Mobilität und Chancengleichheit im 19. und 20. Jahrhundert* (1983); P.G. Lauren, *Diplomats and Bureaucrats* (1976); K. Vondung, *Das wilhelminische Bildungsbürgertum* (1976); M. Lamberti, *State, Society and the Elementary School in Imperial Germany* (1989); C. McClelland, *State, Society and University in Germany* (1980); K.A. Schleunes, *Schooling and Society* (1989); R.J. Evans, *The German Underworld* (1988); W.E. Mosse, *Jews in the German Economy* (1987); G. Cocks and K. Jarausch, *German Professions* (1990).
17. See, e.g., M. Makela, *The Munich Secession* (1990); P. Paret, *The Berlin Secession* (1980); A.T. Allen, *Satire and Society in Wilhelmine Germany* (1985); H. Glaser, *Die Kultur der wilhelminischen Zeit* (1984); K. Roper, *German Encounters with Modernity* (1991); J. Campbell, *The German Werkbund* (1978); V. Lidtke, *The Alternative Culture* (1985); B. Emig, *Die Veredelung des Arbeiters* (1980); S. Gehrmann, *Fußball, Verein, Politik* (1988).
18. See, e.g., D. Blackbourn, *Populists and Patricians* (1987); W.K. Blessing, *Staat und Kirche in der Gesellschaft* (1988); J. Sperber, *Popular Catholicism in Nineteenth-Century Germany* (1984).
19. See, e.g., D. Blackbourn, *Class, Religion and Local Politics in Wilhelmine Germany* (1980).
20. See note 12 above.
21. G. Eley, *Reshaping the German Right* (1980).
22. G. Eley and D. Blackbourn, *The Peculiarities of German History* (1984).

23. G. Eley, 'In Search of the Bourgeois Revolution', *Political Power and Social Theory*, 7 (1988) 105–33. See also Eley's critics: H. -U. Wehler, 'Deutscher Sonderweg oder allgemeine Probleme des westlichen Kapitalismus?', *Merkur*, 35 (1981) 478–87; idem, 'Der deutsche Weg', *Frankfurter Allgemeine Zeitung* (25 March 1991) p. L18; J. Kocka, 'Der "deutsche Sonderweg" in der Diskussion', *German Studies Review*, 3 (1982) 365–79.

24. See also G. Schmidt, 'Innenpolitische Blockbildungen am Vorabend des Ersten Weltkrieges', *Das Parlament* (Beilage) (13 May 1972) pp. 3 ff.

25. See most recently J.C.G. Röhl (ed.), *Der Ort Des Kaisers in der deutschen Geschichte* (1989).

26. U. Bermbach, *Vorformen parlamentarischer Kabinettsbildung* (1967); D. Grosser, *Vom monarchischen Konstitutionalismus zur parlamentarischen Demokratie* (1970); P. Molt, *Der Reichstag vor der improvisierten Revolution* (1963).

27. M. Rauh, *Föderalismus und Parlamentarismus im wilhelminischen Reich* (1972); idem, *Die Parlamentarisierung des Deutschen Reiches* (1977).

28. See S. Suval, *Electoral Politics in Wilhelmine Germany* (1985); G. Eley, 'The Social Construction of Democracy in Germany, 1871–1933', unpublished MS (1992).

29. F. Fischer, *War of Illusions* (1973); J.C.G. Röhl, 'Der militärisch-politische Entscheidungsprozeß in Deutschland am Vorabend des Ersten Weltkrieges', in idem, *Kaiser, Hof und Staat* (1987) pp. 175–20; B.F. Schulte, *Vor dem Kriegsausbruch 1914* (1980); H. Pogge von Strandmann, 'Germany and the Coming of War', in idem and R.J.W. Evans (eds), *The Coming of the First World War* (1988).

30. B. Sösemann, 'Die Tagebücher Kurt Riezlers', *H.Z.*, 236 (1983) 327 ff.

31. K.D. Erdmann (ed.), *Kurt Riezler. Tagebücher, Aufzeichnungen, Dokumente* (1972).

32. F. Fischer, *Juli 1914: Wir sind nicht hineingeschlittert* (1983).

33. K.D. Erdmann, 'Zur Echtheit der Tagebücher Kurt Riezlers', *H.Z.*, 236 (1983) 371 ff.; A. Bläsdorf, 'Der Weg der Riezler-Tagebücher', *Geschichte in Wissenschaft und Unterricht*, 35 (1984) 651 ff.

34. S.R. Williamson, Jr., *Austria-Hungary and the Origins of the First World War* (1991).

35. Ibid., pp. 199 ff., also for the following.

36. See V.R. Berghahn, *Militarism. The History of an International Debate, 1861–1979* (1981) pp. 53 ff.

1.   THE CRISIS OF THE PRUSSO-GERMAN
     POLITICAL SYSTEM

1. B. Tuchman, *The Guns of August—August 1914* (1962) pp. 135 ff.

2. E. Eyck, *A History of the Weimar Republic* (1964).

3. W. Deist, 'Die Politik der Seekriegsleitung und die Rebellion der Flotte Ende Oktober 1918', *V.f.Z.G.* (October 1966).

4. See H. Herzfeld, *Die deutsche Rüstungspolitik vor dem Weltkriege* (1923); S. Förster, *Der doppelte Militarismus* (1985); V.R. Berghahn und W. Deist (eds), *Rüstung im Zeichen der Wilhelminischen Weltpolitik* (1989).

5. K. von Einem, *Erinnerungen eines Soldaten* (1933) pp. 59 ff.

6. V.R. Berghahn, *Der Tirpitz-Plan* (1971) pp. 249 ff.

7. *Kriegsrüstung und Kriegswirtschaft*, 2 vols (1930).

8. Ibid., Vol. I, pp. 65 f.

9. Ibid., Vol. II, pp. 90 ff.

10. Quoted in Berghahn, *Tirpitz-Plan*, p. 269.

11. Quoted ibid., p. 270.

12. For details see, e.g., G.A. Craig, *The Politics of the Prussian Army* (1955); M. Kitchen, *The German Officer Corps, 1890–1914* (1968); K. Demeter, *Das deutsche Offizierkorps in Gesellschaft und Staat* (1964).

13. Thus the report of the Bavarian Militärbevollmächtigte of 23 May 1903, quoted in Berghahn, *Tirpitz-Plan*, p. 264.
14. Ibid.
15. Ibid., p. 266.
16. The text of the Reich Constitution is reprinted in E.M. Hucko (ed.), *The Democratic Tradition* (1987) pp. 119 ff.
17. See G.A. Craig, *The Politics of the Prussian Army*, pp. 136 ff.
18. See below pp. 155 ff.
19. See M. Stürmer, 'Staatsstreichgedanken im Bismarckreich', *H.Z.*, 209 (1969) 566–615. See also below pp. 34 f. and pp. 172 f.
20. See below p. 36 f.
21. See note 19.
22. See, e.g., W. Tormin, *Geschichte der deutschen Parteien* (1968).
23. See, e.g., T. Nipperdey, *Deutsche Geschichte, 1866–1918*, Vol. II (1992) pp. 364 ff.
24. See S. Neumann, *Die deutschen Parteien* (1932).
25. See above p. 9, and below pp. 155 ff.
26. Quoted in H. Boldt, *Rechtsstaat und Ausnahmezustand* (1967) p. 91.
27. Quoted ibid.
28. See below, pp. 183 ff.
29. Quoted in Craig, *Prussian Army*, p. 252 n.
30. A.O.E Klaussmann (ed.), *Kaiserreden* (1902) pp. 218 f.
31. B. von Bülow, *Reden* (1930) III 150.
32. B.A.–M.A., Senden Papers, N 160/5, Tirpitz to Senden, 15.2.1896.
33. Bülow, *Reden* III 18 f.
34. Quoted in K. Saul, 'Der Kampf um die Jugend zwischen Volksschule und Kaserne', *M.G.M.* I (1971) p. 102.
35. Cabinet Ordre of 18 January 1901.
36. B.A.–M.A., Senden Papers, N 160/5, Tirpitz to Senden, 15.2.1896.
37. Quoted in Berghahn, *Tirpitz-Plan*, p. 260.
38. Quoted ibid., p. 261.
39. Quoted ibid., p. 260.
40. See W. Pöls, *Sozialistenfrage und Revolutionsfurcht in ihrem Zusammenhang mit den angeblichen Staatsstreichplänen Bismarcks* (1960); J. Röhl, 'Staatsstreichplan oder Staatsstreichbereitschaft', *H.Z.*, 203 (1966); E. Zechlin, *Staatsstreichpläne Bismarcks und Wilhelms II* (1929).
41. For details see J. A. Nichols, *Germany after Bismarck: The Caprivi Era, 1890–1894* (1958).
42. Quoted in H. Pogge von Strandmann, 'Domestic Origins of Germany's Colonial Expansion under Bismarck', in *P. & P.* (February 1969) p. 142.
43. B.A., Hohenlohe Papers, Rep. 100, XXII, A 12, Völderndorff to Hohenlohe, 9.11.1897. See also the studies by K. Barkin and by H. Lebovics.
44. Quoted in Rosenberg, *Grosse Depression*, p. 271 n.
45. See Wehler, *Bismarck*, passim.
46. G. Schmoller *et al.* (eds), *Handels- und Machtpolitik* (1900) I 135.
47. Quoted in J. Röhl, *Deutschland ohne Bismarck* (1969) p. 147.
48. B.A.–M.A., Senden Papers, N 160/11, Notes by Senden (1896?).
49. Röhl, *Germany Without Bismarck* (1967) p. 157.
50. Quoted ibid., pp. 188 f.
51. Quoted ibid., p. 199.
52. Quoted in Berghahn, *Tirpitz-Plan*, p. 262.
53. Quoted in Röhl, *Germany*, p. 200.
54. Quoted ibid.

55. N. Rich and M.H. Fisher (eds), *Die Geheimen Papiere Friedrich von Holsteins* (1963) IV 17 (no. 605).
56. Quoted in Röhl, *Germany,* p. 202.
57. C. Fürst zu Hohenlohe-Schillingsfürst, *Denkwürdigkeiten der Reichskanzlerzeit* (1931) p. 311.
58. See Pogge, 'Domestic Origins', p. 142.
59. Quoted in H. Schottelius and W. Deist (eds), *Marine und Marinepolitik, 1871–1914* (1972) p. 92.

2. TIRPITZ'S GRAND DESIGN

1. Quoted in Röhl, *Germany,* p. 187.
2. E. Eyck, *Das Persönliche Regiment Wilhelms II* (1948); E.R. Huber, 'Das Persönliche Regiment Wilhelms II', *Z.f.R.u.G.*, 3 (1951); Röhl, *Germany* pp. 220 ff.; O. Graf zu Stolberg-Wernigerode, *Die unentschiedene Generation* (1968).
3. G.W.F. Hallgarten, *Imperialismus vor 1914* (1963) I 422.
4. Wehler, *Bismarck,* p. 48.
5. Ibid.
6. B.A.–M.A., Tirpitz Papers, 16, Ahlefeld to Tirpitz, 18.8.1899.
7. See Berghahn, *Tirpitz-Plan,* p. 144.
8. See below, p. 53.
9. B.A.–M.A., Tirpitz Papers, 16, Ahlefeld to Tirpitz, 18.8.1899.
10. P.A.A.A., A.A. Deutschland, 138, no. 5, vol. 1, Report of the Prussian Ambassador to Mecklenburg and the Hanseatic Cities, 13.2.1900.
11. See E. Kehr, *Schlachtflottenbau und Parteipolitik* (1930) pp. 235 ff.
12. Reprinted in E. Kehr, *Der Primat der Innenpolitik* (1965) pp. 146 f.
13. J. Steinberg, *Yesterday's Deterrent* (1965) p. 38.
14. Quoted in K. Schilling, *Beiträge zu einer Geschichte des radikalen Nationalismus in der Wilhelminischen Ära, 1890–1909* (1968) p. 60.
15. Quoted in Berghahn, *Tirpitz-Plan,* p. 137.
16. Quoted in Schmoller *et al.* (eds), *Handels- und Machtpolitik* (1900) 194 f.
17. Quoted in Wehler, *Bismarck,* p. 116.
18. A. von Tirpitz, *Erinnerungen* (1919) p. 52.
19. B.A.–M.A., Tirpitz Papers, K 63, Maltzahn to Tirpitz, 28.8.1895.
20. Quoted in F. Münz, *Fürst Bülow* (1930) p. 78.
21. Quoted in Schmoller *et al.* (eds), *Machtpolitik,* I 113.
22. Ibid., p. 120.
23. Quoted in Berghahn, *Tirpitz-Plan,* p. 148.
24. Quoted ibid.
25. Rosenberg, *Grosse Depression,* p. 196.
26. Nauticus (1900) quoted in Berghahn, *Tirpitz-Plan,* p. 150.
27. For details see Craig, *Prussian Army,* pp. 217 ff.
28. E.W. Böckenförde, 'Der deutsche Typ der konstitutionellen Monarchie im 19. Jahrhundert', in *Beiträge zur deutschen und belgischen Verfassungsgeschichte im 19 Jahrhundert,* W. Conze (ed.), (1967) p. 80.
29. B.A.–M A , R.M.A., 2051, P.G. 66110, Memorandum by Knorr (Navy High Command), 21.5.1898.
30. Ibid., 2050, P.G. 66103, Navy High Command to the Kaiser, 31.1.1891.
31. Quoted in W. Hubatsch, *Der Admiralstab und die obersten Marine-behörden in Deutschland* (1958) p. 77.
32. B.A.–M.A., R.M.A., 2051, P.G. 66110, Tirpitz to the Kaiser, 3.2.1898.
33. Ibid., 2045, P.G. 66079, Memorandum by Tirpitz, November 1905.

34. Bülow quoted in Berghahn, *Tirpitz-Plan*, p. 153.
35. Ibid.
36. Quoted in Kehr, *Schlachtflottenbau*, p. 117 n.
37. G. von Schulze-Gaevernitz (1898) quoted ibid.
38. B.A.– M.A., Senden Papers, N 160/11, Notes by Senden (1896?).
39. See below, p. 53.
40. Quoted in Wehler, *Bismarck*, p. 465.
41. Quoted in G. Oldenhage, *Die deutsche Flottenvorlage von 1897 und die öffentliche Meinung* (1935) p. 30.
42. For details see Berghahn, *Tirpitz-Plan*, pp. 157 ff.
43. B.A.–M.A., Tirpitz Papers, 16, Ahlefeld to Tirpitz, 12.2.1898.
44. See especially his *The Influence of Sea Power upon History* (1889). On Mahan, see W.E. Livezey, *Mahan on Sea Power* (1954).
45. Quoted in Berghahn, *Tirpitz-Plan*, p. 180.
46. B.A.–M.A., Senden Papers, 160/3, Memorandum by Senden (1899?).
47. Bülow, *Reden*, I 98 f.
48. Klaussmann (ed.), *Kaiserreden* (1902) p. 269.
49. B.A.–M.A., Heeringen Papers, 7619 II, Tirpitz to Miquel, 8.2.1899.
50. Ibid., Tirpitz Papers, K 70, Tirpitz to?, 13.6.1879.
51. Ibid., 8, Tirpitz to Crown Prince William, 15.4.1909.
52. For a detailed discussion of the following see Berghahn, *Tirpitz-Plan*, pp. 192 ff.
53. B.A.–M.A., R.M.A 2036, P.G. 66040, 'Sicherung Deutschlands gegen einen englischen Angriff' (February 1900).
54. Ibid., 2044, P.G. 66074, 'Tirpitz's Notes for his discussions with the Kaiser on 28.9.1899, n.d.
55. Quoted in Berghahn, *Tirpitz-Plan*, pp. 191 f.
56. See esp. his *Deutschland und die Weltpolitik im 20. Jahrundert* (1955), pp. 73 ff.
57. B.A.–M.A., R.M.A. 2044, P.G. 66074, Tirpitz's Notes for his discussions with the Kaiser on 28.9.1899, n.d.
58. Sub-title of Berghahn, *Tirpitz-Plan*.
59. Quoted in Röhl, *Germany*, p. 176.
60. Thus Diederich Hahn of the Agrarian League quoted in Kehr, *Schlachtflottenbau*, p. 198.
61. Ibid., p. 203.
62. Ibid., p. 264.
63. Ibid.

3. THE ANGLO-GERMAN NAVAL ARMS RACE

1. Klaussmann (ed.), *Kaiserreden*, p. 227.
2. Quoted in Schottelius and Deist (eds), *Marine und Marinepolitik*, p. 182.
3. A.J.P. Taylor, *The Struggle for Mastery in Europe, 1848–1918* (1954) p. 397.
4. See also, Berghahn, *Tirpitz-Plan*, pp. 380 ff.
5. For a recent summary of the problem see H.W. Koch, 'The Anglo-German Alliance Negotiations: Missed Opportunity or Myth?', *History* (October 1969). See also the studies by G.W. Monger and J.A.S. Grenville.
6. *G.P.*, vol. 18 (11) 502 f.
7. Ibid., vol. 17, 570 ff.
8. Ibid., 588 ff.
9. Ibid., vol. 19 (1) 46 ff.
10. R. Vierhaus (ed.), *Das Tagebuch der Baronin Spitzemberg* (1961) p. 439.

11. *G P.*, vol. 19 (I) 349 f.
12. Ibid., 312.
13. Quoted in Berghahn, *Tirpitz-Plan*, p. 410.
14. See L.J.R. Cecil, 'Coal for the Fleet that had to Die', A.H.R., July 1964.
15. E.N. Anderson, *The First Moroccan Crisis* (1928), pp. 196 ff.; E.L. Woodward, *Great Britain and the German Navy* (1935) pp. 79 ff.
16. German term: *Auskreisung* (K.E. Born).
17. N.W. Summerton, *The Development of British Military Planning for a War against Germany, 1904–1914* (1970) p. 602.
18. Quoted in A.J. Marder, *The Anatomy of British Sea Power* (1940) p. 274.
19. Quoted ibid., p. 315.
20. See ibid., pp. 291 ff.
21. Ibid., pp. 456 ff. See also Z. Steiner, *The Foreign Office and Foreign Policy, 1898–1914* (1969) pp. 37 ff.
22. Quoted in J.A.S. Grenville, *Lord Salisbury and Foreign Policy* (1964) p. 213.
23. Marder, *Anatomy*, pp. 78 ff.; Steiner, *Foreign Office*, p. 54.
24. B.A.–M.A., R.M.A., 7184, P.G. 68926, Report by Coerper, 27.3.1905. See also Marder, *Anatomy*, pp. 14 ff, 23 ff.
25. See Marder, *Anatomy*, pp. 515 ff.; E.L. Woodward, *Great Britain and the German Navy* (1935) pp. 100 ff.
26. For details see Berghahn, *Tirpitz-Plan*, pp. 458 ff.
27. Reprinted in: Tirpitz, *Erinnerungen*, pp. 143 ff.
28. On the problem of German militarism see G. Ritter, 'Das Problem des Militarismus in Deutschland', *H.Z.*, 177 (1954); L. Dehio, 'Um den deutschen Militarismus', *H.Z.*, 180 (1955); W. Sauer, 'Die politische Geschichte der deutschen Armee und das Problem des Militarismus', *P.V.S.* 6 (1965).
29. B.A.–M.A., R.M.A., 2044, P.G. 66077, Report of the R-Commission, 14.12.1904.
30. See below, pp. 115 ff.
31. B.A.–M.A., Admiralstab, 5641, IV, 5.1., vol. 1, Memorandum by Büchsel (February 1905). See also P. Kennedy 'Maritime Strategieprobleme der deutsch-englischen Flottenrivalität', *Marine und Marinepolitik*, ed. Schottelius and Deist, pp. 178 ff.
32. See Ritter, *Staatskunst und Kriegshandwerk* (1954) II 239 ff.
33. Quoted in F. Fischer, *Krieg der Illusionen* (1969) p. 99.
34   B.A.–M.A., R.M.A., 2044, P.G. 66077, Müller to Tirpitz, 8.2.1905.
35. P. Guillen, *L'Allemagne et le Maroc de 1870 à 1905* (1967) p. 889.
36. See Anderson, *First Moroccan Crisis*, pp. 181 ff.; C. Andrew, *Théophile Delcassé and the Making of the Entente Cordiale* (1968) pp. 268 ff.; G.W. Monger, *The End of Isolation* (1963) pp. 268 ff.; Summerton, *The Development*, pp. 154 f.
37. See Berghahn, *Tirpitz-Plan*, p. 480.
38. A. von Waldersee, *Denkwürdigkeiten* (1922–3) III 181 ff.
39. See Vierhaus (ed.), *Baronin Spitzenberg*, pp. 210 ff.; R. Graf Zedlitz-Trützschler, *Zwölf Jahre am deutschen Kaiserhof* (1924) pp. 33 ff.
40. See Bülow, *Reden*, III 206 ff.; IV 62 ff.
41. See K.E. Born and P. Rassow (eds), *Akten zur staatlichen Sozialpolitik in Deutschland, 1890–1914* (1959), pp. 138 ff.
42. B.A., Bülow Papers, 77, Eulenburg to Bülow, 9.8.1903.
43. Ibid., 107, Stolberg to Bülow, 27.12.1903.
44. Quoted in Berghahn, *Tirpitz-Plan*, p. 263.
45. Quoted ibid., p. 274 n.
46. Ibid., p. 263.
47. For the reasons see below, pp. 86 f.
48. B. von Bülow, *Denkwürdigkeiten* (1930), II 198.

49. Quoted ibid.
50. Schilling (Ph.D. thesis, 1968) p. 267 n.
51. A. von Tirpitz, *Der Aufbau der deutschen Weltmacht* (1924) pp. 24 f.
52. Ibid., p. 23.
53. For details see G.D. Crothers, *The German Elections of 1907* (1941).
54. B.A., Bülow Papers, 153, Note no. 358 (October 1911).
55. See Berghahn, *Tirpitz-Plan*, p. 494.
56. *B.D.*, vol. 3, 397 ff.
57. For details see Berghahn, *Tirpitz-Plan*, pp. 505 ff.
58. See Crothers, *Elections of 1907*.
59. See Berghahn, *Tirpitz-Plan*, pp. 565 ff.
60. B.A.–M.A., R.M.A., 2040, P.G. 66060, Memorandum by Dähnhardt, 4.2.1907.
61. D. Senghaas, *Rüstung und Militarismus* (1972) p. 46.
62. For details see Berghahn, *Tirpitz-Plan*, pp. 580 ff.

4. FROM BÜLOW TO BETHMANN HOLLWEG

1. For details see Berghahn, *Tirpitz-Plan*, pp. 588 ff.
2. See J. Steinberg, 'The Copenhagen Complex', *J.C.H.* (July 1966).
3. See above, p. 93.
4. *G.P.*, vol. 24, 17 ff.
5. Ibid., 21. See also Woodward, *Great Britain and the German Navy*, pp. 155 ff.
6. *G.P.*, vol. 24, 27 f. See also Steiner, *Foreign Office*, pp. 88 f.
7. Reprinted in Tirpitz, *Aufbau*, pp. 58 ff.
8. *G.P.*, vol. 24, 50 f.
9. *B.D.*, vol. 6, 81 f. See also Summerton, *The Development*, p. 634.
10. *G.P.*, vol. 24, 60 f., 68 ff.
11. Reprinted in Tirpitz, *Aufbau*, pp. 69 ff.
12. *G.P.*, vol 24, 131 f. See also ibid., 99 ff.
13. Ibid., 139 ff.
14. Ibid., 136 n.
15. Ibid., 148 ff.
16. See also ibid., vol. 25 (11) 474 ff.
17. For details see ibid. vol.24, 167 ff.
18. Ibid., vol. 28, 5 n.
19. Quoted in Tirpitz, *Aufbau*, p. 96.
20. Ibid., p. 101.
21. See below, pp. 87 ff.
22. Tirpitz, *Aufbau*, p. 102.
23. B.A.–M.A., R.M.A., 2045, P.G. 66081, Tirpitz to Prince Henry, 20.12.1908.
24. *G.P.*, vol. 28, 26.
25. Ibid., 58 f.
26. Ibid., 60 ff.
27. Ibid., 67 ff., 78 f.
28. Ibid., 81.
29. Ibid., 58 f., 66 f.
30. Ibid., 75 ff.
31. Including four optional ships finally approved in the spring of 1909.
32. *G.P.*, vol. 28, 122.
33 Ibid., 168 ff.
34. Ibid., 184 f.

35. Ibid., 178 ff.
36. Ibid., 180 ff.
37. See Berghahn, *Tirpitz-Plan*, p. 219.
38. For details see K.E. Born, *Staat und Sozialpolitik seit Bismarcks Sturz* (1957) pp. 90 ff.
39. P.Chr. Witt, *Die Finanzpolitik des Deutschen Reiches von 1903 bis 1913* (1970) pp. 51 f., 105 ff.
40. It provided for all revenue from tariffs and tobacco over and above 130 mill. marks to be allocated to the federal states.
41. Berghahn, *Tirpitz-Plan*, p. 276. On the Centre Party see the studies by K. Bachem and K. Epstein.
42. Witt, *Finanzpolitik*, pp. 80 ff.
43. Schilling (Ph.D. thesis, 1968) p. 288.
44. Bülow to the Baden Ambassador quoted in Berghahn, *Tirpitz-Plan*, p. 554 n.
45. For details see the studies by G.D. Crothers and K. Epstein.
46. Detailed figures in Witt, *Finanzpolitik*, p. 380.
47. Berghahn, *Tirpitz-Plan*, pp. 540 ff.
48. Ibid., pp. 479 ff.
49. *G.P.* vol. 24, 96 ff.
50. B.A.–M.A., Marinekabinett, 3304, P.G. 667133, Tirpitz to Müller, 5.12.1907.
51. Ibid., R.M.A., 2045, P.G. 66081, Note by Tirpitz, 6.9.1908.
52. Ibid., Note by Tirpitz, 12.12.1908. See also *G.P.*, vol. 28, 21 n, 66 ff.
53. See also *G.P.*, vol. 28, 155 n.
54. Taylor, *Struggle*, pp. 450 ff.
55. E. Brandenburg, *Von Bismarck zum Weltkriege* (1924) p. 279.
56. Quoted in F. Conrad von Hötzendorff, *Aus meiner Dienstzeit* (1921) p. 1404.
57. W. Schüssler, *Die Daily-Telegraph-Affaire* (1952) pp. 13 ff.
58. See F. Fischer, *Krieg der Illusionen* (1969) p. 104.
59. Quoted ibid., p. 106.
60. Zedlitz-Trützschler, *Zwölf Jahre am deutschen Kaiserhof*, p. 226.
61. Quoted in Berghahn, *Tirpitz-Plan*, p. 585.
62. *G.P.*, vol. 24, 117 ff.
63. See above, p. 64.
64. B.A.–M.A., R.M.A., 2045, P.G. 66081, Cabinet Ordre, 9.1.1909.
65. Ibid.
66. Ibid., Marinekabinett, 3443, P.G. 66473, Tirpitz to Müller, 25.4.1909.
67. Ibid., R.M.A., 2045, P.G. 66081, Tirpitz to Holtzendorff, 20.4.1909.
68. Ibid., Cabinet Ordre, 9.1.1909.
69 Quoted in Schottelius and Deist (eds), *Marine und Marinepolitik*, p. 162.
70. Witt, *Finanzpolitik*, pp. 207 ff.
71. Quoted in Schottelius and Deist (eds), *Marine und Marinepolitik*, p. 165.
72. Quoted in D. Stegmann, *Die Erben Bismarcks* (1970) p. 360.
73. For details see Witt, *Finanzpolitik*, pp. 243 ff.
74. Quoted in Schottelius and Deist (eds), *Marine und Marinepolitik*, pp. 165 f.

5. THE CRITICAL YEAR OF 1911

1. K. Jarausch, *The Enigmatic Chancellor* (1972), p. ix.
2. See below, pp. 155 ff.
3. Bülow, *Reden*, I 209.
4. For details see Jarausch, *Enigmatic Chancellor*, pp. 32 ff.
5. H.-G. Zmarzlik, *Bethmann Hollweg als Reichskanzler, 1909–1914* (1957) p. 31 n.

6. Quoted in E. Jäckh, *Kiderlen-Wächter. Der Staatsmann und Mensch* (1924) II 112.
7. Quoted in E. von Vietsch, *Bethmann Hollweg* (1969) p. 105.
8. Ibid., pp. 106 f.
9. For details see Stegmann, *Bismarcks Erben*, pp. 176 ff.
10. Jarausch, *Enigmatic Chancellor*, p. 75.
11. Quoted ibid.
12. Quoted ibid., p. 77.
13. Bethmann Hollweg quoted ibid.
14. Bethmann Hollweg quoted ibid., p. 79.
15. Ibid.
16. Quoted ibid.
17. See Stegmann, *Bismarcks Erben*, pp. 187 ff.
18. Quoted ibid., p. 200.
19. Quoted ibid., p. 213.
20. Quoted ibid., p. 223.
21. Ibid., p. 207.
22. Reprinted in Jäckh, *Kiderlen-Wächter*, II 48 ff., 64 ff.
23. Ibid., 57.
24. Marginal by Tirpitz on: B.A.–M.A., R.M.A., P.G. 69123, Report by Widenmann, 27.7.1909.
25. See the material in *G.P.*, vol. 28, 222 ff.
26. See the diplomatic documents ibid., chapters CCXXIII and CCXXIV. See also Tirpitz, *Aufbau*, pp. 165 ff.
27. See the material in *G.P.*, vol. 28, 281 ff., 347 ff.
28. Quoted in Jäckh, *Kiderlen-Wächter*, II 38.
29. B.A.–M.A., R.M.A., 2045, P.G. 66081, Tirpitz to Müller 24.7.1909
30. Zedlitz-Trützschler, *Zwölf Jahre am deutschen Kaiserhof*, p. 227. On the problem of the Wilhelmine military-industrial complex, see Berghahn, *Rüstung*, pp. 47 ff.
31. B.A.–M.A., Tirpitz Papers, 24, Capelle to Tirpitz, 29.7.1909.
32. Ibid., 8, Tirpitz to Capelle, 19.9.1909.
33. Quoted in Vietsch, *Bethmann Hollweg*, p. 112.
34. Quoted in Stegmann, *Bismarcks Erben*, p. 210.
35. H. Oncken quoted in K. Hildebrand, *Preussen als Faktor der britischen Weltpolitik* (1972) p. 29.
36. *G.P.*, vol. 29, 107 ff.
37. Quoted in K. Wernecke, *Der Wille zur Weltgeltung* (1970) p. 29.
38. *G.P.* vol. 29, 152.
39. Quoted in K. Wernecke, *Der Wille zur Weltgeltung* (1970) p. 32.
40. Quoted ibid.
41. Quoted ibid., p. 33.
42. Quoted in Witt, *Finanzpolitik*, p. 338.
43. Wernecke, *Der Wille zur Weltgeltung*, p. 36.
44. Quoted ibid.
45. Quoted in Fischer, *Krieg*, p. 126.
46. Quoted ibid.
47. See Wernecke, *Der Wille zur Weltgeltung*, p. 66.
48. Quoted in Fischer, *Krieg*, p. 131.
49. Quoted ibid., p. 144.
50. Quoted ibid., p. 131.
51. H. von Moltke, *Erinnerungen, Briefe, Dokumente* (1922) p. 362.
52. W. Görlitz (ed.), *Der Kaiser ...* (1965) p. 88.
53. See Tirpitz, *Aufbau* p. 202.
54. Jäckh, *Kiderlen-Wächter*, II 10.

55. B.A.–M.A., Tirpitz Papers, 24, Notes by Tirpitz, May (1911).
56. Ibid., 8, Note by Capalle, 9.9.1909.
57. See Schottelius and Deist (eds), *Marine und Marinepolitik*, p. 166.
58. B.A.–M.A., R.M.A., 2046, P.G. 66088, Protocol of R.M.A. Meeting of 24.11.1911.
59. For details see Berghahn, *Rüstung*, pp. 47 ff.
60. B.A.–M.A., R.M.A., 2046, P.G. 66088, Protocol of R.M.A. Meeting of 25.8.1910.
61. Ibid., 2041, P.G. 66061, 'Green Paper' Note, n.n., n.d.
62. Quoted in Tirpitz, *Aufbau*, p. 221.
63. See above, p. 93.
64. B.A.–M.A., Tirpitz Papers, 24, Notes by Tirpitz, May (1911).
65. Ibid., R.M.A., 2051, Tagesmeldungen 1911, Tagesmeldung no. 5, 8.7.1911.
66. Tirpitz, *Aufbau*, p. 200.
67. Ibid., p. 213.
68. Ibid., p. 206.
69. Ibid., pp. 207 f.
70. Ibid., p. 209.
71. Ibid.
72. Quoted in Fischer, *Krieg*, p. 140.
73. See Witt, *Finanzpolitik*, pp. 340 f.

6. THE REORIENTATION OF GERMAN ARMAMENTS
    POLICY

1. Tirpitz, *Aufbau*, p. 207.
2. Ibid., p. 210.
3 Ibid., pp. 211 f.
4. Ibid., p. 213.
5. B.A.–M.A., Marinekabinett, 3443, P.G. 67474, Kaiser to Bethmann Hollweg, 30.9.1911 (2.10.1911).
6. Ibid., R.M.A., 2045, P.G. 66082, Müller's Summary of Kaiser/Tirpitz Discussions at Rominten, 26.9.1911.
7. Tirpitz, *Aufbau*, p. 215.
8. Ibid., p. 216.
9. B.A.–M.A., Tirpitz Papers, 24, Capelle's Draft of Notes for Tirpitz's Report to the Kaiser, n.d.
10. Tirpitz, *Aufbau*, pp. 222 ff.
11. Ibid., pp. 218 ff.
12. Ibid., p. 220.
13. Ibid., p. 222.
14. Ibid., p. 212.
15. Ibid., p. 222.
16. On Wermuth's policies see Witt, *Finanzpolitik*, pp. 316 ff., 330 ff.
17. B.A.–M.A., Tirpitz Papers, 24, Wermuth to Tirpitz, 19.6.1911.
18. Tirpitz, *Aufbau*, pp. 226 f.
19. Ibid., p. 227.
20. Görlitz (ed.), *Der Kaiser* ..., p. 96.
21. Ibid., p. 97.
22. Ibid.
23. B.A.–M.A., R.M.A., 2041, P.G. 66061, Notes by Dähnhardt (October 1911).
24. Görlitz (ed.), *Der Kaiser* ..., p. 99.
25. Ibid.
26. Quoted ibid.

27. St.A.H.H., S.K., A IV, c. 6, vol XVIII, Report of 5.12.1911.
28. Ritter, *Staatskunst*, II 273.
29. *Militärwochenblatt*, 12.3.1910.
30. Quoted in Ritter, *Staatskunst*, II 274.
31. B.A.–M.A., Tirpitz Papers, 24, Capelle to Tirpitz, 29.7.1910.
32. Quoted in Fischer, *Krieg*, p. 140.
33. Quoted ibid., p. 139.
34. St.A.H.H., S.K., A IV, c. 6, vol. XVIII, Report of 20.11.1911.
35. Tirpitz, *Aufbau*, p. 266.
36. See Fischer, *Krieg*, pp. 175 ff.
37. H.St.A., Aussenministerium, Acta Flotte, no. 4707, Report of 6.12.1911.
38. Görlitz (ed.), *Der Kaiser …*, p. 95.
39. Tirpitz, *Aufbau*, pp. 265 f.
40. Ibid.
41. Ibid., pp. 261 f.
42. Ibid., p. 266.
43. Ibid., p. 263.
44. Görlitz (ed.), *Der Kaiser …*, p. 101.
45. Tirpitz, *Aufbau*, pp. 263 f.
46. Görlitz (ed.), *Der Kaiser …*, p. 104.
47. Tirpitz, *Aufbau*, p. 268.
48. Vietsch, *Bethmann Hollweg*, p. 137.
49. See G. Schmidt, 'Rationalismus und Irrationalismus in der englischen Flottenpolitik', in *Marine und Marinepolitik*, ed. Schottelius and Deist, pp. 283 ff.
50. Tirpitz, *Aufbau*, pp. 243 ff.
51 Ibid., p. 232.
52. Ibid., p. 239.
53. Ibid., p. 232.
54. Ibid., p. 243.
55. Ibid., p. 252.
56. Ibid.
57. Quoted in Jäckh, *Kiderlen-Wächter*, II 129.
58. Tirpitz, *Aufbau*, pp. 269 ff.
59. Görlitz (ed.), *Der Kaiser …*, p. 106.
60. Ibid., p. 107.
61. Ibid.
62. Ibid.
63. Tirpitz, *Aufbau*, p. 276.
64. Quoted in J. Steinberg, 'Diplomatie als Wille und Vorstellung: Die Berliner Mission Lord Haldanes, im Februar 1912', in *Marine und Marinepolitik*, ed. Schottelius and Deist, p. 266.
65. Görlitz (ed.), *Der Kaiser …*, p. 110.
66. *G.P.*, vol. 31, 98.
67. Quoted in Schottelius and Deist (eds) *Marine und Marinepolitik*, p. 275.
68. *G.P.*, vol. 31, 98.
69. Quoted in Schottelius and Deist (eds), *Marine und Marinepolitik*, p. 278. See also W.S. Churchill, *The World Crisis*, 1911–1918 (1964) p. 74
70. *G.P.*, vol. 31, 102 ff.
71. Görlitz (ed.), *Der Kaiser …*, p. 111.
72. Tirpitz, *Aufbau*, pp. 277 f.
73. Ibid., pp. 227, 278.
74. Ibid., p. 284.
75. B.M.–M.A., R.M.A., 2041, P.G. 66062, Note by Dahnhardt, n.d.

76. See Steinberg's article in *Marine und Marinepolitik*, ed. Schottelius and Deist, pp. 263 ff.
77. Tirpitz, *Aufbau*, p. 269.
78. Ibid., p. 319.

7. RETREAT TO THE EUROPEAN CONTINENT

1. Quoted in Fischer, *Krieg*, p. 209.
2. Tirpitz, *Aufbau*, p. 422.
3. See H.V. Emy, 'The Impact of Financial Policy on English Party Politics before 1914', *H.J.*, March 1972, pp. 103 ff.
4. Tirpitz, *Aufbau*, p. 422.
5. Ibid., p. 365.
6. Ibid.
7. B.A.–M.A., R.M.A, 2041, P.G. 66063, Memorandum by Capelle, 22.5.1912.
8. For details see Schottelius and Deist (eds), *Marine und Marinepolitik*, pp. 111 f.
9. B.A.–M.A., R.M.A., P.G. 69125, Report of 30.10.1913.
10. Ibid., Marinekabinett, 3502, P.G. 67858, Müller to the Kaiser, 8.8.1912.
11. Sec Schottelius and Deist (eds,), *Marine und Marinepolitik*, pp. 112 f.
12. B.A.–M.A., R.M.A., 6024, H. 28a, Reichsschatzamt to Tirpitz, 25.8.1913.
13. Tirpitz, *Aufbau*, p. 423.
14. B.A.–M.A., Tirpitz Paper, K. 7, Müller to Philipp, 27.3.1926.
15. Quoted in K. Jarausch, *The Enigmatic Chancellor. Bethmann Hollweg and the Hubris of Impertal Germany*, p. 96.
16. B.A.–M.A., Capelle Papers, N 170/1, Tirpitz to Capelle, 8.7.1913.
17. See above, p. 117.
18. Churchill, *World Crisis*, p. 79.
19. Berghahn, *Rüstung*, p. 61.
20. See K. Stenkewitz, 'Deutscher Wehrverein', in *Die Bürgerlichen Parteien in Deutschland*, ed. D. Fricke *et al.* (1968) p. 1575.
21. Quoted ibid., p. 576.
22. Ibid.
23. Quoted in Görlitz (ed.), *Der Kaiser ...*, p. 105.
24. *Kriegsrüstung und Kriegswirtschaft*, II 138 f.
25. Ritter, *Staatskunst*, II 277.
26. Ibid., p. 279.
27. Ibid., p. 277.
28. Ibid.
29 Fischer, *Krieg*, p. 251.
30. See below, pp. 156 ff.
31. Tirpitz, *Aufbau*, pp. 370 f.
32. Ibid., p. 375.
33. Ibid., p. 380.
34 Ibid., p. 378 .
35. A. Hillgruber, 'Zwischen Hegemonie und Weltpolitik', in *Das Kaiserliche Deutschland*, ed. M. Stürmer (1970) pp. 196 ff.
36. Quoted in Fischer, *Krieg*, p. 331.
37. F. Fischer, *Weltmacht oder Niedergang* (1965).
38. Th. von Bethmann Hollweg, *Betrachtungen zum Weltkriege* (1919) p. 24.
39. See K. Hildebrand, *Deutsche Aussenpolitik*, 1933–1945 (1970).
40. *Deutsche Volkswirtschaftliche Correspondenz* (heavy industry) quoted in Fischer, *Krieg*, p. 341.
41. Quoted ibid., p. 340.

42. Wernecke, *Der Wille zur Weltgeltung*, p. 298; Fischer, *Krieg*, p. 376.

43. Quoted in Schottellius and Deist (eds), *Marine and Marinepolitik*, p. 316.

44. *G.P.*, vol. 31, 92 ff.

45. J.J. Ruedorffer, *Grundzüge der Weltpolitik in der Gegenwart* (1916), p 106.

46. Fischer, *Krieg*, pp. 289 ff.; W. Gutsche, 'Mitteleuropaplanungen in der Aussenpolitik des deutschen Imperialismus vor 1918', *Z.f.G.*, 5 (1972) 533 ff.; H.C. Meyer, *Mitteleuropa in German Thought and Action* (1955).

47. Quoted in Fischer, *Krieg*, p. 330.

48. Quoted ibid., p. 336.

49. Quoted ibid., p. 334.

50. Quoted ibid., p. 341.

51. F. von Bernhardi quoted ibid., p. 345.

52. Quoted ibid., p. 327; Wernecke, *Der Wille zur Weltgeltung*, p. 290.

53. See R. Poidevin, *Les relations économiques et financières entre la France et l'Allemagne de 1898 à 1914* (1969).

54. See above, pp. 30 ff.

55. Tirpitz, *Aufbau*, p. 376; *G.P.*, vol. 31, 93.

56. Quoted in V.R. Berghahn and W. Deist, 'Kaiserliche Marine und Kriegsausbauch 1914', *M.G.M.*, I (1970) 43.

57. Quoted in Fischer, *Krieg*, p. 1.

58. Quoted in Berghahn, *Tirpitz-Plan*, p. 444.

59. Quoted in Brandenburg, *Von Bismarck zum Weltkriege*, p. 275.

60. Quoted in Taylor, *Struggle*, p. 484.

61. Quoted ibid., p. 485.

62. *D.D.F.*, 3ᵉ série, vol. 4, 315 f.

63. *Ö.U.*, vol. 4, 727 ff.

64. *G.P.*, vol. 33, 276.

65. See Fischer, *Krieg*, p. 229.

66. William's marginal comment on *G.P.*, vol 34 (11) p. 462.

67. J. Röhl (ed.), 'Ein Brief Kaiser Wilhelms II vom 9 Dezember 1912', *M.G.M.*, I (1973).

68. *G.P.*, vol 34 (11) 462.

69. Ibid., vol. 35, 68.

70. Ibid., 115 f.

71. Fischer, *Krieg*, p. 304.

72. *G.P.*, vol. 35, 134 f.

73. Quoted in Fischer, *Krieg*, p. 304.

74. *Ö.U.*, vol. 7, 8 f.

75. *G.P.*, vol. 38, 200.

76. Quoted in Fischer, *Krieg*, p. 486.

77. Quoted in L.F.C. Turner, *Origins of the First World War* (1970) p. 58.

78. Taylor, *Struggle*, p. 508.

79. Quoted in Turner, *Origins*, p. 58.

80. Quoted in Fischer, *Krieg*, p. 498.

81. Taylor, *Struggle*, p. 508.

82. See Wernecke, *Der Wille zur Weltgeltung*, pp. 244 f.

83. Quoted in Fischer, *Krieg*, p. 488.

8. THE PARALYSIS OF MONARCHY AT HOME

1. For a detailed analysis see J. Bertram, *Die Wahlen zum Deutschen Reichstag vom Jahre 1912* (1964).

2. See Stegmann, *Bismarcks Erben*, p. 257.

3. See Fischer, *Krieg*, p. 147.
4. Quoted in Stegmann, *Bismarcks Erben*, p. 261.
5. Quoted ibid.
6. Quoted ibid., p. 431.
7. Quoted ibid., p. 432.
8. Quoted ibid.
9. See Born, *Staat und Sozialpolitik*, pp. 80 ff.
10. Quoted in Stegmann, *Bismarcks Erben*, p. 272.
11. Ibid., p. 275.
12. Published in D. Fricke, 'Eine Denkschrift Krupps aus dem Jahre 1912 über den Schutz der Arbeitswilligen', *Z.f.G.*, 6 (1957).
13. J. Vorster (Cd.I.) quoted in Fischer, *Krieg*, p. 392.
14. Stegmann, *Bismarcks Erben*, p. 267.
15. Quoted ibid., p. 272.
16. For details see Born, *Staat und Socialpolitik*, pp. 242 f.
17. Quoted in Stegmann, *Bismarcks Erben*, p. 339.
18. Quoted ibid.
19. Quoted ibid., p. 326.
20. See below, p. 192.
21. Quoted in Stegmann, *Bismarcks Erben*, p. 287.
22. Quoted ibid.
23. Schweidnitz Chamber of Commerce quoted ibid., p. 374.
24. For details see ibid., p. 283.
25. Quoted ibid., p. 427.
26. Quoted ibid., pp. 332 f.
27. Quoted ibid., p. 294.
28. See, e.g. H. Arendt, *The Origins of Totalitarianism* (1962); E.G. Reichmann, *Hostages of Civilisation* (1950).
29. Quoted in U. Lohalm, *Völkischer Radikalismus* (1970) p. 53.
30. Quoted in Stegmann, *Bismarcks Erben*, p. 294.
31. Ibid., p. 325 n.
32. Ibid., p. 258.
33. H.A. Winkler, *Mittelstand, Demokratie und Nationalsozialismus* (1972) p. 52.
34. Quoted ibid., p. 50.
35. Ibid., pp. 52 f.
36. Quoted in Stegmann, *Bismarcks Erben*, p. 345 n.
37. Ibid., p. 305.
38. Quoted ibid., pp. 308 f.
39. Quoted ibid., p. 310.
40. B. Marwitz (Young Liberal) quoted ibid., p. 310 n.
41. Quoted in Fischer, *Krieg*, p. 257.
42. See Witt, *Finanzpolitik*, pp. 356 ff.
43. Quoted ibid., pp. 362 f.
44. Quoted ibid., p. 359.
45. Quoted ibid.
46. Quoted ibid., p. 361.
47. Quoted in Schottelius and Deist (eds.), *Marine und Marinepolitik*, p. 175.
48. Quoted in Witt, *Finanzpolitik*, p. 364.
49. See Wernecke, *Der Wille zur Weltgeltung*, pp. 190 ff.
50. Quoted in Witt, *Finanzpolitik*, p. 365.
51. See ibid., p. 364.
52. Quoted in Fischer, *Krieg*, p. 258.
53. Quoted in Witt, *Finanzpolitik*, p. 365.

54. For details see Wernecke, *Der Wille zur Weltgeltung*, pp. 193 ff.
55. Quoted in Fischer, *Krieg*, p. 268.
56. Quoted in Stegmann, *Bismarcks Erben*, p. 360.
57. Thus Clemens von Delbrück, State Secretary of the Interior, 18 November 1912 in a memorandum quoted in H. Goldschmidt, *Das Reich und Preussen im Kampf um die Führung* (1931) p. 341.
58. Quoted in Stegmann, *Bismarcks Erben*, p. 369.
59. Quoted ibid., p. 360.
60. Quoted ibid., p. 361.
61. Thus the Report of the General Commission to the 9th Trade Union Congress in June 1914 quoted in D. Schneider and R. Kuda, *Die Arbeiterräte in der Novemberrevolution* (1969) p. 14.
62. Quoted in Stegmann, *Bismarcks Erben*, p. 385.
63. Deutsche Bergwerkszeitung, 31.8.1913, quoted ibid., p. 382.
64. On these certificates see below, pp. 191 f.
65. Quoted in Stegmann, *Bismarcks Erben*, pp. 350 f.
66. Quoted ibid., p. 351.
67. Quoted ibid., p. 441.
68. Quoted ibid., p. 401.
69. A. Feiler, *Die Konjunkturperiode 1907–1913 in Deutschland* (1914) p. 165.
70. G. Schmidt, 'Innenpolitische Blockbildungen in Deutschland am Vorabend des Ersten Weltkrieges', *Das Parlament* (Beilage) 13.5.1972, pp. 3 ff.
71. Ibid., p. 8.
72. Ibid ., p. 14.
73. Ibid., p. 30.
74. Ibid ., p. 31.
75. W. Sauer in *Moderne deutsche Sozialgeschichte*, ed. H.-U. Wehler (1968) p. 434.
76. V. R. Berghahn, 'Zu den Zielen des deutschen Flottenbaus unter Wilhelm II', *H.Z.*, 210 (1970) 100.
77. Schmidt, *Das Parlament* (Beilage) 13.5.1972, p. 4.
78. See W. Rathenaus diary notes on a conversation with Bethmann Hollweg in July 1912 in *Walther Rathenau, Tagebuch 1907–1922*, ed. H. Pogge von Strandmann (1967), pp. 169 f.
79. H. Pogge von Strandmann, 'Staatsstreichpläne, Alldeutsche und Bethmann Hollweg', in H. Pogge von Strandmann and I. Geiss, *Die Erforderlichkeit des Unmöglichen* (1965) p. 16.
80. See his letter to his son ibid., pp. 37 ff.
81. Quoted in Jarausch, *Enigmatic Chancellor*, p. 71.
82. Quoted in Pogge, 'Staatsstreichpläne', p. 19.

9. TOWARDS A MILITARY SOLUTION

1. See C.E. Schorske, *The German Social Democratic Party, 1905–1917* (1955).
2. For further details Berghahn, *Rüstung*, pp. 85 ff.
3. See Röhl, *Kriegsschuldfrage*, p. 10.
4. Fischer, *Krieg*.
5. Quoted ibid., p. 550.
6. Quoted in Jarausch, *Enigmatic Chancellor*, p. 149.
7. See above, pp. 34 f.
8. See above, p 19 ff.
9. *G.P.*, vol. 39, 124.
10. Görlitz (ed.), *Der Kaiser* ..., p. 124.

11. Ibid., p. 125.
12. Ibid.
13. Quoted in J. Röhl, 'Admiral von Müller and the Approach of War, 1911–1914', *H.J.* 4 (1969) 662. Was omitted from Görlitz's edition.
14. Quoted in Fischer, *Krieg*, p. 235.
15. See ibid., pp. 620 f.
16. *G.P.*, vol. 39, 533 ff.
17. Conrad, *Aus meiner Dienstzeit*, III 597.
18. Ibid., p. 670.
19. Quoted in Fischer, *Krieg*, p. 584.
20. Conrad, *Aus meiner Dienstzeit*, III 609 ff.
21. Ibid., p. 597.
22. *Germania*, 3.3.1913, quoted in Wernecke, *Der Wille zur Weltgeltung*, pp. 192 f.
23. Quoted ibid., p. 196.
24. *Hamburger Nachrichten*, 3.12.1912, quoted ibid., p. 185.
25. Quoted ibid., p. 187.
26. Quoted in Witt, *Finanzpolitik*, p. 372 n.
27. Quoted in Schottelius and Deist (eds), *Marine und Marinepolitik*, p. 315.
28. Quoted in Vietsch, *Bethmann Hollweg*, p. 169.
29. For details see Kitchen, *German Officer Corps*, pp. 197 ff.
30. Ibid., p. 204.
31. Quoted in Zmarzlik, *Bethmann Hollweg als Reichskanzler*, p. 131.
32. Quoted ibid.
33. Quoted ibid., pp. 115 f.
34. Quoted ibid., p. 119 n.
35. Quoted ibid.
36. Quoted ibid., p. 117.
37. Quoted ibid., p. 118.
38. Quoted in Vietsch, *Bethmann Hollweg*, p. 168.
39. Quoted in Zmarzlik, *Bethmann Hollweg als Reichskanzler*, p. 119.
40. Quoted ibid., p. 120.
41. Quoted ibid., p. 131.
42. Quoted ibid., p. 117.
43. Quoted in Vietsch, *Bethmann Hollweg*, p. 167.
44. Quoted in Zmarzlik, *Bethmann Hollweg als Reichskanzler*, p. 124.
45. Quoted in Vietsch, *Bethmann Hollweg*, p. 168.
46. Quoted in Zmarzlik, *Bethmann Hollweg als Reichskanzler*, p. 123.
47. Quoted in Vietsch, *Bethmann Hollweg*, p. 169.
48. See Zmarzlik, *Bethmann Hollweg als Reichskanzler*, p. 129.
49. Quoted ibid., p. 125 n.
50. Quoted ibid., p. 124.
51. Quoted ibid., p. 131.
52. Quoted in Vietsch, *Bethmann Hollweg*, p. 172.
53. Quoted in H. Kohn, *The Mind of Germany* (1965) p. 292.
54. Quoted in Wernecke, *Der Wille zur Weltgeltung*, pp. 249 ff.
55. See ibid., p. 255.
56. Quoted in Fischer, *Krieg*, p. 555.
57. See Wernecke, *Der Wille zur Weltgeltung*, p. 250.
58. Ibid., p. 279.
59. Quoted in Fischer, *Krieg*, pp. 580 f.
60. F. Fellner (ed.), *Schicksalsjahre Österreichs* (1953), I 221.
61. Quoted in Wernecke, *Der Wille zur Weltgeltung*, p. 272.
62. Quoted in Fischer, *Krieg*, p. 547.

63. Quoted in Wernecke, *Der Wille zur Weltgeltung*, p. 249.
64. Wehler, *Bismarck*, p. 454.
65. See Fischer, *Krieg*, p. 537.
66. Ibid., p. 540.
67. Quoted ibid., p. 536.
68. Quoted ibid., p. 535.
69. Ibid. p. 536.
70. Quoted ibid., p. 538.
71. See Wernecke, *Der Wille zur Weltgeltung*, p. 270.
72. Quoted ibid., p. 269.
73. See Stegmann, *Bismarcks Erben*, p. 280.
74. Quoted ibid., p. 281.
75. Quoted in Jarausch, *Enigmatic Chancellor*, p. 152.
76. Quoted ibid.

10. THE JULY CRISIS OF 1914

1. Quoted in Jarausch, *Enigmatic Chancellor*, p. 99.
2. Quoted ibid., p. 105.
3. Quoted in Fischer, *Krieg*, p. 583.
4. Jarausch, *Enigmatic Chancellor*, p. 153.
5. I. Geiss (ed.), *Julikrise und Kriegsausbruch* 1914 (1963) I 59.
6. Ibid., 60 f.
7. Ibid., 72.
8. See ibid., 69 ff., 74 f.
9. Ibid., 60.
10. Ibid.
11. See ibid., 105.
12. Ibid., 75.
13. See ibid., 86 ff; V.R. Berghahn and W. Deist, 'Kaiserliche Marine und Kriegsausbruch 1914', *Militärgeschichtliche Mitteilungen* (1970) p. 45.
14. Berghahn and Deist, 'Kaiserliche Marine', p. 45 (on 6.7.1914).
15. Ibid., p. 47.
16. K.D. Erdmann (ed.), *Kurt Riezler—Tagebücher, Aufsätze, Dokumente* (1972) p. 185 (entry of 11.7.1914).
17. Bethmann Hollweg to Clemens von Delbrück, the Vice-Chancellor, on 9.7.1914, quoted in Jarausch, *Enigmatic Chancellor*, p. 160.
18. Quoted in L. Albertini, *The Origins of the War of 1914* (1965) II 154.
19. Hopman to Tirpitz, 6.7.1914, quoted in Berghahn and Deist, 'Kaiserliche Marine', p. 45.
20. Ibid.
21. Ibid.
22. D.Z.A. I, Reichskanzlei, 1261/l, Falkenhayn to Bethmann, 8.7.1914.
23. H. Butterfield, 'Sir Edward Grey und die Julikrise 1914', in *Erster Weltkrieg*, ed. W. Schieder (1969) pp. 411 ff.
24. Erdmann (ed.), *Kurt Riezler*, p. 183.
25. Ibid., p. 185.
26. Ibid., p. 182.
27. Ibid., p. 187 (entry of 20.7.1914).
28. Ibid., p. 183 (entry of 7.7.1914).
29. Ibid., p. 184 (entry of 8.7.1914).
30. Ibid.

31. Quoted in E. Zechlin, 'Bethmann Hollweg, Kriegsrisiko und die S.P.D. 1914', in W. Schieder (ed.), *Erster Weltkrieg. Ursachen, Entstehung und Kriegsziele*, pp. 167 f.
32. Quoted in Fischer, *Krieg*, p. 692.
33. By F. Fischer and his pupils.
34. Geiss (ed.), *Kriegsausbruch 1914*, I 104 ff.
35. Ibid., p. 129.
36. Ibid., p. 144.
37. Ibid., p. 183.
38. Ibid., p. 144.
39. Ibid., p. 174.
40. Ibid., pp. 179 f.
41. Quoted in Berghahn and Deist, 'Kaiserliche Marine', p. 50.
42. Geiss (ed.), *Kriegsausbruch 1914*, I 144.
43. Ibid., 164 f.
44. Ibid., 198.
45. Ibid., 224 ff.
46. Erdmann (ed.), *Kurt Riezler*, p. 188 (entry of 23.7.1914).
47. Geiss (ed.), *Kriegsausbruch 1914*, I 156.
48. Erdmann (ed.), *Kurt Riezler*, p. 185 (entry of 14.7.1914).
49. Geiss (ed.), *Kriegsausbruch 1914*, I 165 f.
50. Quoted in Berghahn and Deist, 'Kaiserliche Marine', p. 55.
51. Erdmann (ed.), *Kurt Riezler*, p. 187 (entry of 20.7.1914).
52. Ibid., p. 188.
53. Geiss (ed.), *Kriegsausbruch 1914*, I 189.
54. Ibid., p. 265.
55. Ibid., p. 200.
56. Ibid., p. 205.
57. Erdmann (ed.), *Kurt Riezler*, p. 189 (entry of 23.7.1914).
58. Geiss (ed.), *Kriegsausbruch 1914*, I 228.
59. Berghahn and Deist, 'Kaiserliche Marine', pp. 52 f.
60. See ibid., pp. 53 ff.
61. See L. Burchardt, *Friedenswirtschaft und Kriegsvorsorge* (1968).
62. Quoted in Fischer, *Krieg*, p. 567.
63. Quoted in Berghahn and Deist, 'Kaiserliche Marine', p. 48.
64. See ibid., p. 56.
65. Ibid., pp. 62 f.
66. See Ruedorffer, *Grundzüge der Weltpolitik in der Gegenwart* (1916) pp. 214 ff.
67. Ibid., p. 222.
68. Geiss (ed.), *Kriegsausbruch 1914*, II 106.
69. Ibid., I 419 f.
70. Ibid., II 297 ff.
71. Erdmann (ed.), *Kurt Riezler*, p. 192.
72. See the article by Zechlin in Schieder (ed.), *Erster Weltkrieg*, p. 173.
73. Ibid.
74. Erdmann (ed.), *Kurt Riezler*, p. 193 (entry of 27.7.1914).
75. See Fischer, *Krieg*, p. 699.
76. Ibid.
77. Jarausch, *Enigmatic Chancellor*, p. 164.
78. Quoted in Schieder (ed.), *Erster Weltkrieg*, p. 174.
79. Ibid., p. 175.
80. Ibid.
81. Ibid.
82. Ibid.

83. Ibid., p. 174.
84. Ibid., p. 172.
85. Ibid., p. 186.
86. W. Görlitz (ed.), *The Kaiser and his Court* (1961) p. 8.
87. Quoted in Jarausch, *Enigmatic Chancellor*, p. 169.
88. Quoted in Fischer, *Krieg*, p. 713.
89. Quoted ibid., p. 717.
90. See Turner, *Origins*.
91. See Fischer, *Krieg*, pp. 704 ff.
92. Geiss (ed.), *Kriegsausbruch 1914*, II 372 f.
93. See Zechlin's article in *Erster Weltkrieg*, ed. Schieder, p. 177.
94. Ibid., p. 178.
95. Quoted in Röhl, 'Admiral von Müller', p. 670.
96. For details see Ritter, *Staatskunst*, II 239 ff.
97. Geiss (ed.), *Kriegsausbruch 1914*, II 283. However, he was rather non-committal with regard to the French colonial empire.
98. Tirpitz's protocol of the meeting in A. von Tirpitz, *Deutsche Ohnmachtspolitik im Weltkriege* (1926) pp. 2 f.
99. Ibid.
100. Geiss (ed.), *Kriegsausbruch 1914*, II 279.
101. Ibid., 373.

Index

Offices are those held during the period covered by the book

strengthening of Army, 127; saves money, 134; resigns, 135; savings of, 164

Westarp, Kuno, Count, Conservative politician, 188

William, Crown Prince of Prussia, 173

William II, German Kaiser and King of Prussia, escapes to Holland, 15; on monarchism, 27 f.; and crisis of 1890s, 33 ff.; and Personal Rule, 38; hopes for colonial empire, 40; and social imperialism, 44; and Iron Budget, 45 ff.; absolution of, 47; admires Mahan, 48 f.; informed of Tirpitz's plans, 51; and *Weltpolitik*, 53; and foreign policy, 57; visits Tangiers, 59; at the crossroads, 62; fears revolution, 67 f.; advocates dictatorship, 69; opposed by Tirpitz, 71; approves 1908 Navy bill, 74; irrationalism of, 75; visits Britain, 79; meets Hardinge at Kronberg, 80; approves publication of *Daily Telegraph* interview, 81; instructs Metternich to inform Britain of German naval plans, 83; reluctant to resort to war, 92; deals with opposition inside Navy, 93; quasi-absolution of, 98; announces reform of Prussian voting system, 100; approves negotiations with Britain, 103; attitude towards Moroccan Crisis, 106; does not want war over Morocco, 110; meets Tirpitz at Rominten, 116; is drawn into struggle over 1912 Navy bill, 123ff.; accepts visit by Haldane, 134; announces Navy bill, 134; hopes for de-escalation of naval arms race, 138; appealed to by Tirpitz, 139; gives Army priority over Navy, 140 f.; critical of colonial expansion, 144; attitude towards Austria-Hungary, 148; attitude towards Bosnian Crisis, 148; on German aims in Balkans, 150; hopes for success of continental policy, 153; tells Liman of German aims in Middle East, 153; depressed by Liman Mission setback, 154; receives letter from Krupp, 159; and *Staatsstreich* plans, 173; warped perception of, 176; exclusive command over Army, 178; and 1912 conference, 179; involvement in Zabern Affair, 186 ff.; and social imperialism, 192; and preventive war, 196; urges war against Serbia, 197; issues 'blank cheque', 198; wants firm action, 202 f.; thinking of arresting socialist leaders, 214; hopes for British neutrality, 219

Williamson, Samuel, American historian, 1, 11 f.

Wirtschaftsvereinigung, 156, 168

Wortley, Stuart, 81

Zabern Affair, 27, 184 ff., 194

Zedlitz und Neukirch, Octavio von, Free Conservative politician, 158

Zedlitz-Trützschler, Robert von, *Hofmarschall*, 93, 104

Ziese, Carl, German industrialist, 159 f.

Zimmermann, Arthur, Under Secretary of State in the German Foreign Office, 210